THE Path OF Emancipation

Other titles of **Thich Nhat Hanh**
from **FULL CIRCLE**

- Planting Seeds
- Under the Banyan Tree
- The Sun My Heart
- The Path of Emancipation
- A Pebble for Your Pocket
- Teachings on Love
- The Stone Boy
- Cultivating the Mind of Love
- Our Appointment with Life
- Being Peace (Pbk)
- Present Moment, Wonderful Moment (Pbk)
- The Heart of Understanding
- Transformation & Healing
- Breathe! You Are Alive
- Interbeing
- The Long Road Turns to Joy (Pbk)
- Present Moment, Wonderful Moment (HC)
- Being Peace (HC)

The Path of Emancipation

Talks from a 21-Day Mindfulness Retreat

THICH NHAT HANH

FULL CIRCLE

THE PATH OF EMANCIPATION

Published by arrangement with the author

First Indian Edition, 2008
First Reprint, 2010
Second Reprint, 2017
Third Reprint, 2018

ISBN-10 81-7621-189-3
ISBN-13 978-81-7621-189-5

Original Cover and text design © Ayelet Maida, A/M Studio
Author photograph by Nang Sao
Edited by Michelle Bernard

FULL CIRCLE

Published by **FULL CIRCLE** *PUBLISHING*
J-40, Jorbagh Lane, New Delhi-110003
Tel: 011-24621011
E-mail: contact@fullcirclebooks.in • *website:* www.fullcirclebooks.in

Print & typesetting : SCANSET
J-40, Jorbagh Lane, New Delhi-110003
Printed at Gopsons Papers Ltd. A-2&3, Sector-64, Noida–201301
PRINTED IN INDIA

Contents

Publisher's Preface

In Spring 1998, Vietnamese Zen master and peacemaker Thich Nhat Hanh led a twenty-one-day retreat in Burlington, Vermont, on the full awareness of *breathing*. Four hundred participants — some quite familiar with Buddhist teachings and practices, and many attending their first retreat — followed a daily schedule of sitting meditation, walking meditation, silent meals, Dharma discussions, and Thich Nhat Hanh's Dharma talks. Practicing mindfully together and listening to Thich Nhat Hanh's lectures, the retreatants were transported from daily concerns to a place of deep peace. We invite you to join them, reading these talks mindfully, while enjoying your breathing and your own true presence.

CHAPTER ONE

Dwelling in the Here and the Now

We are going to invoke the name of the Bodhisattva Avalokiteshvara. We will practice mindfulness of being present in order to produce the energy of healing and transformation. Let us open ourselves and be here so we can be penetrated by the energy of the bodhisattvas for our own healing and transformation.

The brothers and sisters from Plum Village will chant the name of the Bodhisattva of Compassion, and the energy of the Buddhas and the bodhisattvas will be generated by us and around us. It is very beneficial if you can allow yourselves to be penetrated by this energy of healing and transformation. If you feel comfortable, you can join your palms during the chanting and allow the sound of the bell and the chanting to penetrate you. Just follow your breathing, enjoy your in-breath and out-breath, and relax. Do not struggle, do not try to do anything. And please smile.*

[THREE BELLS]

Body, speech, and mind in perfect oneness,
I send my heart along with the sound of the bell.

* This chant is available on the tape and CD *Drops of Emptiness* (Boulder, Colorado: Sounds True, 1997).

May the hearers awaken from forgetfulness
and transcend the path of anxiety and sorrow.

[BELL]

Listen. Listen.
This wonderful sound brings me back to my true self.

[BELL]

Listening to the sound of the bell, I feel the afflictions in me
begin to dissolve.
My mind becomes calm, my body relaxed,
and a smile is born on my lips.
Following the sound of the bell,
my breath guides me back to the safe island of mindfulness.
In the garden of my heart, the flower of peace blooms
beautifully.

[BELL]

The universal Dharma door is already open.
The sound of the rising tide is clear and the miracle happens.
A beautiful child appears in the heart of a lotus flower.
One single drop of compassionate water is enough
to bring back the refreshing spring to mountains and to
rivers.
Namo Avalokiteshvaraya.

[BELL]

Chant in Vietnamese:
Nam Mo Bo Tat Quan The Am (Homage to Avalokiteshvara
Bodhisattva)

Please enjoy the sound of the bell and also your breathing. "Breathing in, I feel I am alive. Breathing out, I smile."

My dear friends, welcome to the first twenty-one-day retreat I have offered in North America. It is a very happy event. Four hundred of us have come to form a Sangha, a community of practice that carries within itself the Buddha and the Dharma. Wherever there is a Sangha, the Buddha and the Dharma are also present.

Among us are experienced meditators who have spent ten, maybe twenty years or more practicing meditation. And among us are also many who are new to the practice. But don't worry. The retreat will benefit all of us, including myself. When the Sangha is here, we have the opportunity to benefit from its collective energy. This is a rare opportunity to receive that energy of the Sangha for our own transformation and healing. Many here are happy practitioners. When you look at such happy people, you know that they are solid in the practice. Their way of walking, sitting, and smiling testifies to their solidity, freedom, and happiness. It is a blessing to have such people among us. They radiate peace, joy, stability, freedom, and happiness. Please make yourselves available to receive the collective energy of the Sangha. Allow yourselves just to be in the Sangha and stop all struggling.

It is so common to struggle in daily life. We are rarely at ease in the here and the now, always struggling, trying to attain something. The first element of the practice is to stop struggling. Just allow yourself to be. The Sangha is like a flowing river. Allow yourself to be a drop of water in the river, and just flow together with that river. If you cannot let go of your anxieties, you won't be able to do that. Taking refuge in the Sangha is not a declaration of faith. It is a practice. It means you allow yourself to be held by the Sangha. You have confidence in the Sangha. When you allow yourself to be in a Sangha the way a drop of water allows itself to be in a river, the energy of the Sangha can penetrate you, and transformation and healing become possible.

If you are a beginner in the practice, don't worry about what is the correct thing to do. What is most important is to allow yourself to be in the Sangha. Just be yourself. Stop struggling. During our retreat, we will practice mindful walking, sitting, and breathing. We will have meals together in mindfulness and Dharma discussions. Please enjoy every minute of our being together. Learn to walk so that each step brings you peace, relaxation, and joy. Learn to breathe in and out in a way that joy and life become possible. You are the only one who knows if you are practicing correctly. No one else can judge. If you take a step and feel peaceful and happy, that is the correct practice. When you practice breathing in and out, if you feel peaceful, if you enjoy your in-breath and out-breath, then you know that you are doing it correctly. Have confidence in yourself. When you do it correctly, there is a feeling of well-being, of peace, and of joy. Whether you stand in the right place or bow at the right moment is not important. Wherever you find yourself, if you feel at ease and peaceful and not under pressure, then you are doing it right. Mindfulness is the energy that helps you be in the here and the now in order to experience this kind of bliss, this kind of peace and joy.

[BELL]

We are not here to do intensive practice. I don't like the word "intensive." What does it mean? Walking meditation is just walking meditation. If you do it correctly, you get the peace, solidity, and freedom you deserve. There is no need to do it intensively. Each step has its own value. If every step can help you cultivate more freedom, peace, and joy, that is good enough. The practice should be pleasant. Don't struggle. Whether you are practicing walking or breathing, it should bring you joy, relaxation, and peace.

You don't need to do anything to prepare for this retreat. We will not give you a lot of things to read. There is only one page of reading for the whole twenty-one-day retreat. It is a sheet of paper that contains the names of the sixteen ways of breathing (see page 14). Also, don't worry about taking notes. The important thing is that you are fully here, and you allow yourself to be penetrated by the energy of the Sangha and the Dharma. The Dharma is a kind of rain, not only in the form of spoken words, but also what you see around you, what you listen to, what you touch. The Dharma comes to you in different forms. When you see a sister walking with peace and joy or sitting with stability, that is the Dharma. When you are greeted by a brother who forms his palms into a lotus flower, smiling, that is the Dharma. He is practicing mindfulness of bowing and mindfulness of smiling. The energy of mindfulness that is radiating from that person is the Dharma.

When you receive the energy of the Dharma from another person, you also radiate the energy of the Dharma from within yourself, because you are also capable of breathing in and out and smiling. Doing this unites your body and mind, and brings you to the present moment. That is already the Dharma. You can touch life from within and without. That is already enlightenment and awakening. If your smile is born from that kind of awareness and awakening, your smile is the living Dharma. You can produce the living Dharma and enhance the quality of your Sangha any time of the day.

We have come together as a Sangha. Each of us can contribute to the quality of the Sangha by enjoying the practice with our own being. We are here, and the quality of our presence is determined by our awareness, our mindfulness. If you let your body and mind get caught in the past or the future, or let your body be caught in worries and fear, you don't have much to contribute to the Sangha. But if you know how to make yourself truly present, body and mind united, how to enjoy your in-breath and out-breath, and how to become aware that being here with the Sangha is a wonderful opportunity, you will improve the quality of your

Sangha. All of us can profit from your presence and your contribution. If you can produce a smile that is authentic and genuine, the crown of enlightenment and mindfulness, it is the Dharma. When you walk with the awareness of each step that you take, you will enjoy more solidity, freedom, and happiness. Each step taken in mindfulness contributes to the quality of the Sangha. If everyone practices like that, then the energy of the Sangha will be healing and transforming. I promise to do my best. The sisters and brothers who sit with me here promise to do their best. And I know that you would like to do the same. The quality of the Sangha depends on every one of us. All of us profit from the collective energy of the Sangha.

In the *Discourse on the Full Awareness of Breathing (Anapananusmriti Sutra)*,* the Buddha shows us how to transform our fear, despair, anger, and craving. The teaching is clear. We are going to learn the teaching and the practice. In order to succeed in the practice, we need the energy of mindfulness. The energy of mindfulness in each person may not be enough for transformation and healing to take place, but if we make use of the energy of mindfulness of other brothers and sisters, we will be able to make it happen. We can profit from the Sangha. In the past, you may have felt that you could not bear to be alone, and when a friend came and sat close to you, you felt better, because you were supported by his or her energy. It is the same case now. Maybe you think that the energy of mindfulness produced by your practice is not enough for your transformation and healing. Look at the people around you who are practicing. Some of them have practiced for a long time, and their happiness is quite solid. With their energy of mindfulness, your transformation and healing is possible. That is why we have to have confidence in the Sangha.

Not only is the Buddha a jewel and the Dharma a jewel, but the Sangha is a true jewel. Taking refuge in the Sangha means we

* See appendix I.

have confidence in the Sangha and know how to profit from the energy it emanates. This is not a five-day or seven-day retreat, it is a twenty-one-day retreat. Let us be intelligent enough to profit from this rare retreat. You have made a great effort to be here. If you allow yourself to be in the retreat one hundred percent, this retreat will be wonderful, and it will profit everyone in the Sangha. Let us concentrate so we can be here in body and mind, one hundred percent, and together we can create a powerful energy to help all of us heal and transform. "I take refuge in the Sangha" is not a statement, it is a practice.

[BELL]

Mindful Eating

I would like to offer now some instructions on walking, breathing, smiling, and eating. When we have breakfast or lunch, we don't all have to eat together at the same time. If we do, we might not have time to do other things, like individual walking meditation.

When you come to the dining hall, after you get your food and sit at a table, and when your table has enough people, you can begin the practice of mindful eating. Mindful eating is very pleasant. We sit beautifully. We are aware of the people that are a part of our Sangha sitting around us. We are aware of the food on our plates. This is a deep practice. Each morsel of food is an ambassador from the cosmos. When we pick up a piece of a vegetable, we look at it for half a second. We look mindfully to really recognize the piece of food, the piece of carrot or string bean. We should know that this is a piece of carrot or a string bean. We identify it with our mindfulness: "I know this is a piece of carrot. This is a piece of string bean." It only takes a fraction of a second. When we are mindful, we recognize what we are picking up. When we put it into our mouth, we know what we are putting into our mouth. When we chew it, we know what we are chewing. It's very simple.

Some of us, while looking at a piece of carrot, can see the whole cosmos in it, can see the sunshine in it, can see the earth in it. It has come from the whole cosmos for our nourishment. You may like to smile to it before you put it in your mouth. When you chew it, you are aware that you are chewing a piece of carrot. Don't put anything else into your mouth, like your projects, your worries, your fear, just put the carrot in. And when you chew, chew only the carrot, not your projects or your ideas. You are capable of living in the present moment, in the here and the now. It is simple, but you need some training to just enjoy the piece of carrot. This is a miracle.

I often teach "orange meditation" to my students. We spend time sitting together, each enjoying an orange. Placing the orange on the palm of our hand, we look at it while breathing in and out, so that the orange becomes a reality. If we are not here, totally present, the orange isn't here either. There are some people who eat an orange but don't *really* eat it. They eat their sorrow, fear, anger, past, and future. They are not really present, with body and mind united. When you practice mindful breathing, you become truly present. If you are here, life is also here. The orange is the ambassador of life. When you look at the orange, you discover that it is nothing less than a miracle. Visualize the orange as a blossom, the sunshine and rain passing through it, then the tiny green fruit growing, turning yellow, becoming orange, the acid becoming sugar. The orange tree took time to create this masterpiece. When you are truly here, contemplating the orange, breathing and smiling, the orange becomes a miracle. It is enough to bring you a lot of happiness. You peel the orange, smell it, take a section, and put it in your mouth mindfully, fully aware of the juice on your tongue. This is eating an orange in mindfulness. It makes the miracle of life possible. It makes joy possible.

The other miracle is the Sangha, the community in which everyone is practicing in the same way. The woman sitting next to me is also practicing mindfulness while eating her breakfast. How wonderful! She is touching the food with mindfulness. She is enjoying every morsel of her breakfast, like me. We are brother and sister on the path of practice. From time to time we look at each other and smile. It is the smile of awareness. It proves that we are happy, that we are alive. It is not a diplomatic smile. It is a smile born from the ground of enlightenment, of happiness. That smile has the power to heal. It can heal you and your friend. When you smile like that, the woman next to you will smile back. Before that, maybe her smile was not completely ripe. It was ninety percent ripe. If you offer her your mindful smile, you will give her the energy to smile one hundred percent. When she is smiling, healing begins to take place in her. You are very important for her transformation and healing. That is why the presence of brothers and sisters in the practice is so important.

This is also why we don't talk during breakfast. If we talk about the weather or the political situation in the Middle East, we can never say enough. We reserve our time to do the things we want to do during our retreat — mindful eating, breathing, smiling, and being here with our Dharma brothers and sisters. Talking takes away the precious time that we share here. We are not depriving ourselves of the joy of talking or imposing silence on ourselves so that we can become a Buddha. We need the silence to enjoy our own presence and the presence of our Dharma brothers and sisters. This kind of silence is very alive, powerful, nourishing, and transforming. It is not oppressive or sad. Together we can create this kind of noble silence. Sometimes it is described as "thundering silence" because it is so powerful.

When we listen to a Dharma talk and when we practice, questions are born within us. I suggest that you write them down in a small notebook. Write down every question that you have. Don't be too eager to ask the question. In my experience, if the question is answered by someone else, even by the teacher, the answer is not as good as when you find it by yourself. In the beginning, you may have a million questions. But you'll discover, with surprise, that through looking deeply and touching deeply, you can answer most of the questions by yourself by the end of the retreat. During the retreat, we will have three question-and-answer periods. I need these sessions in order to offer appropriate teachings. In these sessions, please only ask questions connected with your practice. In your practice, if you find something that you don't understand, that you have some difficulty with, or if you discover something wonderful, but you're not sure if it reflects the true teachings of the Buddha, please ask me.

[BELL]

Your notebook will be like a friend. When we have some insight or question, we write it in the notebook. It is a kind of conversation with ourselves. Some days we will practice in complete silence. When we want to communicate with someone, we write a note. Many of us find the practice of complete silence very rewarding. Last fall in Plum Village, we had a twenty-one-day interfaith dialogue retreat that was almost totally silent. During the Dharma discussions, people were encouraged to express themselves, but apart from that, there was total silence. Everyone in the retreat loved it. They felt very safe and powerful, and they felt the energy of healing and solidity.

Mindful Walking

I would like to speak a little now about walking. Please make every step you take during the retreat a mindful step. When you move from one place to another, please practice mindful walking, no matter how short the distance. We will learn mindful walking with the Sangha, and we will walk mindfully together every day.

Perhaps you have used a seal before. When you stamp a seal

onto a piece of paper, you make sure that the whole seal prints on the paper, so that when you remove the seal, the image is perfect. When we practice walking, we do the same thing. Every step we take is like placing a seal on the ground. Mindfulness is the ink. We print our solidity and peace on the ground. In our daily lives, we don't usually walk like that. We print our hurry, worry, depression, and anger on the ground. But here, together, we print our solidity, peace, and freedom on the ground. You know whether you succeed or not with each step. Bring all of your mindfulness to the soles of your feet and walk. Enjoy every step you take, not only when you walk together with the Sangha, but when you walk alone to the dining room, the meditation hall, or the Dharma discussions. Allow plenty of time to walk. Every step can be healing and transforming. Every step can help you cultivate more solidity, joy, and freedom.

We have only one style of walking in Plum Village: mindful walking. Whether we are having a retreat or not, everyone always walks the same way. That is why when our friends come to Plum Village, they naturally join in the practice and are supported by everyone else in their walking meditation. Walking meditation is a wonderful way to learn how to live deeply each moment of our daily life. You will be surprised to find out that, when you return home, it is possible to implement this practice in the busy city. There are ways to put into practice what we learn during a retreat. When we leave Plum Village and go to the airport or the train station, we practice the same way. Everywhere is Plum Village. When I board an airplane, I walk in exactly the same way, printing peace and joy with every step.

Fifteen years ago, I led a mindfulness retreat in a center called Cosmos House in Amsterdam, where people practiced Tai Chi, Yoga, Zen, and so on. Our meditation room was on the top floor, and the staircase was quite narrow, especially up to the third and fourth floors. But I have only one style of walking. I cannot walk otherwise. My students and I blocked the stairs for hundreds of people behind us. On the third day of the retreat, everyone in Cosmos House had learned to walk like us.

I also remember when I marched for nuclear disarmament in New York City in 1982. There were a million Americans walking together that day. We were a group of thirty people. A Zen teacher, Richard Baker-roshi, asked me to join the march, and I said, "Will I be allowed to walk peacefully in the peace walk?" He said, "Yes, of course." So I joined, and our group walked mindfully, and we blocked more than two hundred thousand people behind us. Strangely enough, people accepted that, and they slowed down. Then the peace walk became more peaceful.

It is not difficult for us to walk peacefully here, because we are a Sangha practicing mindfulness. Please enjoy every step you take. Every mindful step is not only for your sake, but for the sake of the whole Sangha, the whole world. When you take a peaceful step, all of your ancestors in you take that step at the same time. You also walk for your children, whether they are born or unborn. Do not underestimate the strength, the value, of one step taken in mindfulness. One mindful step can produce healing and transformation for many generations. I promise to do my best. Peace is every step. All of us can do it. By the third or fourth day, you will have seen the difference. The presence of our brothers and sisters in the Sangha reminds us of the practice of peaceful walking.

[BELL]

The Bell of Mindfulness

Every time we hear the sound of the bell, it is an opportunity for us to go back to our mindful breathing. We may lose our mindful breathing, get lost in our thinking, in our projects and worries. The sound of the bell is the voice of the Buddha inside us calling us back to our true home, the here and the now. The practice of mindfulness is, foremost, to produce our true presence in the here and the now, so that everything becomes real and alive. During our meals, from time to time, you will hear the sound of the bell. It is for our enjoyment. When you hear the bell, remember to come back to the here and the now, and to recognize your food, and the Sangha. Learn to welcome the sound of the bell like a friend, like the Buddha smiling to us and wanting us to enjoy each moment of our retreat. I know that you all just arrived today, and are still tired, so I will continue tomorrow.

[BELL]

The Sixteen Ways of Breathing

FORM

1. in/out
2. long/short
3. experiencing body
4. calming body

FEELINGS

5. experiencing joy
6. experiencing bliss
7. experiencing mental formations
8. calming mental formations

MENTAL FORMATIONS

9. experiencing mind
10. gladdening mind
11. concentrating mind
12. liberating mind

PERCEPTIONS

13. contemplating impermanence
14. contemplating non-craving
15. contemplating nirvana
16. contemplating letting go

CHAPTER TWO

Enjoying Our Breathing

[BELL]

Good morning, dear friends. Today is the twenty-fourth of May, 1998, the first day of our twenty-one-day retreat.

The Four Foundations of Being

The practice of mindful breathing brings us back to the four foundations of our being, so we can take care of them and bring about healing and transformation. As you can see on page 14, the first foundation of our being is our body. The practice of mindful breathing is to bring us back home to our body, to reconcile ourselves with our body, to take care of our body, to look deeply into our body, to understand our body, and to allow transformation and healing to take place.

The second foundation of our being is our feelings. Very often, we leave our feelings unattended. Mindful breathing helps us go back to our feelings to recognize them, reconcile ourselves with them, and look deeply into their nature so that understanding is possible. By practicing mindful breathing, we take good care of our feelings; we can calm them, transform them, and heal them. Our feelings are very much interconnected with our body. We cannot take our feelings out of our body, and we cannot take our body out of our feelings. They inter-are.

The third foundation of our being is our mental formations.

Formation means a thing that is conditioned by different kinds of elements. A flower is a physical formation. It is made of several elements. When these elements come together, a flower manifests itself. Among its elements, we can see the sunshine. If we touch the being of a flower deeply, we touch the sunshine. We know that we cannot take the sunshine out of a flower. If we did, the flower would collapse. There would be no flower. The flower and the sunshine inter-are. When we touch a flower deeply, we also touch a cloud. There is a cloud in the heart of a flower, and we cannot take the cloud out of the flower. The cloud and the flower inter-are. If we continue to look deeply, we can see the earth, the minerals, the air, and everything in a flower. All these elements have come together to bring about the formation called "flower." All formations are impermanent. When one of the conditions is no longer sufficient, the formation dissolves. There is no flower.

There are other kinds of formations that are not physical, like fear. Fear is a mental formation; it is made of several elements, including the element of ignorance. Despair, anguish, attachment, love, and mindfulness are all mental formations. In the teaching of my tradition, there are fifty-one categories of mental formations. Mindful breathing brings us close to our mental formations as they manifest within ourselves. Sometimes fear manifests, and our mindful breathing brings us back to our fear so that we can embrace it. We look deeply into the nature of our fear to reconcile ourselves with it. If we do well, we can calm our fear, look deeply into it, and discover its true nature. Insight into our fear helps us transform it. This is true with all mental formations — such as anger, despair, agitation, and restlessness. Sometimes restlessness is present as a form of energy, and it prevents us from being peaceful. It prevents well-being. When restlessness manifests itself within us, we can practice mindful breathing in order to come back to it, to hold it mindfully, tenderly, and lovingly. The practice consists of two parts: the first part is calming; the second part is looking deeply. We calm down our mental formation, look deeply into it, and see its deep roots.

As soon as you use the energy of mindfulness to hold your mental formation, there is a tendency in that mental formation to calm down. As you continue holding your mental formation, you are capable of looking into it, and you begin to have the insight you need regarding what kinds of conditions have brought that mental formation to you. This is the practice of looking deeply, which we call *vipassana* in Pali, or *vipashyana* in Sanskrit.

The fourth foundation of our being is our perception. Most of our suffering comes from our wrong perceptions. We do not have correct insight about the nature of reality. Mindful breathing brings us back to ourselves to investigate the nature of our perceptions. Looking deeply into the nature of our perceptions, we discover the reasons why we suffer, or why our fear or despair are born. If we know how to practice looking deeply into the nature of our perceptions, the insight we get liberates us from our suffering, grief, and fear. We practice looking deeply into the true nature of reality, the true nature of a flower, the true nature of our body, of our feelings, or of our mental formations. Form, feelings, and mental formations are all the objects of our perceptions.

We have seen that form and feelings inter-are. We cannot take form out of feelings nor take feelings out of form. The same is true of mental formations and perceptions. These four foundations of our being — form, feelings, mental formations, and perceptions — inter-are. We cannot take one out of the other three. If we know the art of looking deeply, we will discover reality as it really is. By doing so, we remove all errors and wrong perceptions. This is liberation through understanding, salvation by knowledge. If we speak in terms of grace, grace is understood here as wisdom, as knowledge, as understanding. We know that sometimes we suffer because of our ignorance, jealousy, and anger. At the base of our jealousy and anger is ignorance, because we don't understand why we suffer. The moment we begin to understand our jealousy, our anger begins to dissolve. That is why understanding is the liberating factor, and the aim of the practice of meditation is to get this liberating insight. That is why our perceptions are so important. We have to go back to them and inquire about their nature.

[BELL]

The Art of Self-Healing

About fifteen years ago I met a young person in Montréal. He told me that he was going to die. He had cancer. The doctors said that he had about three weeks to live, maybe less, maybe more. I was sitting next to him at the breakfast table. I ate my breakfast mindfully, not thinking about how to help him; I just ate my breakfast mindfully. When I finished my breakfast, I turned to him and talked to him about living deeply in the present moment. Even if you only have one or two weeks to live, you can still practice living deeply in each moment of your life. I told him that some people live for sixty, seventy, or eighty years, but they do not know how to live deeply each moment of their daily lives. They have not had the chance to do that. Seventy or eighty years may not mean a lot. If you know how to live deeply each moment of your daily life, three weeks is a lot. He was interested in what I told him, and I gave him instructions on how to enjoy breathing and walking. Even with his diagnosis, he continued to live for another eleven years. He received the Five Mindfulness Trainings,* and I gave him the Dharma name "True Life."

The Buddha said that if you have a wound within your body or within your mind, you can learn how to take care of it. There are many ways of taking care of your wound. You allow the wound in your body and soul to heal. You do not stand in the way of its healing. But very often we do just that. We forbid our

* See appendix 2 and Thich Nhat Hanh, *For a Future to Be Possible: Commentaries on the Five Mindfulness Trainings* (Revised Edition) (Berkeley: Parallax Press, 1998).

body to heal itself; we do not allow our mind, our consciousness to heal itself, because of our ignorance. We know that our body has the capacity to heal itself. When we cut our finger, we don't have to do much. We just clean it and allow it to heal — maybe for one or two days. If we tamper with the wound, if we worry too much or do too many things to it, it may not heal. Especially when we worry too much about it.

The Buddha gave the example of someone who is hit by an arrow. The person suffers. If soon afterwards a second arrow strikes him in exactly the same spot, the pain is not just double, it is ten times more intense. If you have a wound within your body and you magnify it with your worry and your panic, the wound will become more serious. It would be helpful to practice breathing in and breathing out and understanding the nature of the wound. Breathing in, we think, "I am aware that this is only a physical wound. It can be healed if I allow it to do so." If you need to, you can ask a friend or a doctor to confirm that your wound is only minor, and that you shouldn't worry. You should not panic, because panic is born from ignorance. Worry and panic are mental formations. They make the situation worse. You should rely on your knowledge of your own body. You are intelligent. Do not imagine that you are going to die because of a minor wound in your body or soul.

We know that when an animal is wounded, it looks for a quiet place to lie down. Wisdom is present in the animal's body. It knows that rest is the best way to heal. It does not do anything, not even eat or hunt; it just lies down. Some days later, it can get up. It is healed. Human beings have lost confidence in their body. We panic and try to do many different things. We worry too much about our body. We do not allow it to heal itself. We do not know how to rest. Mindful breathing helps us to re-learn the art of resting. Mindful breathing is like a loving mother holding her sick baby in her arms saying, "Don't worry, I'll take good care of you, just rest."

We have to re-learn the art of resting. Many of us do not know how to make use of our vacations. Very often we are more tired after a vacation than before it. I hope we can bring together our insights on how to rest in our Dharma discussions. We will learn the art of relaxation and resting during this retreat, and practice deep relaxation together.

[BELL]

We have to believe in our body's capacity to heal itself. The power of self-healing is a reality, but many of us don't believe in it. Instead, we take a lot of vitamins and medicine that may sometimes be more harmful to our body than not. An animal knows that four or five days without food will not harm it, it will help. But we are afraid of fasting. We think that if we don't eat, we will be weakened, and that healing will not take place. That is not true. In ancient times, people often fasted for several weeks. It is a wonderful way to begin the healing in our body and in our consciousness. In Plum Village we have fasting retreats. We do not eat for two or three weeks. This is something we can all do. During our fast, we follow our normal schedule. I continue to give Dharma talks and practice walking meditation outdoors with the Sangha. I continue to practice sitting and doing daily work. If you are afraid, you cannot do it. You need confidence. Your body can go without food for several weeks. You begin by skipping dinner and using that time for total relaxation or slow walking meditation. When you have experienced the joy of fasting, you will have faith in the practice. The capacity for self-healing is a reality in your body and your consciousness.*

We have to trust the power of understanding, healing, and loving within us. It is our refuge. It is the Buddha. It is the Kingdom of God existing within us. If we lose our faith and confidence in it, we lose everything. This is not abstract, it is very real.

* For more information on fasting, see chap. 11.

We can touch it, hold it, and take refuge in it. Instead of panicking or giving ourselves up to despair, we practice mindful breathing and put our trust in the power of self-healing, self-understanding, and loving within us. We call this the island within ourselves in which we can take refuge. It is an island of peace, confidence, solidity, love, and freedom. Be an island within yourself. You don't have to look for it elsewhere. Mindful breathing helps you go back to that precious island within, so that you can experience the foundation of your being.

When you find yourself in a dangerous or difficult situation, or when you feel like you are losing yourself, mindful breathing helps you go back to the island of self. We have a song that we sing. It appears on the following page.

As you sing this song, you take refuge in the safe island of mindfulness, and you recover your calm and serenity. You feel much better.

Our practice is based on the insight that mindfulness is the energy of the Buddha that is within us. To be mindful means to be here, fully present, with body and mind united, not in a state of dispersion. Mindfulness is the energy we generate in mindful walking, mindful breathing, sitting, and even washing dishes. It is a protecting agent, because within mindfulness is the energy of concentration and insight. Mindfulness makes it possible for us to understand, to accept, to love, and to relieve suffering. That is why the island of mindfulness is our best refuge. Before passing away, the Buddha recommended to his students that they take refuge in the island of mindfulness within themselves.

Our Appointment with Life

The practice of resting, of stopping, is crucial. If we cannot rest, it is because we have not stopped. We have continued to run. We began to run a long time ago. We even continue to run in our sleep. We think that happiness and well-being are not possible in the here and the now. That belief is inherent in us. We have

Being an Island Unto Myself

Thich Nhat Hanh

Arrangement by Betsy Rose and Children

received the seed of that belief from our parents and our grandparents. They struggled all of their lives, and believed that happiness was only possible in the future. That is why when we were children, we already had the habit of running. We believed that happiness was something to seek in the future. But the teaching of the Buddha is that you can be happy right here, right now. The conditions for your well-being and happiness can be found in the here and the now. This is the teaching of living happily in the present moment *(Drstadharmasukhavihari)*.

If you can stop and establish yourself in the here and the now, you will see that there are many elements of happiness available in this moment — more than enough for us to be happy. Even if there are a few things present that we dislike, there are still plenty of positive conditions for our happiness. When we walk in the garden, we may see that a tree is dying. We may feel sorry about that and may not be able to enjoy the rest of the garden that is still beautiful. We allow one dying tree to destroy our appreciation of all the other trees that are still alive, vigorous, and beautiful. If we look again, we can see that the garden is still beautiful, and we can enjoy it. We look into the four foundations of our being — form, feelings, mental formations, and perceptions — and we know that we contain elements that are beautiful, refreshing, and healing. We allow these elements to be present for us. Let us look at our eyes:

Breathing in, I am aware of my eyes.
Breathing out, I smile to my eyes.

This is mindfulness of our eyes. When we generate the energy of mindfulness, we embrace our eyes and smile to them. We touch one of the conditions for happiness that exists. Having eyes that are still in good condition is a wonderful thing. A paradise of form and colors is available to us at any time. We need only to open our eyes. Yet many of us are not capable of enjoying this paradise because we allow our worry, suffering, and anger to overwhelm us, and we lose our paradise. So, take the hand of your little boy or little girl and invite him or her to walk in paradise and to recognize the beautiful forms and colors that surround you. This is an easy exercise to do.

Breathing in, I am aware of my heart.
Breathing out, I smile to my heart.

When you use the energy of mindfulness to embrace your heart and smile to it, you see that your heart is still functioning normally, and that is a wonderful thing. Many people wish they had a heart that functioned normally. It is the basic condition for our well-being, another condition for our happiness. When we hold our heart with the energy of mindfulness, our heart is comforted. We have neglected our heart for a long time. We think only of other things. We run after things that we believe to be the true conditions for happiness, while we forget our heart.

We even cause trouble for our heart in the way we rest, work, eat, and drink. Every time we light a cigarette, we make our heart suffer. We commit an unfriendly act towards our heart when we drink alcohol. We know that our heart has been working for our well-being for many years, day and night. Because of our lack of mindfulness, we have not been very helpful to our heart. We do not know how to protect the conditions of well-being and happiness within us. We can continue to do this practice with other parts of our body, like our liver. Embrace your liver with tenderness, love, and compassion. Generate mindfulness with mindful breathing and hold your body with mindfulness. When we direct the energy of mindfulness to the part of our body that we are embracing with love and tenderness, we are doing exactly what our body needs. If a part of our body does not feel well, we have to spend more time holding it with mindfulness, with our smile. We should do this once or twice each day.

[BELL]

Mindful Breathing

The first exercise of mindful breathing that the Buddha proposed is "In/out." It means "Breathing in, I know I am breathing in. Breathing out, I know I am breathing out." In this teaching, we consider our breath as part of our body. Our breathing is a physical formation. It is the door through which we go home to our self and reconcile ourselves with our self. The object of our mindfulness is our in-breath and out-breath, nothing else. We identify our in-breath as our in-breath and our out-breath as our out-breath. It is easy. Then, instead of reading to ourselves, "Breathing in, I know I am breathing in," we just use the word "in." When breathing out, we say "out." The words "in" and "out" are instruments in order to maintain our mindfulness. While breathing in, we are aware that we should nourish our in-breath. "In" is no longer a word; it is the reality of our in-breath. If we do this, all our thinking will stop.

We don't suppress our thinking at all. There is no effort to stop thinking. If we really enjoy our in-breath one hundred percent, then thinking suddenly stops. Sometimes we try to force ourselves to be mindful. That is not good. Mindfulness is very enjoyable. When our practice is pleasant, concentration is easy. It's like a Dharma talk. If the Dharma talk is interesting, we are very awake, and if the Dharma talk is boring, we try and try but still we remain sleepy. The key is to make it interesting. The secret is to make it pleasant. We breathe so that our in-breath and out-breath are pleasant, so that we are awake and mindful, and our concentration is strong. If concentration is here, then insight will be born. Mindfulness, concentration, and insight give birth to one another. Mindfulness carries the energy of concentration within itself, and concentration carries the energy of insight within itself.

During sitting meditation, you can sit and enjoy your in-breath and out-breath and nothing else. Make your in-breath mindful and genuine. This is already resting and healing. Sometimes you may like to lie down and enjoy your in-breath and out-breath. Please sit in such a way that your body can rest. You can sit erect like this, and yet your muscles are completely relaxed. Your head and spinal column form a straight line. Do not slouch. Sit erect and release all your muscles. Sit in a lotus or half-lotus position with or without a cushion. The cushion may be thick or thin. You need to find a cushion that suits your physical condition. Find a way of sitting that allows you to sit for at least twenty minutes without feeling tired or stiff. As soon as you sit down, begin mindful breathing and pay attention to your breath. Then pay attention to your sitting position. Relax the muscles in your face — there are about three hundred muscles in your face. Every time you get angry, worried, or afraid, these muscles are tense. People can see the tension in your face. If you breathe in mindfully and become aware of your face, and breathe out mindfully and smile lightly, you relax the hundreds of muscles in your face. Then you move down to your shoulders and also let go. Do not try hard to practice. If you struggle, you are using effort, and you cannot relax. Very soon you will feel the tension in your shoulder muscles, and you may get a headache.

When you sit and watch television, you don't make any effort. That is why you can sit there for a long time. When you sit in meditation, you struggle a lot, and that is why you cannot sit for very long. Please imitate the way you sit in the living room. Effortlessness is the key to success. Don't fight. Don't try hard. Just allow yourself to sit. This relaxing way of sitting is also resting. Allow your body to rest.

When you pour fresh juice into a glass and let it stand for fifteen minutes, all the pulp and particles sink down to the bottom of the glass. If you allow your body to sit in a relaxing, peaceful way, it calms your body and also your mind. Sitting like this allows you to enjoy your in-breath and out-breath, to enjoy being alive, to enjoy sitting here. To enjoy your in-breath and out-breath is a miracle, the miracle of being alive. And you are sitting with many people who are practicing in exactly the same way. Just sit there; don't try to become someone else. Your thinking will stop. You will touch the wonders of life that are available in the here and the now. This period of sitting is time worth living.

[BELL]

The second exercise of mindful breathing proposed by the Buddha is "Long/short." "Long/short" means to be aware of the whole length of your in-breath and out-breath. It does not mean we intentionally make a long in-breath or a short out-breath. It is not like that. The idea is nonintervention. The object of mindfulness in the first two exercises proposed by the Buddha is just your breath, your in-breath and out-breath, nothing else. The effect of these exercises is enormous.

We should not interfere with our breathing. This is very important. We know that breathing happens by itself. Our practice is to light the lamp of mindfulness and shine it on our breathing. We do not modify, bend, or make our breathing the way we want it. We cannot describe the practice as breath work. We are not working on our breath. We allow our breath to enjoy itself. This is mindfulness of breathing. It is like the vegetation and the sunshine. The sunshine just embraces the vegetation. It has an impact on the vegetation, but the work of the sunshine is to shine on the vegetation, embracing it. We do the same thing with our breathing. We don't try to mold our breathing. We just become aware of our in-breath and out-breath as our in-breath and out-breath. If our in-breath is short, we let it be short; if our out-breath is long, we let it be long. We don't try to make them shorter or longer.

When we touch our breathing with mindfulness, the quality of our breathing improves, and a feeling of well-being is born in our body and mind. The calm and harmony of our breathing helps our body be calm and harmonious, too, and the calm and harmony of our body affects our mind.

Sometimes we think and worry nonstop. It is like having a cassette tape continually turning in our mind. It is like leaving a television set on for a long time. It becomes hot. Our head also becomes hot because of our thinking. We cannot sleep well; we cannot stop. Because we cannot stop or sleep, we worry about that, and we go to a doctor who is ready to give us a prescription. Even if we use sleeping pills, we cannot rest, because in our dreams we continue to run, think, and worry. The alternative medicine is mindful breathing. If we practice mindful breathing for five minutes, allowing our body to rest, then we can stop thinking for five minutes. During that time, we don't think at all. The words "in" and "out" are not concepts; they are not thinking. They are a guide for mindfulness of breathing. When we think too much, the quality of our being is reduced. If we can stop thinking, we increase the quality of our being. There is more peace, relaxation, and rest. That is why we cannot say, "I think, therefore I am." I think, therefore I am not.

I Have Arrived

We might like to use a *gatha* (mindfulness verse) to enjoy the practice of breathing and walking, like: "I have arrived. I am home." Yesterday I spoke about slow walking. We take one step with our in-breath and one step with our out-breath. We can also walk more quickly. We can take two or three steps with one in-breath, "I have arrived, arrived. I am home, home." (two steps) "I have arrived, arrived, arrived. I am home, home, home." (three steps) We practice arriving in the here and the now.

About fifteen years ago, I went to India to visit the Buddhist community of the untouchables. A friend organized this teaching tour for me. He belonged to that caste, which has been discriminated against for many thousands of years. He was sitting with me in the bus, next to me on my right. I was enjoying the Indian countryside very much. When I looked at him, I saw that he was very tense. He had done everything to make my visit pleasant, but he continued to worry. This habit energy had been transmitted to him from many generations of ancestors. They had struggled all their lives, for many generations, against discrimination. It is very hard to transform that kind of habit. I said, "Dear friend, why are you so tense? There is nothing to do now here on the bus. We can enjoy the countryside. When we arrive, our friends will come to the station to get us. Sit back and enjoy the countryside and smile." He said, "OK." But just two minutes later, he looked exactly as before, very tense, thinking about the future, and not being able to be at ease in the here and the now.

Our practice is to be aware that all the wonders of life are available in the here and the now, and that we should stop running. While practicing walking meditation, we should stop. While practicing sitting meditation, we should stop. While enjoying our breakfast, we should stop. There are some people who sit down to have a meal but continue to run inside. They are not capable of stopping, being in the here and the now, and just enjoying a slice of tomato or a carrot. Let us support each other in order to really stop. The Buddha said, "The past is already gone. The future is not yet here. There is only one moment for you to live. That is the present moment." We have an appointment with life in the present moment. If we miss the present moment, we miss our appointment with life. We can all understand this.

But our habit energy is so strong. That is why we need each other in order to stop and establish ourselves in the present moment. Eating together is an occasion for us to stop. W[illegible]ing [illegible]gether is also an opportunity to stop. Sitting together, enjoying our in-breath and out-breath, is another opportunity to stop. Every time the horse of habit energy shows its head, pushing us on, we breathe in and out and say, "My dear friend, I know you, the habit energy of running." We smile to it, and it is not able to push us any more. It will go away. Sometime later, if it manifests itself again as a mental formation, we breathe in and out and say, "My dear friend, I know you." We simply recognize a mental formation. Every time we practice like this, it loses some of its strength. We don't have to fight. All we have to do is recognize it and smile to it. Our true home is in the here and the now. It is in the island of self within. We can only touch life in all its wonders in the here and the now. It's like when we hear the bell. We practice, "Listen, listen. This wonderful sound brings me back to my true home."

Later, you might want to use the second line of the gatha, "In the here and in the now." "In the here" is for your in-breath; "in the now" is for your out-breath. "The here and the now" is the address of your true home, its zip code. "In the here and in the now" means the same as "I have arrived. I am home." They are just different words. It is up to you how long to enjoy each exercise. Later on, you may use the third line, "I am solid. I am free." This is not autosuggestion. If you have arrived, then you have cultivated more solidity and freedom. As you walk mindfully, you touch your true home, and you become more solid, because you are not running anymore. You have reclaimed the freedom to be yourself. Before that, you were a victim of the past and the future, both pulling you in different directions. Now you are more yourself; you have reclaimed some of your liberty. "I am solid. I am free." You are no longer a victim.

In the teachings of the Buddha, solidity and freedom are the two characteristics of nirvana. You begin to touch nirvana when you cultivate mindfulness of walking or breathing. At the same time, you cultivate the elements of solidity and freedom. Happiness is possible on the ground of solidity and freedom.

[BELL]

This solidity and freedom introduces us to the world of the ultimate. The last line of the gatha is, "In the ultimate I dwell." This is best understood when we practice the last four exercises on mindful breathing concerning our perceptions. So let us help each other enjoy our sitting. Sitting is an enjoyment, not hard labor for enlightenment. Mindful walking is an enjoyment, and eating breakfast is an enjoyment. If we enjoy the practice, then the practice becomes pleasant, nourishing, and healing for us. Shall we sing "I have arrived. I am home" together so that everyone can memorize it? Then we will practice walking meditation together.

I Have Arrived

Thich Nhat Hanh
Arrangement by Betsy Rose

[REPEAT]

[BELL]

CHAPTER THREE

Embracing Our Body

[BELL]

My dear friends, my dear Sangha, today is the twenty-fifth of May, 1998, and it is the second day of our twenty-one-day retreat. For those of you who have just arrived, and who were not here for the orientation, I would like to remind you that the convening of the Sangha is a great opportunity, and that we should allow ourselves to be in the Sangha, to surrender to the Sangha, to allow the energy of the Sangha to penetrate our body and our consciousness. We trust the Sangha, because the Sangha is practicing, and the collective energy of mindfulness is strong. We profit a lot from that collective energy.

Of course, we also rely on the energy of mindfulness that we generated in our personal practice. But sometimes that is not enough. If we know how to use that energy in order to receive the collective energy of the Sangha, we will have a powerful source of energy for transformation and healing. Again, we can return to the example of a smile. Maybe a lady will sit next to you who has practiced well, but the smile on her face has not fully bloomed. She has arrived at eighty or ninety percent of her capacity to smile. You can produce the energy of mindfulness and support her. You can smile your wondrous smile of mindfulness and supply her with the ten percent that she lacks. Suddenly she is able to smile, and when she smiles like that, all the ancestors in her smile at the same time. It is wonderful. A smile is not an individual product; it is a co-product.

Whatever transformation and healing we receive during this retreat is a co-product of the Sangha. Please allow the Sangha to be in you, to hold you like a mother holding a baby. Allow yourself to trust the Sangha and profit from its collective energy. This is how we can best profit from our retreat.

Yesterday we learned about the first exercise of mindful breathing, "Breathing in, I know I am breathing in. Breathing out, I know I am breathing out." We can also say, "Breathing in, I know that this is my in-breath. Breathing out, I know that this is my out-breath." We identify our in-breath as our in-breath and our out-breath as our out-breath. We also learned that we should not interfere with our breathing. We should just allow our breathing to unfold naturally. We produce the energy of mindfulness to become aware of our in-breath and our out-breath. If we continue breathing in and out like this, the quality of our breathing will improve naturally. Our breathing will become deeper and more harmonious. Mindful breathing influences our body and mind without trying to influence them.

The second breathing exercise is, "Breathing in a long breath, I know I am breathing in a long breath. Breathing out a long breath, I know I am breathing out a long breath. Breathing in a short breath, I know I am breathing in a short breath. Breathing out a short breath, I know I am breathing out a short breath." We do not make our breath long or short. Our mindfulness is nourished throughout the duration of our in-breath and out-breath. We know how long or short it is. The words "long" and "short" do not mean much. Between long and short is mid-length, pretty long, and somewhat short. We cannot really call our breath long or short. The practice is to be aware of the length of our in-breath and out-breath. This can also be called our breath body.

When we look into these two exercises, we see that when we practice the first exercise well, we are also practicing the second one well. "Breathing in, I know I am breathing in." We are aware throughout our in-breath. Practicing with awareness, we are already doing the second exercise. And when we practice the second exercise well, we are also doing the first exercise. As we go along, we will see the nature of interbeing of all sixteen exercises.

[BELL]

We can train ourselves to see the nature of interbeing. Our first breath is made of the second. If we practice the first exercise well, we are practicing the second exercise at the same time. If we bring forth the second exercise from the first, the first is no longer the first. It's wonderful. The nature of interbeing can be seen in everything, including one breathing exercise.

Experiencing Our Body

Now we come to the third exercise of mindful breathing, "Breathing in, I am aware of my whole body. Experiencing my whole body, I breathe in. Breathing out, I am aware of my whole body. Experiencing my whole body, I breathe out." First, we have to understand that this is an attempt to go back to our body and reconcile ourselves with it. We may have the feeling that our body is us. It is very close to us, very dear to us. Sometimes we believe that. But sometimes we believe our body is a stranger to us. We hate our body and wish that we didn't have one. We don't want our body anymore; we want to get rid of it. These attitudes show that we are alienated from our own body, and that is why we have to go home to our body and reconcile ourselves with it. Our breathing is part of our body. Our breath is the door through which we can go back to our body, our perceptions, and so on. We have come to the door to embrace our breathing. Mindfulness is thus born. Mindfulness is the energy that embraces our in-breath and our out-breath. We have become one with our in-breath and out-breath. As our practice continues, our in-breath and out-breath become deeper, more harmonious, more peaceful.

Then we go a bit deeper and touch our body, "Experiencing my whole body, I breathe in. Experiencing my whole body, I breathe out." We go home to our body and embrace it. We reconcile ourselves with our body. We might do this in a sitting position or lying down. It is very important to go back to our body and show our concern, attention, and love. Our body might be suffering. It might have been abandoned for a long time. That is why we generate the energy of mindfulness and go back to embrace our body. This is the beginning of the practice of love. We become aware of our body; we are determined to take good care of our body. And our body will feel much better when we are able to do so.

Sabbakaya means the whole body. During our in-breath we become aware of our body as a whole. We embrace our body in its entirety. The object of our mindfulness is no longer our in-breath alone. It now includes our body. We embrace our body tenderly during our in-breath and out-breath with the intention to reconcile ourselves with it, to take care of it, and to show our concern and loving kindness. You may want to modify the language a little, but the content of the practice is the same: "Breathing in, I am aware of my body. Breathing out, I smile to my body." This is a smile of awareness, a smile that shows your concern and loving kindness.

How much time do we spend going back to our body, holding it tenderly with the energy of mindfulness, and smiling to it? Each of us knows that we need to do this a lot. We need to spend time just doing that, holding our body with our awareness very tenderly, with a lot of compassion, and smiling to it, with the smile of recognition, "Oh, my body, I know you are there. I will take good care of you." Let us now practice holding our body with mindfulness and smiling.

[BELL]

Now we pay attention to each part of our body — our eyes, lungs, heart, and liver — in the way I suggested yesterday: "Breathing in, I am aware of my eyes. Breathing out, I am aware of my eyes." As you continue to do this, many kinds of insights will come, bringing you a lot of happiness, and liberating you. In the *Discourse on the Four Establishments of Mindfulness,* the Buddha said, "A farmer goes down into his cellar and brings up a bag of seeds. He opens one side of the bag and lets all the seeds flow out onto the floor. He is able to recognize, 'These are kidney beans. These are mung beans. These are corn kernels.'" The farmer can identify the different types of seeds because his eyes are still in good condition.

When you go back to your body, first you may want to embrace your body as a whole, in its entirety. Afterwards, you can pay attention to the different parts of your body, like the farmer identifying the seeds. In the discourse, the Buddha mentions thirty-six parts of the body. Each part should be embraced by our mindfulness, and we should smile to it. First we enjoy relaxing, either sitting or lying down. Please do total relaxation at least once a day during our retreat. We can do it together as a Sangha, but if you have five, ten, or fifteen minutes available, please lie down on the grass and do it on your own. This is the practice of compassion, of love, directed to your body. After a few minutes of relaxation with the help of mindful breathing (total relaxation cannot be perfect without mindful breathing), then you direct your attention to each part of your body. In the *Discourse on the Four Establishments of Mindfulness,* these parts of the body are listed: bone, marrow, kidneys, blood, and so on. You breathe in and embrace each part of your body with mindfulness, like a mother holding her baby in her tender arms. And smile to it. This is very healing, very important.

When you practice "Breathing in, I am aware of my liver. Breathing out, I smile to my liver," your liver might react right away, "Oh, I have been waiting for this for a long time. I have been sending SOS messages for help, day and night. But he just neglected me. He continued to drink and smoke. And it gives me a hard time. I could not tell him how hard it is for me to bear all that. I suffer so much day and night, and I work so hard day and night, and my message has been neglected." If we practice mindful breathing, we will get a lot of relief. If we pay attention to our liver and smile to it, we will get some insight into the condition of our liver. Our liver has been trying its best to maintain our well-being, but we have been neglectful.

Forgetfulness is the opposite of mindfulness. We have been forgetful, and we didn't know it. For the first time, we pay attention to our liver. Our liver is comforted at that moment. If we continue for three, four, or five breaths, then insight will come. There is the intention to be kind to our liver, to protect it, because we know that our liver is a condition for our well-being. When that awareness is born, we know what to do and what not to do. We don't need anyone to tell us to stop drinking alcohol. We just embrace our liver and stop drinking and ingesting the poisons that harm it. Each part of our body should be embraced and taken care of in exactly the same way.

[BELL]

Awareness of the Four Elements in the Body

According to the *Discourse on the Four Establishments of Mindfulness,* we can begin to look into our bodies and recognize the basic elements that have helped to make our bodies possible. "Breathing in, I am aware of the earth element within myself. Breathing out, I smile to the earth element within myself." There are four basic elements *(mahabhuta):* earth, fire, water, and air.

The earth element is the element of solidity in us. If we recognize the earth element within us, we can also recognize the earth element outside of our body. We know that they both belong to the earth. There is a constant exchange between the earth element inside and outside. It happens in every second of our daily life.

"Breathing in, I am aware of the fire element within my body." This is heat. We know that life is made of combustion. We breathe in air and use the oxygen for combustion. This process takes place every second, every fraction of a second, within us. Thanks to this process, life is possible. Birth and death are also taking place simultaneously in every moment. We know that the cells in our body continue to die and continue to be born. If there is no death, there can be no birth. We might get the insight that death contains birth and life, and life contains death. If you take death out of life, life collapses. If you take life out of death, death will collapse.

It is like the example of the flower, the cloud, and the sunshine — looking at the flower we can see the cloud and the sunshine. We have to train ourselves to look in this way. We are used to a dualistic way of looking. We think that death is the enemy of life. When we practice looking deeply (and not only meditators practice looking deeply, scientists also practice looking deeply, but with different kinds of instruments), we see that life carries death within herself, and death carries life within herself. Without one, the other is not possible. It would be naive to think that we could only take one half and not the other. From observing the elements within ourselves, we know that birth and death inter-are; they make each other possible. We begin to see something wonderful that we have never seen before.

Through deep looking, we can dissipate our fear, anguish, and despair. We know that fear, anguish, and despair can flourish only on the ground of ignorance. It is like this pencil. We think of this end as being the left, and the other end as the right. Sometimes we want only the left side, and not the right. Politically, you might prefer the left, and you might want to eliminate the right, but is it possible to have only the left? You want to eliminate the right side, so you take a knife and cut the pencil. But as soon as you cut it, this part becomes the right side. As long as the left remains, the right remains, also. We are caught in pairs of opposites, and we have to train ourselves to look in a non-dualistic way if we want reality to reveal itself to us.

"Breathing in, I see the water element in me. Breathing out, I smile to the water element in me." The words "in" and "out" are also a pair of opposites. I have written a book called *The Sun My Heart.* I was inspired by the image of the sun as my second heart. I used to think that I just had a heart inside my body. If it stopped functioning, I would die right away. But if my other heart, the sun, collapsed, I would also die right away. My second heart is outside of my body. I might think that my lungs are just inside my body, but the mountains and the forests around me are also my lungs. If they don't breathe, there will be no oxygen for me to breathe. I have lungs inside my body and outside of my body. The idea of the body vanishes if you recognize the four elements both within and without. The idea of self, identified with the body, will also vanish. You need only to look deeply like this in order for your illusions to be dissipated. We touch the realm of no-birth and no-death. Self is possible only with nonself.

Awareness of the Positions of the Body

According to the teachings of the Buddha in the *Discourse on the Four Establishments of Mindfulness,* after contemplating the four elements in the body, you direct your mindfulness to the position of your body. There are four basic positions: sitting, standing, walking, and lying down. You become aware of the position your body is in. If you are sitting, be aware that you are sitting. If you are walking, be aware that you are walking. You shine the light of mindfulness upon the body's positions. The monks and nuns are trained very carefully in this. We can see that they are aware of the four basic positions by the way they sit, stand, walk, and lie down.

This teaching is not just for monks and nuns. It is for everyone. It belongs to the realm of contemplation of the body in the body. We begin by embracing our breath and becoming aware of our breath. Then we become aware of our body, and embrace our body. We become aware of each organ in our body, and embrace and smile to each part of our body. We are aware of each of the four elements within our body, and smile to each element within our body. Then we practice being aware of the position our body is in: standing, sitting, walking, or lying down. Please let us do this together during our retreat. If you sit, sit beautifully. If you walk, walk beautifully. If you stand, stand beautifully, with peace. And if you lie down, relax beautifully, also.

[BELL]

Awareness of Each Movement of the Body

Awareness of our body leads to awareness of each movement of our body. When you bend down to pick something up, be mindful of doing that. "Breathing in, I know that I am bending down to pick up that pen on the floor. Breathing out, I am picking it up now. Breathing in, I have already done that." You become aware of each movement and action that your body makes.

Suppose you are boiling water to make coffee in the morning. You can use that time as a practice. You become aware of each act, each movement, during the whole time you are making coffee. You smile to every act, however small it is. It is a joy, because you are living your daily life, knowing how to light the lamp of mindfulness and shine it on each moment, each act of the day. You do everything in the light of mindfulness. Mindfulness is the presence of God, is the energy of the Buddha within us, is the element of holiness within us. It is not something abstract. The seed of mindfulness lies deep in our consciousness. It is possible for each of us to touch the seed and invite it to manifest as energy. We know that we can cultivate the energy of mindfulness.

[BELL]

When I was a novice (I became a novice at the age of sixteen), one day my teacher asked me to do something for him. I loved my teacher very much, and I wanted to do it. I was motivated by the desire to make him happy. I went out, and I did not open the door and close it behind me mindfully. My teacher called me back. He said very quietly, "My child, this time go out more mindfully. Do better than last time." I bowed to him, and I knew what to do. I practiced walking meditation to the door. I held the doorknob mindfully, opened it, stepped out, closed the door behind me mindfully, and went out. My teacher did not have to ask me a second time.

I never forgot that teaching. In 1966, I went to Kentucky to visit Thomas Merton, the Trappist monk. We had a nice time together. Later, he spoke to his monks, and on one of the tapes, he said, "You only need to look at Thich Nhat Hanh opening and closing a door, and you know that he is an authentic monk." One year ago in Plum Village, a lady visited us from Germany. She stayed with us for one month. On the day she left, she told us that she had come to Plum Village because she had heard the tape by Thomas Merton. She had been curious to know how I opened and closed the door. She had had a good time being with us, observing us opening and closing doors for a month. Opening and closing the door is part of our practice that brings peace within. Please practice opening and closing the door mindfully for the joy and happiness of many people, and for the joy and happiness of my teacher. He is still here today.

What we have learned about mindful breathing regarding our body is important. We don't need to be a Dharma teacher to organize this practice. We can have a weekend practice to enjoy taking care of our body and reconciling ourselves with our body. We may invite a number of friends to come and practice giving their bodies a chance to rest and restore themselves. We can see the compassion of the Buddha clearly when we study the exercises on breathing with our body.

The fourth exercise of mindful breathing is, "Calming the activities of my body, I breathe in. Calming the formation called body, I breathe out." Our body deserves this kind of treatment. We should learn to be kind, to be understanding of our body. If one part of our body is ailing, we have to spend much more time holding it tenderly with the energy of mindfulness. And we smile to it. This will speed up our healing. No one questions a doctor's prescription. But it is not enough. If we don't allow our body to rest and heal, it may not heal with a prescription alone. We have to help it. Sometimes our body will heal itself without the prescription if we know how to allow our body to rest and restore itself.

"Experiencing my body, I breathe in. Smiling to my body, I breathe out. Calming my body, I breathe in. Smiling to my body, I breathe out." This is a wonderful practice that everyone can enjoy. We have to learn the art of mindful breathing, mindful living, mindful smiling, and mindfully taking care of our body. Students can set up mindfulness practice groups in their schools, because students are under stress; their bodies are under stress. Teachers are also under stress. They suffer because of their students. They can also set up a group to take care of their bodies. Psychotherapists can do the same. They take care of many people who suffer. If they don't take good care of themselves, they might become exhausted and give up. They can practice with other therapists or with a group of their clients. The police also suffer. They are victims of fear and stress. There is so much violence and suffering. They, too, can practice in a group and take good care of themselves. People living in correctional houses can also start a group. Anyone can practice mindfulness. You don't need to be a Buddhist. You don't need to be a Dharma teacher. You don't need transmission from a teacher in order to start a practice group. You can start a mindfulness practice group anytime, anywhere.

[BELL]

Three Discourses of the Buddha

Before I continue, I would like to introduce the three discourses of the Buddha, which may help you to learn more about this practice. During the Dharma talks I will refer to them often. The first one is called the *Discourse on the Full Awareness of Breathing.* Sister Annabel will read it with you. The heart of this discourse is the sixteen exercises of the practice of mindful breathing that we are learning (see page 14). I have written commentaries on this discourse in my book, *Breathe! You Are Alive.*

The second text is the *Discourse on the Four Establishments of Mindfulness:* form, feelings, mind, and objects of mind. It is important to use both discourses together, because they complement and complete each other. We should study the first discourse in the light of the second discourse, and the second discourse in the light of the first discourse. It has been translated from both the Chinese and Pali versions and published in my book, *Transformation and Healing.*

The third text is the discourse on living happily in the present moment, titled the *Discourse on Knowing the Better Way to Live Alone.* I have written commentaries on this text in my book, *Our Appointment with Life.* This is the most ancient text telling us how to live in the here and the now. You can use these three discourses as materials for further study. It is not necessary to read them during the retreat. It's better to use our time to practice together.

Mind and Body Inter-Are

In the teachings of the Buddha, the expression *namarupa* is sometimes used to refer to our person. *Nama* means "mental," and *rupa* means "physical." We make a distinction between the physical and the mental. We think that our body is physical, and our feelings, perceptions, mental formations, and consciousness are mental. This is a kind of discrimination. We tend to believe that nama is not rupa, and rupa is not nama. We should learn to look in the light of interbeing. If you take nama out of rupa, rupa will collapse, and if you take rupa out of nama, nama will collapse. Namarupa, body and mind, are two aspects of the same reality. Sometimes we call it nama, and sometimes we call it rupa. That is why instead of writing two words we can write namarupa.

This way of thinking is a little difficult in the beginning, but you will get used to it, like the nuclear physicist who says that elementary particles sometimes reveal themselves as waves and sometimes as particles. Yet it is the same reality. In the beginning, we think that if something is a wave, then it cannot be a particle, and if something is a particle, it cannot be a wave. In fact, an elementary particle sometimes manifests as a wave and sometimes as a particle. That is why scientists have created the word "wavicle." The same is true with our body and mind. We think that mind and matter are opposites, but mind can manifest as matter, and matter can manifest as mind. They are the same thing. It is strange, but it is the truth.

The Five Skandhas

The Buddha presents different ways of analyzing our being, sometimes as namarupa, sometimes as the Five Skandhas. The Five Skandhas are the five elements of our being. The first element is form; the second is feelings; the third is perceptions; the fourth is mental formations; and the fifth is consciousness. If we use the concept of namarupa to analyze our being, then the first element is physical and the other four are mental.

We have already spoken about formations. Formation means anything that is made of different kinds of elements. A flower is a formation. We can call it a physical formation. It belongs to the realm of rupa. Clouds and trees are also physical formations. Anger, fear, love, and hate are mental formations. In the teaching of my tradition, there are fifty-one categories of mental formations. When I was sixteen, I had to learn them by heart. Two of the *skandhas* — feelings and perceptions — are also mental formations. They are two of the fifty-one categories of mental formations. Because the practice of embracing and looking deeply into our feelings is so important, the Buddha singled out feelings as one skandha, or element, on its own. And because perception plays a very important part in our practice, it is also singled out as a separate category.

[BELL]

The fifth skandha is consciousness. What is consciousness? Consciousness means the ground of all mental formations. In the teaching of my tradition, sometimes we call it the store consciousness. Lying deep down in the bottom of the store consciousness are all kinds of seeds *(bijas)*. All of the fifty-one mental formations are buried in the form of seeds in the soil of our store consciousness and are ready to manifest themselves on the upper level of our consciousness. When we look at our consciousness, we see two layers. The upper part is the mind consciousness, the place in which all the mental formations manifest themselves. One, two, or three seeds can manifest themselves at the same time in the mind consciousness. The lower part is the store consciousness, storing all the seeds. Consciousness here is the base, the ground of all mental formations, including feelings and perceptions.

There are times when we are not angry. We laugh and have a good time. We are not angry because the seed of anger is lying deep in the bottom of our consciousness. Yet the seed of anger is always there. If someone says something that provokes us, he or she touches the seed of anger in our store consciousness, and it will manifest itself on the higher level of our consciousness and become a mental formation. That burning energy of anger makes our landscape ugly. The energy of anger pushes us to do and say destructive things.

The Four Establishments of Mindfulness

The Four Establishments of Mindfulness are the four foundations for looking deeply in our meditation. The first establishment of mindfulness is the contemplation of the body in the body; the second establishment of mindfulness is contemplation of the feelings in the feelings; the third establishment of mindfulness is contemplation of the mind in the mind; and the fourth establishment of mindfulness is the contemplation of objects of mind in objects of mind (dharmas). Here, "dharma" does not mean the Buddha's teaching, it means phenomena or formations, like a flower, a cloud, a tree, or anger. Dharmas are described as objects of mind. What is not an object of mind? Mountains, rivers, flowers, trees, anger, love, and our body are all objects of our mind. Dharmas are the phenomenal world.

Why does the Buddha say in the *Discourse on the Four Establishments of Mindfulness* that we contemplate the body in the body, the feelings in the feelings? Why this repetition? Because in order to practice mindfulness and looking deeply, we cannot remain as an observer, standing outside the object of our inquiry. This is important. When we breathe in mindfully and embrace our body, our breathing has to become one with our body in order for the practice to be successful.

Mind can manifest itself in fifty-one ways. Sometimes it manifests itself as love. Love always needs an object. Loving is always loving something or someone. There cannot just be love without an object. Consciousness is always consciousness of something. To be mindful means to be mindful of something. You cannot be mindful without an object. When you are mindful of your body and breathing, your body becomes the object of your mindfulness. This means it becomes mindfulness. When you breathe in and embrace your body, your body is your mindfulness. Your mindfulness has become your body, and your body has become your mindfulness. There is no more distinction between the subject and the object, the knower and the known. This is very important in the teaching of the Buddha and in our practice.

The French word *comprendre* means to understand, to comprehend. "Com" means "to be one with" and "prendre" means "to pick up," so comprendre means to pick something up and become one with it. When we want to really understand something, we have to be that thing. In deep meditation, the distinction between subject and object vanishes. There is no longer a distinction between the subject and object of cognition.

We have to train ourselves to be able to do this. We are used to saying that the body is not the mind, and that the mind is the subject of inquiry, the knower. The mind wants to know the body, and the body is the object. But according to the principle I mentioned, cognition is possible only with subject and object together, and both are born at the same time. It is like the moment you have the right side, you have the left side. That is why the Buddha said, "Contemplation of the body in the body. Contemplation of the feelings in the feelings." The frontier between subject and object is removed, and then understanding, penetration, becomes possible. The word "penetration" is good because it means that you no longer stay outside in order to observe. Scientists of our time have recognized this. In order to really understand an electron, you cannot be an observer. You have to be a participant.

[BELL]

When we say "mind," we mean both the subject of cognition and the object of cognition. When we say "mindfulness," we mean both the subject of mindfulness and the object of mindfulness. Mindfulness is not possible without the subject and object being present at the same time. Mindfulness is always mindfulness of something. When we distinguish mind and dharmas (objects of mind) as two separate establishments of mindfulness, that is only for the sake of our practice. They are objects for our practice, for our contemplation and deep looking. The same is true with the establishments of our body and our feelings. When we look deeply, we will recognize that the mind doing the looking and the object being looked at (our joy and pain, a tree, a cloud, our body, etc.) are all one. We can not have one without the other.

As I mentioned, in the *Discourse on the Full Awareness of Breathing,* the Buddha proposes the sixteen exercises of mindful breathing that we are learning together. The first four are for contemplating the body in the body. The first is "Breathing in, I know I am breathing in. Breathing out, I know I am breathing out. In/out." The second is "Long/short." The third is experiencing the body, "Awareness of the whole body, I breathe in and I breathe out." The fourth is "Breathing in, I calm my whole body. Breathing out, I calm my whole body."

The next four exercises are for contemplation of the feelings in the feelings. We are going to learn about them in the next few days. The third tetrad — exercises nine, ten, eleven, and twelve — are for contemplating the mind in the mind. Mind here means mental formations. The last tetrad — exercises thirteen, fourteen, fifteen, and sixteen — help us inquire about the true nature of the dharmas — reality as it is, or suchness. Because of our wrong perceptions, we do not see reality as it is. These four exercises help us to dissipate our ignorance so that reality can reveal itself to us. This is the kind of insight that liberates us from our ignorance, suffering, and fear.

All of our fifty-one mental formations are the concrete manifestation of consciousness. When we touch the fifty-one mental formations, we touch consciousness. Consciousness is the base of them all. It is the ground of all mental formations. It is like when we touch a wave, we cannot help but touch the water, because a wave is the water.

It is important to remember that our body is also a manifestation of our consciousness. In Buddhist psychology, we learn that our collective and individual consciousnesses are the ground for the manifestation of everything, including mountains, rivers, animals, vegetables, minerals, even our society. Everything is a product of our consciousness. The stock market is a product of our collective consciousness. The stock market has its ground in our mind, with all its fear and craving. The stock market does not rely on any objective thing. Our consciousness, both collective and individual, is the ground of manifestation of everything that is interbeing: rupa and nama. Consciousness is omnipresent. It is helpful to train ourselves to look in this way so we can understand the teachings of the Buddha more easily.

The last time I was in North America, I offered a retreat on the *Fifty Verses on the Manifestation of Consciousness* in Key West, Florida. We had the opportunity to discuss this aspect of the teaching: the world as a manifestation of our consciousness, collective and individual.* The collective and individual inter-are. If we take the individual out of the collective, the collective collapses. If we take the collective out of the individual, the individual consciousness collapses. Interbeing can be touched in every teaching.

This morning I spoke to you about living and dying. Many of us have not had the opportunity to look deeply into living and dying. We think that dying is the opposite of living. If we know how to practice deep looking in the ways the Buddha suggested, we discover that life and death inter-are. Death makes life possible, and life makes death possible. Both are the same reality. Sometimes reality manifests itself as death, sometimes it manifests as birth and life. When you have touched this reality, you are no longer subject to fear.

[BELL]

* See Thich Nhat Hanh, *Transformation at the Base: Fifty Verses on Buddhist Psychology* (Berkeley: Parallax Press, 2000).

CHAPTER FOUR

Questions and Answers Session One

Today is the twenty-seventh of May, 1998. We have time for questions and answers. I would appreciate it if you ask questions related to the Dharma talks I have offered — especially those concerning walking, breathing, sitting, and eating. I have read the questions and know that most of them will be addressed by the Dharma talks. When we come to a retreat, the noble silence and the quiet sitting may touch our seeds of pain and cause them to manifest. We have to be with our pain, and this is difficult. I can understand that.

About fifteen years ago, at a retreat in Denver, there was a man who resisted the practice and the teachings until the last day of the retreat. Six hours before the end of the retreat, he surrendered himself to the Sangha, and only then was he able to be happy.

I have a question from a lady who says that she cannot stop or rest in the present moment; she doesn't feel at rest.

There is a strong energy pushing us to move ahead. I know this habitual energy is very strong in this lady. No matter what she does, she doesn't feel at rest. That is exactly why we are offered the practices of sitting, eating, and breathing. While eating, we enjoy every morsel of food that we chew. If we are successful with one morsel, we can be successful with the second and the third. The practice of eating helps us stop. The practice of walking also helps us stop. If you feel that you cannot stop, practice walking meditation, taking one step at a time. If you can take one step that brings solidity and rest, then you can take another step.

The energy of restlessness within you may be very strong. As I have mentioned before, if you are agitated or restless and don't know how to cope with that energy — it does not allow you to be peaceful — you should recognize and name that energy as restlessness or agitation. Breathing in, you say, "I know you, the energy of restlessness." Just use your in-breath and out-breath to recognize it and smile to it. A few practitioners have already left the retreat because they did not succeed in walking or breathing like this. I know the first few days are always difficult. But if we find ourselves capable of being in the Sangha, we will receive its energy and be able to continue the practice. I am certain that by the end of the retreat, all of us will feel much better. The degree of healing and transformation will be different for each of us, but we will all have made progress in the direction of peace and healing. Let us have faith in the practice. Let us begin with one morsel of food, one in-breath, and one step. This is the only freedom that we have. It is through our in-breath, our morsel of food, and our step that we can reclaim the freedom we have lost. Whatever you are doing, scrubbing the floor or taking a step, breathe in and reclaim the liberty to become yourself. Then you will no longer be a victim of the energy of restlessness.

I would like to have a question directly from the Sangha.

Question: Thank you, Thây. This is a question from my Sangha back home. There are more and more Christian and Jewish practitioners who share the practice with us in the Order of Interbeing*

* The Order of Interbeing was established by Thich Nhat Hanh in Vietnam in 1966 as a way to help alleviate suffering through the practice of mindful living. The Order is guided by the Fourteen Mindfulness Trainings.

— not only laypeople, but also rabbis, priests, ministers, and pastors. The Fifth Precept presents a barrier for them. Our understanding of the Fifth Precept when it is taken for membership in the Order or in preparation for the Fourteen Precepts* for full membership in the Order is that not one drop of alcohol should pass our lips. Is it appropriate for people who consume small quantities of alcohol — such as wine at a Seder, wine at a Mass, or within the context of a sacred ritual — to receive the Fifth Precept, become a formal member of the Order, and receive the Fourteen Precepts?

Thầy: Now we use the phrase Mindfulness Trainings instead of Precepts, because they are really trainings in mindfulness. Every day, we have to learn to understand the Mindfulness Trainings more deeply and find ways to apply the teachings in our daily lives. No one can be perfect as far as the Five Trainings are concerned. When we speak about the Five Trainings or the Fourteen Trainings, we think about the direction we are going in. The North Star helps us face north, but just looking at the North Star does not mean we will go in a northerly direction. You have to take daily steps to go in that direction. The practice of the Mindfulness Trainings requires intelligence and skill. You should not be dogmatic. You cannot practice well if you are dogmatic. Those of us who practice not drinking alcohol know it is best not to drink any alcohol at all. If you drink a little, you may drink more and get drunk. In France, the Ministry of Health's advertisement on television says: "One glass of wine is OK, but three glasses are harmful." I tell young people, "If you don't drink the first glass, you will never drink the third glass."

Once, I proposed to a group of Catholic monks and nuns who came to a retreat that instead of using wine for the Eucha-

* For a commentary on the Fourteen Precepts, now called the Fourteen Mindfulness Trainings, see Thich Nhat Hanh, *Interbeing: Fourteen Guidelines for Engaged Buddhism* (Third Edition) (Berkeley, Parallax Press, 1998).

rist, they could use grape juice. Most of them accepted the idea. If you celebrate the Eucharist using wine, and you know that performing the rite will not harm your observance of the Mindfulness Trainings or cause any kind of destruction, I think it is OK to do it. You should not be too dogmatic about this. If consuming wine and alcohol causes destruction, that is another matter. We should not be dogmatic and we should be diligent in our practice. We follow the Mindfulness Trainings because we don't want to cause harm, damage, or destruction.

Question: Dear Thây, my daughter is twenty-four years old. When she gets upset or angry, and slams the door, I try to breathe and be mindful, but I feel her pain, and become very sad. I feel guilty that she doesn't cultivate mindfulness to help herself. What can I do to help?

Thây: We know that slamming doors is not pleasant. We know that it is not just a habit or due to a lack of skill or respect for other people. The seed of suffering may come from deep within a person, and manifests in different ways. Talking to the person — especially when he or she is not in a fresh state — is not very helpful. In order to understand, we should look deeply into the person's seeds of suffering and try to help the person practice to transform those seeds. We use loving speech to help him or her to see and practice. We cannot help transform anyone by using reproach. If we look deeply into ourselves, we may see that we have the same seeds of suffering. The practices of deep, mindful breathing and walking help us to recognize and transform our seeds. We can practice with our loved one. We go to her and say, "Dear one, I have the same seed of irritation in me, and when it manifests, I sometimes do things that make other people suffer. I have tried my best to recognize these seeds and transform my habitual energy." Then we tell her about our practice and our success in the practice. That alone can help. If she is able to understand, you can go further and invite her to practice with you. Practicing together is much more pleasant than practicing alone.

Question: My question concerns my own suffering. It's a little hard to talk about it. When I was very small, my father, who was an alcoholic, insisted on teaching me everything about sex for five years. I couldn't talk to him about this and decided to end my life when I was twenty. I was in a coma for several months and in hospital for a year. That was thirty years ago. I have done a lot to recover, but I still don't know how to trust life. I live through my mind and not my heart. When I am with a group of people, [crying] I want to scream. How do I surrender to other people's love? How do I trust them?

Thây: Many of us have a wounded child within. Many! And because we are so busy, we don't have time to go back to our wounded child and be with her or him to help with the healing. When we have been deeply wounded as children, it is hard for us to trust and love, and to allow that love to penetrate us. I always advise my friends to arrange their daily lives so that they have time to go back to themselves and take care of their wounded child. This is a very important practice.

There is an obstacle. Many of us know that we have a wounded child within us, but we are afraid to go back to ourselves and be with that child. The block of pain and sorrow in us is so huge and overwhelming that we run away from it. We run in the opposite direction. Even if we have time, we do not walk home to ourselves. We run away by reading novels, watching television, and having conversations. But in this practice, we are advised to go home and take care of our wounded child, even though this is difficult. We need instructions on how to do this so that we are not overwhelmed by the pain inside. We practice cultivating the energy of mindfulness to become strong enough. With this energy, we can go home and embrace our wounded child within. The practices of mindful walking, mindful sitting, and mindful breathing are crucial. Also, our friends' energy of mindfulness can help us. Maybe the first time we go home, we need one or two friends — especially those who have been successful in the practice — sitting next to us, to lend us their support, mindfulness, and energy. When a friend sits close to us and holds our hand, we combine his or her energy with our own and go home to embrace our wounded child within.

Some of my students have been wounded as children. I tell them to go home and talk to their wounded child within, to embrace that child with the energy of mindfulness. "Darling, I am here for you. I will take good care of you. I know that you suffer so much. I have been so busy and neglectful of you, and now I have learned a way to come back to you." You have to talk to your child several times a day. Only then can healing take place. The little child has been left alone for so long. That is why you have to begin the practice right away. Embracing your child tenderly, you reassure him that you will never let him down again or leave him unattended. If you have a loving Sangha, then your practice will be easier. To practice alone, without the support of brothers and sisters, would be too difficult for beginners. Taking refuge in the Sangha and having brothers and sisters to assist you, give advice, and support you in difficult moments is very important.

Your wounded child may represent several generations. Maybe your parents and grandparents had the same problem; they also had a wounded child within that they did not know how to handle, so they transmitted their wounded child to you. Our practice is to end this vicious cycle. If you can heal your wounded child, you will liberate the person who abused you. That person may also have been the victim of abuse. If you generate the energy of mindfulness, understanding, and compassion for your wounded child, you will suffer much less. People suffer because they have not been touched by compassion and understanding. When we generate mindfulness, compassion and understanding become possible. Then we can allow people to love us. Before, we were suspicious of everything and everyone. Compassion helps us relate to others and restore communication.

Question: Dear Thây, I have begun to hate our silent meals. They are not joyful but joyless. How can we draw energy from the Sangha when we, mostly strangers, are stopped from developing the relationships we need to be a Sangha? We are not, as in Plum Village, a monastic community. Maybe some meals should be silent and some should not.

Thây: Dear friends, you have been eating and talking for many, many years. We only have twenty-one days to practice together. We shouldn't believe that talking is the only way to communicate; talking may be an obstacle to communication. Television producers sometimes say, "We bring people together" — meaning that they bring information from one place to another, show us things that we haven't seen. The purpose of television or radio is to talk, but that is not necessarily communication.

A reporter from *Elle* magazine in Paris came to Plum Village. After interviewing the sisters and the lay practitioners, she wanted to interview me. She asked for a complete description on how to begin the practice. I said, "Young couples should turn off the television, and, instead of looking at the screen, look at each other." There is a background to this comment. A famous French writer, Antoine Saint Exupéry, said that to love each other means not to look at each other but to look in the same direction. He may be right, but not if you are looking in the direction of the television. I advise the opposite: Turn off the television and look at each other. Then you can ask, "Darling, are we a happy couple?" That is the real question. Then ask, "If not, why?" Start looking into your real situation. "We have jobs, a house, a television, everything, yet we are not happy. We don't feel at ease looking at each other, so we look at the television." That is the first meditation exercise: Turn off the television, look at each other, and ask the real question. If the couple spends half an hour discussing why they aren't happy, then they will see the cause of their unhappiness and be able to work together toward real happiness.

When we share a meal in mindfulness, the object of our mindfulness is the food. We communicate with the cosmos and recognize the food as a gift from the cosmos. If we are careful, we can communicate with the sunshine, the clouds, the earth, with everything. I eat my breakfast in the Upper Hamlet in Plum Village with an attendant, a novice monk. I usually have a piece of bread and a little yogurt sprinkled with salt. Looking out at the hills, I see the cows eating grass. Looking at the yogurt, I see that I am like a calf. My mother is a cow, and I am drinking her milk. I see the cow eating the grass, making yogurt for me. I look at the yogurt, and I know that the next Dharma talk that I will give is made of the yogurt I am eating. That kind of silent eating is very communicative and deep — and I don't need to say anything.

While we are eating, the second object of our mindfulness is the person sitting with us. Are we aware that they are sitting there? Each person has hope, fear, suffering, and happiness inside them. That person is willing to transform his or her suffering and to develop his or her capacity of understanding and of being joyful for the sake of many other people. Sitting with that person, looking at him or her, and knowing that he or she is a co-practitioner, a brother or sister in the Dharma, is very communicative. You don't need to talk to communicate. If you sit and radiate peace, stability, and joy, you are offering something very precious to the other person. If the other person is sitting and producing his or her true presence with solidity and peace, you can receive a lot of energy from him or her. True communication is possible in silence. Silence can be very elegant. It is a method of training.

Question: I had just begun to work with pride as an issue for healing when I saw your quote on a T-shirt, "In true love, there is no place for pride." Please speak about how to recognize and transform pride.

Thây: When someone you don't know hurts you by doing or saying something, you suffer. But when the person you love does the same thing, you suffer more. When you suffer, you want relief. Generally, you go to the person you love the most to tell him or her of your suffering. But in this case, it is impossible. You have pride, and you do not go to him and ask for help. You prefer to go to your room, lock the door, and cry. You are not capable of telling him how much you suffer and asking him to please help you. You are too proud. I say that in true love there is no place for pride. You know that your love is not true love when pride stands in the way. To love each other means to trust each other. If you don't go and tell the person you love the most of your suffering, it means you do not love him enough to trust him, to realize that he is the best person to help you. We should be able to get help from the person we love. That is why we must not let pride stand in our way.

[BELL]

CHAPTER FIVE

Experiencing Our Body

Today is the twenty-eighth of May, 1998. We have learned from the previous talk about experiencing the body: "Experiencing the body, I breathe in and I breathe out." When we are aware of our body and practice breathing in and out, we embrace our body with mindfulness. We have a chance to be with our body and look deeply into its nature. Out of this deep looking, we discover wonderful things, such as how life and death inter-are. There can be no life without death, and vice versa. We might also discover that each cell in our body contains all of our ancestors. A single cell can provide us with all the information we need concerning many of our past generations. This Dharma hall is large, but it could not contain the archives of all our ancestors.

We know that we can clone our body from just a single cell. This means that the teaching of the Buddha, that the one contains all, is correct. Our ideas of small and large, one and many, are just ideas. The infinitely large can be seen in the infinitely small. Each cell in our body is a wondrous manifestation of life, of our collective consciousness. We know that death takes place every second in our body and in our consciousness, but we don't mind. When a cell is dying, we don't mourn and organize a funeral. If we organized a funeral each time a cell died, there would be no time left to live! Thanks to our constant dying, life is possible.

Even though we see that life and death inter-are, we cling to our ignorance and say, "I only want to live. I don't want to die." Why? This is naive. In the *Satipatthanasutta,* the *Discourse on the Four Establishments of Mindfulness,* the Buddha advises us to look into our living body as well as our decaying body. We begin by holding our body mindfully and trying to look into it. We need to discover our consciousness and the many wonderful things that we don't know about our body, our feelings, our perceptions, and our mental formations. Meditation is a very exciting practice because it allows us to see, contemplate, and admire the wonders of life that are always available. Often, we are so busy that we miss them.

Calming Our Body

Let us look again at the fourth exercise of mindful breathing proposed by the Buddha: calming our body. We breathe in and breathe out. Through holding our body with the energy of mindfulness, we calm it; mindfulness has the capacity to calm and heal. The text says, "Calming the body formation, I breathe in" *(kayasankhara).* It means, "Calming the formation called body — or calming the body as a formation — I breathe in." A formation is a conditioned phenomenon, like a flower. If the right conditions come together, a formation manifests itself. Our body is a formation that manifests itself because conditions are sufficient and favorable. One day, when a certain condition is no longer present, our body will no longer manifest itself. That does not mean that our body goes from being to nonbeing. When conditions are sufficient and our body reveals itself, we think of it as existent, as being. When one condition is lacking, and our body does not manifest itself, we say it is nonexistent or nonbeing. Deep looking helps us to transcend the notions of being and nonbeing. When we strike a match and conditions are sufficient, a flame appears. We say that the flame exists. After we've blown it out, we say that the flame no longer exists. But the reality is that the flame is always there. Sometimes it manifests itself and sometimes it doesn't, and we cannot say the flame is existent or nonexistent. We can only say that sometimes the flame manifests itself, and sometimes it hides itself. When we can't see the flame, we say it doesn't exist. According to this teaching, the question is not "To be or not to be" — rather, "To manifest or not to manifest."

When we embrace our body and look deeply into it as a formation, we discover many things, such as fever, or lack of peace and harmony. We don't know how to take good care of our body. That is why our body holds suffering, instability, and disharmony. We have to go back to our body, hold it tenderly and mindfully, and calm it.

The Seven Miracles of Mindfulness

The energy of mindfulness has many functions. Calming is one of them. To practice meditation is, first of all, to generate and cultivate the energy of mindfulness. As we already know, the first function of mindfulness is to produce our true presence and make us alive in the present moment. Sometimes our body is here, but we are not really here.

In our daily lives, our body and mind seldom work together. Mindfulness brings us back home to the present moment, with body and mind united. This is why meditation is not just for meditators. In order to be truly alive, we have to practice mindful driving, mindful smiling, mindful eating, and mindful walking. Mindfulness allows us to do things well and avoid accidents.

Everyone needs mindfulness, and everyone is able to cultivate mindfulness. We breathe, smile, and bring our body back to our mind and our mind back to our body. We should practice like this and help our children to practice like this, so that we can be here for each other. When you love someone, the most precious gift you can make to that person is your presence. How can you love without being present? Being present is not difficult. You need only to breathe in, breathe out, smile, and become fully present. Then you go to your beloved and say, "Darling, I am really here for you." This is the best gift you can offer to your beloved. This is meditation.

The second function of mindfulness is to recognize that life is already here, that you can have real contact with it and make it meaningful and deep. When you are present, life is also present. Suppose you are watching a beautiful sunset with a group of people. Many of them are concentrating on the wonders of the sunset and contemplating them. But maybe one or two people, obsessed by their worries and fears, are not really present. For them, the beautiful sunset is not available as it is to the other people in the group. That is why we say that when you are truly present, life is also present. As I have mentioned before, we have an appointment with life in the present moment. We have to be in that moment so we don't miss our appointment.

When you are really present, you are able to recognize the presence of your beloved. To be loved means to be recognized as existing. It's very simple. When you are driving, you might think about everything except the person sitting by your side. You might completely ignore her. Your forgetfulness — not your presence or mindfulness — embraces her. A person who is ignored, whose presence is not acknowledged, slowly dies. Only mindfulness can bring her back to life. That is why when you are really present, you can look at your beloved and declare, "Darling, I know you are there, and I am very happy." Embraced by your mindfulness, your beloved will bloom like a flower. When two beings are real, there is authentic contact. I can touch a flower with my presence and my mindfulness. The flower will smile at me, and I will smile at the flower. Life is authentic and possible in that moment.

The third function of mindfulness is to touch and embrace. This function has two effects: to receive nourishment and healing, and to provide healing and calming. In this way, you and your beloved are both nourished. If the object of our mindfulness is fresh, refreshing, and healing, then we are freshened and healed by that contact, and vice versa. It says in the New Testament that everyone Jesus touched was healed, because the energy of the Holy Spirit lived in Jesus. To me, the Holy Spirit is the energy of being alive and fully present, and having the capacity for understanding and compassion. Similarly, wherever mindfulness exists, the ability to be fully alive and fully present, to recognize and touch, also exists. Nourishment becomes possible.

[BELL]

Please enjoy a few deep breaths before continuing.

Touching life helps you to be more alive, and makes life more real for you. Imagine that you're practicing mindful eating while eating an orange. If you are present one hundred percent, the orange, which is nothing short of a miracle, will reveal itself to you. You will also reveal yourself. This is orange meditation. The Dharma becomes a living Dharma, and life is deeply present.

We benefit from touching the refreshing, beautiful, and healing elements in life. The things we touch also benefit from this act. You and your beloved benefit from the refreshing and healing elements within both of you. If the object of your mindfulness is experiencing suffering, your mindfulness will help calm and relieve him or her. That is why the fourth exercise of mindful breathing is, "Calming our body, we breathe in." Since suffering, disharmony, and instability exist in our body, we embrace our body with mindfulness. Through deep touching and mindful embracing, we help our body suffer less and calm itself. "Calming the body as a formation, I breathe in. Calming the body as a formation, I breathe out." This is a time for healing. If you are not present, who will heal your body? You have to attend to your body's needs. If you have a therapist, the therapist can support you with his or her mindfulness, adding to your mindfulness. The touching may be deeper and the healing may take place more quickly if you are supported by co-practitioners.

When we practice walking meditation together, we use the energy of mindfulness we have generated to touch the Earth, healing both ourselves and the Earth. We have caused a lot of suffering to the Earth. The Earth needs healing, just like we do. That is why when we touch the Earth with peace and compassion, we help her heal. At the same time, we receive the Earth's healing power. This is the power of walking meditation. The energy of one or two hundred practitioners walking together is powerful, because the Sangha's collective energy strengthens our steps and makes them more solid and peaceful. The sight of a Dharma brother walking in front of us with stability and freedom helps us go back to ourselves. Suddenly, our steps become firmer, more peaceful. This is why we need the energy of the Sangha.

The fourth function of mindfulness is concentration. If we are mindful of something, we can concentrate on it. If we succeed in eating an orange mindfully and our mindfulness is solid, we can concentrate solely on the orange. We don't let our mind wander in other directions, worrying about the past or the future, or taking care of other things. We do only one thing — we get in touch with the orange. The energy of mindfulness carries within it the energy of concentration, much like a flower carries its particular color and perfume. We are concentration. Life can only become deep through concentration. By being concentrated in your daily life, you will come to understand and look more deeply into what is there. This is called deep looking, looking deeply into the nature of whatever is there — your body, your love, your hate, a flower, or a cloud. Deep looking concerns itself with insight and understanding, which will liberate you from your fear, despair, and suffering.

The fifth function of mindfulness is that when you are concentrated, you can practice living deeply. The sixth function is looking deeply. The seventh function is that the insights you gain can liberate you. As we continue to practice and generate this energy, we receive many benefits. The energy of mindfulness is the energy of the Buddha, because a Buddha is someone who is inhabited by such energy.

We do have some mindfulness, however we are not full-time Buddhas. We are only part-time Buddhas, because sometimes we are completely overwhelmed by forgetfulness. We know that the energy of the Buddha — mindfulness — is not abstract. Each one of us possesses the seed of mindfulness. For those of us who practice daily, this seed is important. Every time we touch it, it provides us with a lot of energy. If we have not had a chance to practice, the seed is small, but still there. This is the baby Buddha in us. If we practice, we give the baby Buddha a chance to grow. Every time we breathe in and smile, the Buddha in us grows. If we are too busy and always running in the direction of our habitual energy, the Buddha in us suffocates. She has no chance to grow and help us.

Wherever there is mindfulness, there is life, understanding, and compassion. That is why the energy of mindfulness, the energy of the Buddha, is equivalent to the Holy Spirit. The Holy Spirit is the energy of love. We have that energy within us. When we say, "God is in my heart," we mean exactly that. Mindfulness is there if we know how to nurture and develop it. We know that we have the source of the light of God to help us to heal, transform, and bring happiness to people around us.

"Calming the formation called body, I breathe in. Calming the formation called body, I breathe out."

[BELL]

Experiencing Joy and Bliss

The fifth exercise of mindful breathing is: "Experiencing joy, I breathe in, and I breathe out." The sixth is: "Experiencing bliss, I breathe in, and I breathe out." These exercises concern both our body and our feelings. Our body and feelings inter-are. We cannot remove our body from our feelings or our feelings from our body. Without one, the other cannot be. Before he became enlightened, the Buddha had many experiences and made many mistakes. Mistakes are nothing special; everyone makes them. The Buddha almost died because of his mistakes. That is why in the *Discourse on the Full Awareness of Breathing,* he teaches us to take good care of our body so that we may go far in the practice. We should learn how to nourish our body with joy and well-being. We can see the compassion and loving kindness in his teaching on experiencing and calming the body, and experiencing joy and bliss. The Buddha taught us not to simply regard our body as an instrument, but to take good care of it in order to go far.

In the teaching of my tradition, we speak of joy and bliss as our daily food. Meditation should provide you with joy, peace, and happiness. If it doesn't, you are not practicing correctly. Meditation is a source of food to nourish your body and consciousness. It should not be laborious, but nourishing and healing. The message is clear, but many of us don't understand it. We work our bodies hard, saying we have to learn from physical suffering — as if our bodies have not suffered enough. Our bodies have suffered so much; they don't need to suffer anymore. Meditation helps us to suffer less and to restore peace, solidity, and harmony to our bodies so that we can make progress on our spiritual paths.

The joy and bliss of meditation sustain us. "Experiencing joy, I breathe in. Experiencing joy, I breathe out." This should not be an ideal. It's not wishful thinking, but a real practice. The Buddha told us that we need to produce joy, beauty, bliss, and happiness in order to nourish ourselves. We need certain conditions in order to produce true joy and true happiness. If we don't have joy and happiness, then just saying the words, "Experiencing joy, I breathe in" won't mean anything. We will sit here stiffly, without joy. We have to learn the art of generating joy mindfully, with concentration and insight.

Releasing Our Cows

A lot of joy and happiness comes from getting away or leaving something behind. Suppose you are suffering from the noise, pollution, and stresses of the city. It is Friday afternoon, and you want to get away. You get in your car and drive away. Once you're in the countryside with the beautiful trees, the blue sky, and the bird song, you feel joy. The joy you experience from being in the countryside is born from having abandoned the city, from leaving something behind.

There are many things we are unable to leave behind, which trap us. Practice looking deeply into these things. In the beginning, you may think that they are vital to your happiness, but they may actually be obstacles to your true happiness, causing you to suffer. If you are not able to be happy because you are caught by them, leaving them behind will be a source of joy for you. The Buddha and many of his disciples experienced this, and have handed down their wisdom to us. Please look at the things you think are necessary to your well-being and happiness, and find out whether they bring you happiness or are almost killing you.

One day the Buddha was sitting with a group of monks in the woods near the city of Sravasti. They had just finished a mindful lunch and were engaged in a small Dharma discussion. Suddenly a farmer came by. He was visibly upset and shouted, "Monks! Have you seen my cows?"

The Buddha said, "No, we have not seen any cows."

"You know, monks," the man said, "I am the most miserable person on earth. For some reason, my twelve cows all ran away this morning. I have only two acres of sesame seed plants, and this year the insects ate them all. I think I am going to kill myself." The farmer was really suffering.

Out of compassion, the Buddha said, "No, sir, we have not seen your cows. Maybe you should look for them elsewhere."

When the farmer was gone, the Buddha turned to his monks, looked at them deeply, smiled, and said, "Dear friends, do you know that you are the happiest people on Earth? You don't have any cows to lose." [laughter]

So, my friends, if you have cows [laughter], look deeply into the nature of your cows to see whether they have been bringing you happiness or suffering. You should learn the art of releasing your cows. The key thing is to let go and free yourself. A monk or nun is supposed to leave everything behind in order to be a free person. A monk or nun should have only three robes and one bowl, because freedom is the most valuable possession.

There is a poem that describes the Buddha in this way: "The Buddha is like a full moon sailing across the empty sky." The Buddha had a lot of space around him because he did not possess anything. He didn't have any cows. That is why his happiness was immense. The monks and nuns who follow him today should follow his example of not possessing anything, not owning a lot of cows. I know a monk who was very busy trying to build a big temple. He said, "Before I became a monk, I was very busy, and thought that once I was a monk, I would be less busy. But in fact, I am busier than ever." His temple had become a cow. When he told this to a friend, his friend laughed and asked him, "Why don't you become a real monk?"

Freedom is the base of our happiness. We cannot be happy if we are trapped. Solidity and freedom are the authentic grounds of our happiness. That is why we have to practice to restore our freedom and create space around us. Also, when you love and are loved, if there is no freedom, your love can be suffocating. You cannot be happy with the kind of love that deprives you of freedom and doesn't allow you to be yourself. That kind of love is not authentic love; it is a cow. You must find the courage to let your cow go.

We cherish freedom. As monks and nuns, we cannot exchange our freedom for anything — not even a temple. Joy and happiness are born from releasing our cows. This is real happiness. We all have to look into the nature of our cows and see whether they are making us miserable. After meditating profoundly on their nature, we can make a decision. When we have made the correct decision, we gain freedom and experience incredible joy. We are much happier than before, and we enjoy the fact that we have been able to release our cows.

I have a friend in Germany who is a businessman. He had a lot of cows. He attended one of my retreats and loved it. However, he said he couldn't come to the second retreat because he had to go to a meeting in Frankfurt. I said, "Be careful with your cows." That night he left for his meeting. However, during sitting meditation at the second retreat, I was surprised to see him in the meditation hall. I approached him after the session and asked, "Why are you here? Didn't you go to Frankfurt?" He said, "Thây, halfway to Frankfurt, I began to release my cows, and I made a U-turn back to the retreat." I said, "Congratulations! You are a good practitioner, because you can easily release your cows."

Now it is time to sit down and practice looking deeply. I am sure that with each cow you release, your happiness and freedom will grow. This is the kind of joy and happiness the Buddha recommends. You have the Dharma, and it is liberating.

Mindfulness and Concentration

Some of us feel that our lives make no sense nor hold any meaning. When we don't see a meaningful path in our lives, we suffer greatly. We are unhappy because we do not know where to go. Our confusion makes us suffer, no matter how rich and powerful we are. If we see a direction in our lives, find meaning in our lives, and live with compassion, we will know how to help ourselves and others around us to suffer less. We know the Dharma, have practiced it, and know that in difficult moments the Dharma can rescue us and the people we love. We have been freed by the Dharma. Just by touching the Dharma within us and touching our confidence in it, joy and happiness are born in us, making us truly happy.

You might think that happiness means having a lot of money, being physically fit, being famous, or having as much sex as you like whenever you want to. Many of us have traveled these paths and recognize that the more we get caught up in cravings and sensual desires, the more we suffer. We used to think of these things as elements of our happiness, but now we have learned that true happiness lies in letting go and restoring our freedom. That is why the Buddha advised us to nourish ourselves by cultivating joy and happiness through the practice of looking deeply.

"Experiencing joy, I breathe in." This isn't wishful thinking. It means you look deeply and touch the elements that bring about true joy and happiness. Joy can be born from concentration. We have already learned about the benefits of concentration. The amount of happiness we get from eating an orange depends on our mindfulness and concentration. The more concentrated we are on the orange, the greater our pleasure and happiness will be. Conditions for happiness are everywhere — inside and around us — but because we do not concentrate, we do not recognize them.

One of my students lives in Paris and practices mindful walking. Sometimes she is so busy that she has to run. One day she was in an elevator with an older lady. Looking at the lady, she said, "This is not life, always running. *Ce n'est pas une vie.*" The lady looked her over and said, "Yes, but you can run. I cannot; I'm too old. If I run, I'll fall over." Having strong legs and feet, being able to run, is happiness — not a reason to complain — because some people would like to run and can't. You know that you are young and have good feet. Your awareness and mindfulness yield an insight that brings you happiness. "Breathing in, I know my feet are solid. I can run. Breathing out, I smile." Mindfulness and concentration are grounds for happiness.

Old age also has its advantages. If older people are aware, they can be very happy, because they realize how quickly life passes. They are mature and capable of savoring each moment of their lives, wisely appreciating the positive elements within themselves.

They don't run, but sit quietly and live each moment of their lives more deeply. When you are young, you are like a stream of water running from the top of the mountain to its base. As you grow older, you become more like a river that flows peacefully and reflects the blue sky and the earth. The young stream of water running from the top of the mountain cannot do that. If older people are able to recognize the positive elements in their lives, they, too, can be happy. We need mindfulness to recognize what is there, and concentration to be with that element deeply. Concentration helps our happiness to be born; it is the ground of happiness.

If we know how to manage all twenty-four hours in a day, we realize that a day is a long time. What makes it long is our concentration. Older people live in a more concentrated way than the young, establishing themselves more in the present moment. With mindfulness and concentration, older people can appreciate each moment that is offered to them. Each moment of daily life can become a story for their children and grandchildren. This is possible. The Buddha did it. He didn't leave behind a set of dogmas and theories; he left behind his life. Every step he took was peaceful and solid. His compassion penetrated not only the living beings of his time, but also of our time.

In Asia, people release animals on their birthdays. This is thanks to the compassion and teachings of the Buddha. I have proposed to our Christian friends to practice releasing birds instead of killing them on Christmas Day. Also, I am sure that Jesus will be happy if, instead of cutting a tree, you plant one. As Christians, you need to realize your capacity for living deeply, and speak out. On the day of Wesak, the birthday of the Buddha, in Sri Lanka, Thailand, and other Buddhist countries, no one goes hungry because food is cooked and offered in every front yard. I hope that we can celebrate Wesak every day so that no one will ever go hungry in the world. This tradition also springs from the compassion of the Buddha. Each step, each breath, each word of the Buddha conveys and transports the energy of mindfulness, understanding, and compassion. From this source, his students continue to inherit compassion and knowledge. If they practice well, they can transmit this source of compassion, healing, and happiness to future generations.

The practice is to live every moment of your daily life mindfully and deeply. When you drink a glass of water, while you hold your baby in your arms or sit in front of your beloved, if you concentrate and are mindful, life is real, and happiness and joy are born. That is why the Buddha spoke about the birth of joy and happiness from concentration.

[BELL]

Sometimes we need a friend to help us realize the elements of happiness. This is why we need a Sangha. We already know that the Sangha can give us a lot of support and guidance. From time to time, with all our heart, we can ask the Sangha to shed light on our practice. We say, "Please, dear Sangha, be compassionate with me. Please shine your light on me and help and guide me in my practice." While sitting together, the Sangha will practice looking deeply and tell you about your strengths and weaknesses. This offering of guidance is a wonderful practice that benefits both the person who requests it and those who offer it. The Sangha looks deeply with love and care, which is why we progress rapidly when offered guidance by them.

Being reminded of your strengths can make you happy. You think, "I am equipped with these positive elements for the joy of my practice and the joy of those who come into my life. I practice not only for my sake but for the sake of my family and society." Every time you achieve transformation and healing, you know that it is for the benefit of many. Practice cultivating the energy of the Buddha in yourself and touch it every day — not as a vague concept or an abstraction — but as the energy of mindfulness. This energy will act as a source of light to guide and nourish you.

The Dharma is not a set of dogmas or a collection of scriptures. It is a living entity. We create the living Dharma in the Sangha through mindful walking, mindful eating, mindful speaking, and mindful listening. The Dharma is alive and wonderful. Mindful listening makes understanding possible. If your brothers and sisters know how to listen to you with compassion, you suffer much less. Their ability to walk and sit in peace and to transform the suffering within means the Sangha is cultivating the Dharma within. The Dharma is in every minute of your daily life — while you breathe, walk, wash dishes, or make coffee. The living Dharma is what the world, your family, and your society needs. Cultivating the Dharma helps you and your society to be more stable, free, happy, and joyful.

Nobody can take away your faith in the Dharma because it is born from experience, not a set of dogmas. Suppose you have learned how to make tofu. You know that by using certain ingredients and utensils, you can make tofu. When someone asks you to make it, you are confident that you can do it. No one can take this confidence away from you. The same is true for the Dharma. You have cultivated the living Dharma within. You know that, thanks to the Dharma, you have overcome difficult moments and restored your peace and stability. No one can shake your confidence in the Dharma because of this direct experience. You will continue to cultivate the living Dharma for your sake and for the sake of the Sangha.

The Sangha does not have to be perfect. The Buddha's Sangha was not perfect, but the Buddha was happy enough with it. He had some problems with the Sangha, but he used his compassion and talent to solve them. I have some difficulties with my Sangha, too, but, overall, I am very happy, because everyone tries to practice. Everyone breathes, walks, and cooks dinner in the holy element of mindfulness. The Sangha is infused with holy energy. The Holy Spirit is within the Sangha because everyone is doing his or her best to be mindful.

Sangha-building is our practice. The collective energy of the Sangha is a source of support that we all need, and, if we want to continue our practice, we have to build a Sangha wherever we are. Many elements can help create our Sangha, like a beautiful walking path or a good cushion. Your little boy can be a co-practitioner. You can hold his hand and invite him to practice five minutes of walking meditation. Look around you and identify the elements of your future Sangha. When you go home, try to build a Sangha to support you in the practice. Psychotherapists, teachers, students, and doctors all need their own Sanghas. "I take refuge in the Sangha" is not a statement of faith or an abstract notion, but a practice. Cultivate your Sangha for your own protection and support.

Experiencing Feelings

The seventh exercise of mindful breathing is: "Breathing in, I am aware of my mental formations. Breathing out, I am aware of my mental formations." Mental formations refer here to feelings. There are four kinds of feelings: pleasant, unpleasant, neutral, and mixed. When someone practices acupressure on you, you may experience both a painful and a wonderful feeling at the same time; this is called a mixed feeling. We have to learn to look at our body and our feelings as rivers. In the river of the body, each drop of water is a cell, always changing; birth and death take place in it in each moment. The same is true with the river of feelings. Feelings are born, stay for a while, and then die. To practice contemplation of the feelings in the feelings means that we sit on the bank of the river of feelings, observe them, and become these feelings. Sitting mindfully, we do not allow ourselves to drown in our feelings. Mindfulness helps us to embrace and identify our feelings.

In the *Discourse on the Four Establishments of Mindfulness,* the Buddha said, "If it is a painful physical feeling, you recognize it as a painful physical feeling. If it is a pleasant mental feeling, you recognize it as a pleasant mental feeling." We call it by its true name and identify it, just as we do with our in-breath and out-breath. This is called simple recognition of what is there. We say "hello" to the feeling and recognize its presence. When it is a pleasant feeling with the body as a base, we recognize it as such. When it is a pleasant feeling with perceptions as a base, we recognize that. The body is not the only ground for our feelings. Our sensations, perceptions, and other mental formations are also birthing grounds for our feelings. Our task is to identify the feeling, embrace it, and look deeply into its nature.

When you embrace a pleasant feeling, you discover more about its nature. If you take the time, you may see whether it is a truly pleasant feeling or one that contains an unpleasant feeling. Suppose you are drinking liquor, and it gives you a pleasant feeling. If you hold on to that pleasant feeling mindfully, you may find many other things in it. You are sensitive to reality and open to it. Looking deeply, you can see that lots of grains and cereals were used to make the liquor. We know that many people die because they do not have enough to eat. Forty thousand children throughout the world die daily because of lack of food and malnutrition. When you drink liquor and embrace your feelings, you may have these kinds of insights.

You may also see the resistance of your liver. Your tongue may like the pleasant feeling, but your liver may have sent you a message for help, which you neglected. Since you are inhabited by the energy of mindfulness, the energy of the Holy Spirit, you listen to your liver and know that this so-called pleasant feeling contains a lot of misery, and that later it will give birth to unpleasant feelings. This insight helps you to stop and look into the true nature of your so-called pleasant feelings.

With mindfulness, a so-called neutral feeling can become a pleasant or an unpleasant feeling. It depends on your way of handling it. Suppose you are sitting in the garden with your little boy. You feel wonderful. The sky is blue, the grass is green, there are many flowers, and you are able to touch the beauty of nature. You are very happy, but your little boy is not. First, he has only a neutral feeling but, since he doesn't know how to handle it, it turns into boredom. In his search for more exciting feelings, he wants to run into the living room and turn on the television. Sitting with the flowers, the grass, and the blue sky is not fun for him. The neutral feeling has become an unpleasant feeling.

We can be extremely happy while sitting and touching the deep source of joy and happiness within us. We can touch the energy of the Buddha, the Dharma, and the Sangha, release our cows, and enjoy deep concentration. Our joy is immense. The person sitting next to us may be waiting for the meditation to end because he does not know how to handle his feelings. The difference is that when we handle our feelings with mindfulness, using concentration and looking deeply, great joy and happiness are born.

Suppose you have a toothache at midnight. Since there is no dentist available, you have to bear that unpleasant feeling. When you discover that not having a toothache is a wonderful feeling, you will become enlightened. Before your toothache, you did not appreciate this feeling and called it neutral. Now you know that an apparently neutral feeling may, in fact, be a wonderful feeling. The meditator should be smart and know how to transform neutral feelings into wonderful feelings. All you need is mindful breathing and looking deeply. This is the nourishment you give yourself as a practitioner.

First, you recognize, touch, and embrace the feelings you are experiencing. You look into them before transforming them. This is especially important when you are dealing with painful feelings. You have to learn to take care of them in the face of the strong emotion emerging from the depth of your consciousness. You have to hold on to the insight that you are more than your emotions. While saying, "This is only an emotion," you recognize what is there. "Breathing in, I know that this is only an emotion.

It is not the whole of me. I am more than my emotions." This is a very basic insight. Emotions will manifest, stay for a while, and then leave. Why should you die because of one emotion? We have to teach young people to remember to practice every time they are caught in the throes of a strong emotion. Breathing in and out, they should concentrate on the rise and fall of their abdomen, and remind themselves that this is only an emotion, and that it will go away at some point.

After a few minutes of this practice, the storm will die down, and you will see how easily you have survived. You should start your practice before the storm begins or you might forget to do it. Suppose you practice daily for three weeks. If a strong emotion comes in the fourth week, you will remember the practice and ground yourself in it. If you have practiced, you will have enough energy of mindfulness to recognize, embrace, and remain yourself — not be blown away. If you haven't practiced, you may not remember, and may get carried away by the storm. This is why our daily practice is important. In difficult times, we also need the presence of our Dharma brothers and sisters to help us withstand the storm. After you have succeeded in dealing with your emotions and taking care of them, you can help young people do the same. First, you might hold your young daughter's hand and say, "My darling, breathe in and out with me. Pay attention to your abdomen." You are bringing your mindfulness and solidity to support her in the practice. Of course, your presence will make her practice much easier; you are her Sangha. If we educate our young people to do this, one day they will be able to practice on their own and deal with their emotions. They won't resort to committing suicide.

Mindfulness helps us to identify a feeling as a feeling and an emotion as an emotion. It helps us hold our emotions tenderly within us, embrace them, and look deeply at them. If your son or daughter succeeds even once, you will have succeeded. Later, he or she will have the confidence to deal with these emotions when they come again. This is faith in the Dharma. Touching this faith brings a lot of joy and happiness.

The eighth exercise of mindful breathing is: "Calming my mental formations, I breathe in and out." Calming is the work of mindfulness. Mindfulness is like the sun. When it touches something, it brings about a transformation. Just as all vegetation is photosensitive, every mental formation is mindfulness-sensitive. If there is joy, mindfulness will make the joy greater. If there is grief, mindfulness will calm and relieve the grief. Mindfulness is the energy of the Buddha, the energy that we all need.

Now it is time for walking meditation. I will wait for you outside and we will enjoy walking together.

[BELL]

CHAPTER SIX

Embracing Our Feelings

Dear Sangha, today is the twenty-ninth of May, 1998. We will continue our inquiry into "contemplating the feelings in the feelings." When we experience a pleasant feeling, we embrace it and touch the ground of that feeling. Embracing the feeling, we have a growing sense of enjoyment. If we continue to touch the feeling deeply, we will discover its base; the base may be the body, a perception, or any other mental formation. Physical well-being can produce a pleasant feeling. Mental and spiritual well-being are produced by one of the mental formations. By being with the feeling, we touch and recognize the physical, spiritual, or mental elements lying underneath it. Once we discover the element that serves as the base for the feeling, we embrace that, too.

Touching Positive Elements

Those of us with allergies suffer from blocked noses and other unpleasant symptoms. After it has rained, when the pollen is washed away, we can breathe more easily and have a vaguely pleasant feeling. If we are mindful, we know that the pleasant feeling comes from the fact that there is no pollen in the air causing our bodies to suffer. Because of awareness and mindfulness, that pleasant feeling is amplified. We smile at it, knowing how wonderful it is. It is like not having a toothache, which is actually a feeling of physical well-being. If we never touch it, we may say it does not exist. Mindfulness helps us to recognize the well-being available to us, then suddenly joy and happiness become possible.

The same is true of a pleasant feeling created by a positive mental formation. If you make someone smile, you, in turn, will feel wonderful. If you look deeply and touch what is underneath this pleasant feeling, you will become aware of the mental formation called compassion or loving kindness within you. It is this which has motivated you to do or say something to make the other person smile. When he or she smiles, you feel wonderful and recognize why. If you know how to embrace this feeling, recognizing the presence of loving kindness and compassion, your pleasant feeling will grow. Your happiness and joy will also grow. This is the practice of nurturing joy and happiness. We need to do this daily in order to nourish and heal ourselves. We can do it with or without the help of someone close to us. If we are surrounded by people who are practicing in a similar way and supporting us, our practice is easier and more effective.

Touching the positive elements within us is important. We need to remember that our garden has many trees, bushes, and flowers in it. As I have mentioned before, if one tree is dying, we have not lost the whole garden. We can see our body as a garden. There may be one ailing part, but the other parts are still healthy and solid. We have to touch both the ailing and healthy parts to really touch the truth. The truth will help us to be happy and joyful. We have to embrace the unhealthy parts tenderly and mindfully, weaving them into the fabric of our otherwise healthy bodies. Generally, we pay too much attention to what is wrong and not enough attention to what is right. You might ask a Dharma brother or sister to tell you what is not wrong in you. This is important. You should enjoy the positive elements within your body and consciousness. In a Sangha, there may be a few people who are sometimes not strong enough to be themselves. Then, the stronger parts of the Sangha hold and support them.

If the weaker Sangha members allow themselves to be cradled in the net of the Sangha and surrender to it, the Sangha can support them. Because of their solidarity with the Sangha, they will never be too weak, too down, or too slow.

If you are a psychotherapist, you might like to add this extra dimension to your practice. Sitting with and facing your client, you can help him or her touch the positive elements within. Don't just talk about what is wrong, talk about what is right, and encourage him or her to touch what is right. Invite her for a walking meditation session and touch the wonderful things within and around you. If you can do this for yourself, you can do it for your clients as well.

Now we come to the other part of the practice — "Experiencing an unpleasant feeling, I breathe in." You cannot ignore unpleasant feelings — suffering, pain, or sorrow — within you. They surface, wanting to be recognized, and mindfulness recognizes them. "I know you are there. I'm here for you. I will take good care of you." That is the work of mindfulness. Try not to run away from your pain or suffering. Be there for them, recognize that they are there, and practice embracing them tenderly with your arms of mindfulness. Embracing the unpleasant, painful feelings, you calm them and touch what is underneath — the base of that unpleasant feeling, that pain. The base may be physical or mental. The feelings are all formations — whether physical or mental — and should be recognized and embraced.

The First and Second Noble Truths

The Buddha's first Dharma talk is about *dukkha,* the First Noble Truth, which is translated as ill-being, suffering, or pain. Ill-being, the opposite of well-being, is a good choice of words. In the Buddhist tradition, ill-being — suffering — is seen as a holy truth. You may ask, "Why? What is so holy about suffering and ill-being?" The answer is that by looking into the nature of your ill-being — not by running away — you find the way out of it.

If you try to run away, instead of confronting or embracing your ill-being, you will not look deeply into its nature and will never have the chance to see a way out. That is why you should hold your suffering tenderly and closely, looking directly into it, to discover its true nature and find a way out.

When you look into dukkha, you see the Second Noble Truth — *samudaya,* the roots or creation of suffering. Samudaya can be only discovered through the practice of looking and touching deeply. Suppose you are depressed. Depression is ill-being. The practice is to look into the nature of your depression and hold it tenderly in your arms. Don't try to run away from it. Look into it to see the truth of samudaya, the roots and making of your ill-being. While sitting, walking, or lying down, we practice deep looking to identify the source of our ill-being. The Buddha said that nothing can survive without food, and that includes depression. You may have been feeding your depression a lot in the past few months.

One way of identifying or understanding our ill-being is to find out what kind of nutriment has caused it and sustained it. Nothing is born in isolation. Our depression must come from somewhere. Our physical ill-being is linked to the ill-being of our consciousness, and vice versa. Therefore, we have to look into what and how we have been feeding our body and our consciousness.

The Four Nutriments

The Buddha spoke of four kinds of nutriments — edible foods, sense impressions, volition, and consciousness. The first kind, edible foods, is what you eat and drink. It is responsible for your physical and mental well-being or ill-being. Different foods contain different toxins, and certain types of food may be inappropriate for your body. That is why we have to look into the nature of our body and the food that we eat to see whether they are compatible. Breathing in and out mindfully, we ask, "Is this food compatible with my body and consciousness?" Follow the prescription of mindfulness and you will know what to consume.

The First Nutriment: Edible Foods

In the teaching of my tradition, when we begin to eat, we meditate on the Five Contemplations. The first two contemplations are: "This food is a gift of the earth, the sky, and the whole cosmos. I want to be worthy of this food." To be worthy of our food, we have to eat it mindfully. If we do not eat it mindfully, we do not feel gratitude, and can damage our body and consciousness. If we eat our food with gratitude and mindfulness, we are worthy of it. The third contemplation is being aware of our negative mental formations, especially our tendency to eat without moderation. The Buddha always reminded his disciples to eat moderately. The fourth contemplation is to see whether the food you are eating is healthy and will keep your body healthy. Food is a kind of medicine. It should be balanced in terms of yin and yang. Looking deeply and mindfully into your food, you know what types of food you can eat and what you must abstain from eating. The fifth contemplation is: "I receive this food because I want to nurture, live, and realize the ideal of compassion and understanding."

[BELL]

Some of us have a feeling of emptiness, restlessness, and ill-being within. We do not know how to handle these unpleasant feelings, and, because there is always something in the fridge, we eat and drink to forget our pain. Many of us do this. The monastics advise us to always eat with our Sangha, unless we are sick. This practice is very helpful. You can do it with your family, which is also your Sangha. At dinnertime, when all the family members are sitting around the table, we can practice the Five Contemplations. We may invite the children to say the contemplations out loud. Each of us can look deeply into our food to see whether it is appropriate for us. In this way, we create a collective energy in the family that helps us to eat properly and not contaminate our bodies.

The Buddha used the following image to illustrate the first nutriment. A couple set out with their little son for a journey through a desert. Halfway through the desert, they realized that their provisions had come to an end. They knew that they would all die before they could cross the desert. After a very painful discussion, the couple decided to kill the little boy. Each day they ate a little bit of the boy's flesh as they continued to walk through the desert. Finally, they got out of the desert alive. The Buddha asked his monks, "Dear friends, do you think the couple enjoyed eating the flesh of their own son?" The monks answered, "no." If we do not eat properly, if we destroy our health, if we eat and drink in such a way that deprives other living beings of having the chance to live, then we are eating the flesh of our parents and our own children in us and around us.

The Second Nutriment: Sense Impressions

The second kind of nutriment is sense impressions. We consume food through our eyes, nose, ears, and body. When we drive across the city, we hear sounds, see images, and smell scents, all of which are considered food. When we watch a movie, we are consuming a certain kind of food. Many of the items we consume contain toxins. A television program or a novel can be highly toxic. The news we read in the newspaper can bring toxins into our consciousness. Our fear, distress, and despair are nourished by such news, information, sights, and sounds. Advertising always promises that if we buy a certain product, we'll be happy: "Happiness is easy — just buy this." The sights and sounds used to capture our attention and draw us in contain toxins. We have to protect ourselves and guard our six senses against these toxins while driving through the city.

The Buddha said that the eyes are a deep ocean — he spoke

like a poet — with hidden waves and sea monsters beneath. If you are not mindful and do not know how to protect and guard the doors of your senses, you will be drowned in the ocean of forms — sometimes several times a day. With the boat of mindfulness, we sail across the ocean of forms and hold on tight so that our boat does not sink. The Buddha also said that the ear is a deep ocean with many hidden waves and sea monsters. If you are not mindful, you might sink into the ocean of sounds.

Depression is also nourished by sights and sounds. It does not come about by itself. It is created and nourished daily by our way of consuming. Walking mindfully through the airport in Paris, I saw many advertisements for perfumes called "Samsara," "Scorpion," and "Poison." They dare to call them by their true names. We know that perfume is an item of consumption and a bait. In the bait there is a hook, and we are the innocent fish. The products are advertised so skillfully and the bait is so appealing that, with one bite, we're caught. What do we have as self-defense? Nothing except our mindfulness.

Mindfulness is the only agent that can guard the door of our six senses and protect us. The Five Mindfulness Trainings are the insights of those who have practiced mindfulness. They are concrete prescriptions for our daily protection. If we live by the Five Mindfulness Trainings, we will protect ourselves, our families, and our society. The Five Mindfulness Trainings were not created by a god and imposed on us; they are the fruit of our deep looking. Being aware of the suffering caused by our unmindful consumption, we are determined not to consume items that bring toxins, disharmony, pain, and sorrow into us, destroying our physical and mental well-being. The Five Mindfulness Trainings are not a set of rules, but guidelines for the practice of mindfulness. We need to train ourselves to live accordingly. This is the wisdom of self-protection.

The Buddha used the image of a cow with a skin disease that has destroyed most of its skin to represent the second kind of nutriment: sense impressions. If the cow stands close to an old wall or an old tree, all the insects in the wall or tree bark will come out, fix themselves upon its body, and suck its blood. Without mindfulness, the sense impressions that we are exposed to destroy us a little more every day, and the toxins penetrate our body and consciousness. Just as the cow needs healthy skin to protect it, we need the practice of mindfulness to guard our six senses.

[BELL]

The Third Nutriment: Volition

The third kind of nutriment is volition — our deep desire. This kind of energy pushes us to do things in our daily lives. We have to look deeply into ourselves to see what kind of energy motivates our daily actions. We are constantly working hard in order to go somewhere or realize something. What is the purpose of this kind of active life? The third nutriment motivates us and can bring us a lot of happiness or a lot of suffering.

What kind of energy did Mother Teresa have in her daily life? She had a desire to help the poor people without resources, supporters, or protection. The willingness to relieve the suffering of many people is a tremendous source of energy. If you have the same intention — volition — within you, your life will be filled with happiness. When compassion — the willingness to relieve the suffering of others — is within you and motivates you, you can relate to people easily and lead a simple life. The relief and happiness you bring to people will be your reward. When you can make a person smile, you feel wonderful. You don't want the reward, but it comes to you anyway. There are people filled with hatred who only want to live in order to punish the person they hate. Such a person cannot be happy because his or her sole intention and source of energy is hatred. If we are motivated by negative energy, our life will be full of suffering.

Siddhartha Gautama had a vital source of energy within him.

That is why for forty-five years, he worked diligently and helped many people — kings, ministers, beggars, and prostitutes. He helped everybody because he was motivated by the desire to relieve people's suffering. All of us need to be aware of the nature of our source of energy, because it determines the quality of our life. If that energy is only craving — for fame, wealth, or sex — then it will make us suffer.

The Buddha used the following image to illustrate the third kind of nutriment. He described a person who wants to live, who does not want to suffer, but who is carried off by two strong men and thrown into a fire. The two strong men represent a volition, an energy, that pushes us in the direction of suffering and death. As meditators, we must take the time to sit and look into ourselves daily to identify the source of the energy that is pushing us, and the direction in which we are going. We must see whether our intention is bringing us suffering and despair. If so, we must release it and find another source of energy.

The Fourth Nutriment: Consciousness

The fourth kind of nutriment is consciousness, the base for the manifestation of our body, our mental states, and our environment (living conditions). Consciousness represents the sum of all actions that have been done: thoughts, speeches, and bodily acts. The maturity of consciousness brings forth the manifestation of our present body, our present mental state, and our present environment. Consciousness here is described in terms of the deluded mind, the mind characterized by wrong views, and afflictions that result from unwholesome volitions. The suffering of the three realms (the realm of desire, the realm of form, and the realm of non-form) is the retribution of our actions that determine the nature and quality of our consciousness. If consciousness gets the wholesome kind of food (Right View, Right Thinking, Right Mindfulness, Right Speech, Right Concentration, etc.), it will undergo transformation and become *true mind,* which will serve as the base for the manifestation of a healthy body, wholesome and happy mental states, and a sane and beautiful environment.

The Buddha used the following image to illustrate the fourth kind of nutriment. A criminal was arrested. The king gave the order to stab him with one hundred knives. The criminal did not die. The same punishment was repeated at noon, and in the evening. Still he did not die. The punishment was repeated the next day, and the day that followed.

We allow our consciousness to be fed every day with the poison of ignorance, craving, unwholesome speech, and unwholesome desires. Our consciousness continues to grow in the direction of the *deluded mind*, and brings forth much suffering. We should change our consciousness food and help it grow in the opposite direction, the direction of the *true mind*. In the light of the teaching concerning the Twelve Links of Interdependent Co-Arising, consciousness is the result of ignorance and unwholesome impulses.

We know that understanding and compassion are sources of energy that can bring us and the people around us a lot of happiness, so we practice cultivating them. The Buddha said, "If you look into ill-being and identify the source of the nutriment that has brought it into you, you are already on the path of emancipation." You have already begun to be released. You need only to cut off the source of these nutriments to be free of them. A few weeks later, you will notice the difference. Nothing can survive without food; if you cut off its source, your depression, sorrow, or despair will die.

By identifying the source of the nutriments, you realize the Second Noble Truth: samudaya, the creation of ill-being. You know that the opposite of samudaya — well-being — is possible. You know that to reach well-being, you must cut off the source of wrong nutriments and find the right ones — Right View, Right Understanding, Right Speech, Right Livelihood, Right Concentration, and so on. The Noble Eightfold Path can bring about well-being and end ill-being. The other path is the ignoble path of consuming without mindfulness. Of the Four Noble Truths, two truths concern ill-being and its creation, while the other two concern well-being and the path leading to its restoration. This is the content of the first Dharma talk that the newly enlightened Buddha offered to the five monks in the Deer Park.

Experiencing Mind

Now we come to the ninth exercise of mindful breathing: "Experiencing mind, I breathe in." Mind means mental formations. We are present for the mental formations. We are present for the mental formations that we have neglected in the past. This is equivalent to the first tetrad or group of four exercises of experiencing the body, and the second tetrad of experiencing feelings. The practice is the same — we go home and take care of ourselves. First our body, then our feelings, and now our mental formations.

First, we simply recognize the presence of a mental formation. We do not try to grasp it, possess it, or be attached to it. We do not try to push it away, either. This is called simple recognition of a mental formation. Recognize it, call it by its true name, and say, "I am here to take care of you because you are myself."

We already know that many of us do not want to go home to ourselves. We are afraid. There is a lot of internal suffering and conflict that we want to avoid. We complain that we do not have time to live, but we try to kill our free time by not going back to ourselves. We escape by turning on the television or picking up a novel or magazine; we go out for a drive. We run away from ourselves and don't attend to our body, feelings, or mental formations.

We have to go home. If we are at war with our parents, friends, society, or church, it may be because there is a war raging within us. An internal war facilitates other wars. The five elements — forms, feelings, perceptions, mental formations, and consciousness — comprise a large territory. Each of us is the king or queen of his or her territory of the Five Skandhas, but we have not been responsible monarchs. We don't want to survey our territory or to govern over it, we just want to abandon it. There are many wars being fought in it. It has turned into a mess, because we just want to escape and are afraid of going back to our own kingdom. The Buddha advised us to go home and tidy up, restoring our peace and harmony.

As I have mentioned before, we are afraid of going home because we lack the tools or the means of self-protection. Equipped with mindfulness, we can go home safely and not be overwhelmed by our pain, sorrow, and depression. Going home mindfully, we can talk to our wounded child within using the following mantra: "Darling, I have come home to you. I am here for you. I embrace you in my arms. I am sorry that I left you alone for a long time." With some training, with mindful walking and mindful breathing, we will be able to go home and embrace our pain and sorrow.

[BELL]

Meditation as Nourishment and Healing

Meditation practice does not mean that you transform yourself into a battlefield, with good and evil sides fighting each other. This is not true to the Buddhist tradition. There are no battles to be fought. Our positive and negative elements are all organic parts of us. If we are skilled in the art of embracing and transforming, we can transform the negative elements into positive ones. We don't throw anything away either; we transform our garbage into compost. Mindfulness is organic and can be fed by other energies. When the energy of mindfulness embraces any other mental formation, it brings about transformation. The many functions of mindfulness include recognizing, calming, nourishing, transforming, and attending to the mental formations that manifest. Suppressed mental formations always try to emerge, to be recognized and embraced by us. First, we recognize the visible part — like an iceberg with just its tip showing above the water. After we have identified it, we touch the huge part that is underwater. Every time there is a manifestation, we produce mindfulness to recognize and embrace it.

We all know that we prefer not to recognize our wounded inner child. Instead, we want to send him or her to a deep, deep place, where we never have to go. But our wounded child always tries to come up and say, "I'm here. I'm here. You cannot avoid me. You cannot run away from me." Our practice is to go home and recognize the different aspects of our wounded child. We embrace each aspect until finally we can embrace the whole child. Our Sangha can support us in this practice.

If mental formations manifest during sitting meditation and prevent you from meditating, you may have to practice recognizing them one by one. This is also meditation. When a thought, feeling, perception, pain, or sorrow manifests itself, practice breathing in and out and recognize it for what it is. Say, "I know you. I know you are there. I am here for you," and embrace it. The object of our practice in the ninth exercise is any kind of mental formation — jealousy, fear, hatred, despair, restlessness — positive or negative.

When you are meditating on an interesting subject, your power of concentration is sufficient to quiet your mental formations. This is called guided or directed meditation. You choose a special subject for meditation, and look deeply into it to discover something. The more interesting the subject, the stronger your concentration. If it is not interesting, then, even if you try hard, you will still feel sleepy, and other things will continue to come up. One guided meditation is identifying and writing down the names of all our cows. Another is to write down what we can do for ourselves every day to bring ourselves joy. At first, you may think that there aren't many things, but when you sit and look deeply, you will discover dozens.

Another way of working with your mind is to allow things to

come up and handle them with mindfulness. You nourish your mindful breathing and recognize each mental formation that manifests. Every time you embrace a wholesome mental formation, your joy and happiness grow, and the wholesome mental formation grows. You realize your compassion and faith in the Dharma, and use the happiness you receive to nourish yourself. Every time negative, unwholesome, and painful mental formations manifest themselves, you recognize and embrace them to calm them and look deeply into them.

Gladdening Our Mind

Now we come to the tenth exercise of mindful breathing: "Gladdening the mind, I breathe in. Gladdening the mind, I breathe out." This exercise also brings us nourishment, joy, and happiness. We touch our wholesome mental formations. It is like the garden that I spoke of earlier, with many beautiful trees that are still alive. We touch and recognize what is not wrong in our consciousness — our capacity for being joyful, mindful, and forgiving.

In each of us there is the seed of loving kindness — *maitri*. We are all capable of love. Even if we are afraid to love, we have the capacity to love in the form of a seed. At the beginning of the week, someone wrote me a long letter saying that he was afraid to love again because he had loved in the past and suffered so much. He had told himself, "Never again, never again." But because he followed my teaching, that day, for the first time, he touched the seed of love in himself and knew that he was capable of loving, and was no longer afraid of saying, "I love you." Our seed of loving kindness needs to be touched and recognized. We have the means to make our beloved happy, and if we can make him or her happy, we will be happy, too. Maitri is the ability to offer joy and happiness. It is not just our good intention to make someone happy. Often, we have good intentions, but because we don't know how to love, we make our beloved suffer. We should also love ourselves. When we practice deep relaxation, loving kindness is directed to our body and self. When we embrace our mental formations of joy and equanimity, we direct our love toward ourselves. Our capacity of loving — making a person happy — is maitri, and we can cultivate that love every day.

Karuna is compassion — the ability to relieve and transform someone's suffering. We have the seed of karuna within us. As we practice cultivating maitri and karuna, our energy of loving kindness and compassion will grow, and we can relate more easily to other living beings. Communication becomes easier, and we suffer less. Joy and happiness become possible. Gladdening our mind means going back to and recognizing our wholesome mental formations — first, in the form of seeds, and then, in the form of mental formations manifested on the upper level of our consciousness.

Please remind yourselves that you are on a retreat with a good Sangha. Not many people have the opportunity to take time off for a retreat and to practice with a Sangha. Together we are practicing the way of awareness, touching things that make us happy and gladdening our mind. There are people who do not know where to go. We know the path of transformation and healing. Each time we have taken it, it has helped us. We have faith in the Dharma. If we touch that seed of confidence within us, we will gladden our mind and bring ourselves peace and joy. The practice of self-nourishment is to grow stronger and go far for our sake and the sake of those around us.

[BELL]

CHAPTER SEVEN

Cultivating Joy

Dear Sangha, today is the thirty-first of May, 1998, and we are beginning the second week of our twenty-one-day retreat. Today we will continue the practice of cultivating joy. The Buddha wants to help us get the nourishment we need in order to be stronger and go further in the practice. He encourages us to relax our bodies, to embrace our pleasant feelings, and to create joy and happiness for our nourishment. Cultivating joy means to strengthen our happiness and nourish ourselves.

Deep in our consciousness there are many wholesome, positive seeds. If we know how to touch them and water them, they will manifest themselves on the upper level of our consciousness — the mind consciousness. We have to practice looking deeply to recognize our wonderful seeds — the seeds of mindfulness, enlightenment, understanding, joy, and loving kindness. We might think that we cannot love because we have not been able to touch the seed of love within us. Through our practice, and with the support of a brother or a sister, we are able to touch our seeds of love, forgiveness, compassion, and joy. Some people say, "I don't know what joy is. I have absolutely no joy within me." That is because that person has not been able to touch the seed of joy within himself. The practice is to touch it and recognize it. This is the practice of cultivating joy.

We need to organize our daily lives so that the positive seeds are watered every day, and the negative seeds are not watered. We all have seeds of suspicion, despair, and anger. In one person, they are stronger; in another person, they are weaker. We do not want the people who live around us to water our negative seeds. Every time a negative seed is touched and watered, we suffer. That seed manifests itself on the upper level of our consciousness in the form of destructive energy — hatred, anger, and despair. Our practice is not to water these seeds, and to tell the people around us, "Darling, if you really love me, please don't water these seeds in me every day."

We have to sign a contract, a treaty, with ourselves and with the people we love: "I vow not to be unskillful. I vow not to water the negative seeds of anger, confusion, hatred, and violence in you, my darling. Please help me. If, out of forgetfulness, I start to water those seeds in you, you can remind me not to do that. I need your help and support not to water those negative seeds." After you have signed a treaty, when the other person is about to say or do something that waters your seed of suffering, you can say, "No, no, please, you promised." You can raise your hand, show your palm, or make any sign that functions as a signal to honor the mutual promise made by you and the other person who signed the contract. We can all do this as couples and families. When we are on very good terms — living joyfully together — we can sit down and sign an agreement about not watering our negative seeds.

Flower Watering

But we can do better than simply not watering our negative seeds; we can water our positive seeds of happiness, loving kindness, forgiveness, and joy. We call this the practice of selective watering. We water the flowers, not the garbage, so that the flowers will bloom in the other person. When we make the other person smile, we benefit as well. It does not take long to see the result of our practice.

Suppose you have a sister who is skillful at arranging flowers. For some time, she hasn't been her usual self, is withdrawn, and does not smile or show any joy. There is a lack of balance within her; she has too little joy and too much grief. By practicing selective watering, you increase her joy and help her become more balanced. Sometimes you need only a few days to do this.

You can go to your sister and say, "My dear sister, it has been a long time since you have arranged any flowers for us. Every time you offer us a vase of flowers that you have arranged, the whole house brightens, and there is a lot of joy. Why have you recently deprived us of that joy and happiness?" By sitting close to your sister, looking at her, smiling, and speaking like this, you are watering her seed of happiness, because she has a talent for flower arranging. She may begin by saying, "No, we don't need flowers. I am not happy enough to do it." But after you leave, she fetches a pair of scissors and goes to the garden, where she contemplates the branches and flowers. She cuts a few, brings them into the house, and spends half an hour arranging them. During that time, she is watering the seed of happiness within her. It is a joy for her to arrange flowers for people she loves. You began to water her seed of happiness, then she continued on her own by practicing flower arranging. When you next see her, she may appear different. She can smile because you have helped her to be happy. If we love someone, we should practice this. It is not difficult to look into a person and recognize his or her positive seeds. They exist in every one of us.

[BELL]

Flower watering should be authentic and based on the truth. You only say things that you believe to be true. When you see the positive seed in the other person, you express it: "Darling, I see a wonderful seed in you. That seed can bring you and many people happiness." If she does not practice, she does not know that the seed is in her. You can help her to water that seed. You recognize the seed and tell her that it is very precious. She is happy, and so are you.

I remember when we were celebrating Wesak, the Buddha's birthday, in the Lower Hamlet in Plum Village. There were many couples and families there from Bordeaux and Toulouse. During the Dharma talk, when I was giving instructions on how to water positive seeds, I noticed a lady crying in the audience. After walking meditation, I approached her husband and simply said, "Dear friend, your flower needs to be watered." He listened, and on the drive home to Bordeaux — which takes about an hour and a half — he practiced flower watering. By the time they arrived in Bordeaux, she was completely transformed into a joyful and happy person. He knew the teaching, but was not practicing. He needed someone to remind him to practice. He practiced for an hour and a half and the situation changed.

Flower watering is not difficult. You need only be sincere. You know that you are responsible for the person you love. He may be your father, your son, or your brother. She may be your mother, your daughter, or your sister. Happiness is not an individual matter. If the person you love is not happy, there is no way that you can be happy. That is why we practice. We bring back the smile to our loved one's face. We can do it. We have lived with her for a long time and know her weaknesses, strengths, and positive seeds. Why hesitate? Touch the positive, not the negative things in each other.

Your well-being is crucial for the stability and happiness of the people around you. Sometimes the person you love is in a contemplative mood. She is absorbed in her sorrow and worries, allowing them to overwhelm her. You can't just leave her; you have to release her from her self-imprisonment. You can say, "A penny for your thoughts, my darling. What are you doing? What are you thinking? Are you watering your negative seeds? That's not healthy for you or me. So please don't." Sometimes you don't need to ask; you just practice flower watering and release her from that state of being. You take good care of her, and she will take good care of you. If you sink into a state of sorrow and allow yourself to be overwhelmed, she will try to help you. This is the art that we have to develop.

Psychotherapists should master flower watering so they can help their clients restore their balance. Their clients can go home and practice with their family members. But first, therapists have to apply this discipline to themselves, to their own lives, before they can really help other people. A therapist can also be a Dharma teacher by living and sharing the Dharma in this way.

Touching the Past

A young man came from America to visit us in Plum Village. One day, he was asked to write down his mother's beautiful qualities. Other people were also given the assignment. Richard did not believe that he could write more than three lines. He said, "My father has many good qualities, but not my mother." However, he practiced like the others and, to his surprise, discovered after a few days that the list had grown quite long.

I think his mother had, at one time, made Richard suffer, and that suffering prevented him from seeing her other wonderful qualities. Let us think again of the image of the dying tree. When you see one tree dying in your garden, you might think that all the trees are dying. This is not true. We are often caught up in our perceptions. This is not wise. We have to be objective and touch all aspects of reality. We mustn't allow one aspect to prevent us from seeing the whole picture.

With the support of the Sangha, Richard completed the exercise. Afterwards, as part of the assignment, he wrote his mother a very sweet, healing letter, saying how proud he was to have a mother like her. Richard's wife told him that when his mother received the letter, she was incredibly moved. Richard had never talked to his mother with such loving words before. She had found a new son born of the Dharma, full of understanding and love, and Richard had found a new mother. The new mother was born from Richard's deep looking. When he practiced deep looking, his true mother began to reveal herself to him.

His mother cried a lot after reading the letter. She told Richard's wife that she wished her own mother were alive so she could write a similar letter. Richard was still practicing at Plum Village. When his wife told him this news, he wrote his mother another letter. "Mommy," he wrote, "don't think that Grandma no longer exists. She is still alive in you and in me. I can touch her anytime I want, just like I can touch you. I am a continuation of Grandma and of you. So write the letter. Grandma will receive it right away and read it. You won't even have to post it." This is the insight he got from the teaching and from the practice, which corresponds to the deep teaching of the Buddha.

We all have to practice like that. Our presence here means the presence of all our ancestors. They are still alive in us. Every time we smile, all the generations of our ancestors, our children, and the generations to come — all of whom are within us — smile too. We practice not just for ourselves, but for everyone, and the stream of life continues.

Richard's mother wrote a healing letter to her own mother. She cried tears of happiness while composing it. In the past, when her mother was alive, Richard's mother did not know the art of mindful living. Mother and daughter both made mistakes and created suffering for each other. Later, Richard's mother regretted this suffering, and it became an obstacle to her happiness. Writing this letter removed that obstacle from her path.

If you have made mistakes and caused your beloved to suffer, and if he or she is no longer alive, don't be frustrated. You can still heal the wound within you. The person whom you think has passed away is still alive in you. You can make him or her smile. Suppose, while your grandma was alive, you said something out of forgetfulness that made her unhappy, and you still regret it. Sit down, breathe in and out mindfully, visualize your grandma sitting with you, and say, "Grandma, I am sorry. I will never again say anything like that to you or anyone else I love." If you are sincere, focused, and utterly mindful, you will see her smiling in you and the wound will be healed. Mistakes come from unskillfulness and forgetfulness, which are in the mind. Because everything comes from the mind, everything can be removed and transformed by the mind. That is the teaching of the Buddha.

Although we think the past is gone and the future is not yet here, if we look deeply, we see that reality is more than that. The past exists in the guise of the present, because the present is made from the past. In this teaching, if we establish ourselves firmly in the present and touch the present moment deeply, we also touch the past and have the power to repair it. That is a wonderful teaching and practice. We don't have to bear our wounds forever. We are all unmindful at times; we have made mistakes in the past. It does not mean that we have to always carry that guilt without transforming it. Touch the present deeply, and you touch the past. Take care of the present, and you can repair the past. The practice of beginning anew is a practice of the mind. Once you realize what mistake you made in the past, you are determined never to do it again. Then the wound is healed. It is a wonderful practice.

A Vietnam War veteran in America told me this story. When he was in Vietnam, he saw many of his friends killed in an ambush. He was so mad and vengeful that he decided to kill some people from the village where the ambush had taken place. He poisoned a bag of sandwiches, left them at the entrance to the village, and hid to watch. A group of children passed by and saw the sandwiches. They happily shared them. Once they had eaten them, they began to cry and say that they had been poisoned. Their parents tried to find a car to take them to the hospital, but the nearest hospital was far away. The GI knew that there was no hope, that the children would die. He had done a terrible thing out of anger, ill-will, and vengeance; he had killed five children.

After he was released from the army and returned home, he did not have any peace. He bore this wound within himself for ten years. Then he came to a retreat in Santa Barbara that we offered to Vietnam War veterans. The veterans were encouraged to speak of their suffering, though it was difficult for them to do so. Only one person — his mother — had heard this man's story. She had said, "Don't suffer too much, my son. In war, these things happen." But that did not help him. Every time he found himself sitting in a room with children, he could not bear it and had to leave. That day, with the strong support of the Sangha — monks, nuns, psychotherapists who work with war veterans, and other friends in the practice — he was able to tell the story to a group of about nine people. Sometimes we had to sit and breathe for a long time — an hour or so — waiting for him to continue. He just sat and cried and was unable to say anything.

After I heard the story, I invited him to my room. I said, "Dear friend, it's true that you killed five children. But there is something you can do to repair that. There are many children today who are dying from lack of food and medicine. Forty thousand children die every day from starvation and malnutrition. Why don't you do something to save the dying children today, instead of letting yourself be imprisoned by the memory of those five children? You have to begin anew. You have to use your life to do the opposite of what you have done in the past. Make a vow to receive the Mindfulness Trainings, and, from now on, do your best to protect and save the lives of children. Go into the world and save the children. Why imprison yourself in guilt when you can repair the past?"

The door was unlocked, and he was transformed, beginning anew. We get powerful energy from the practice, the Sangha, and from our determination to follow the right path. It can wipe away the suffering of the past and transform our guilt.

[BELL]

Untying Our Knots

The eleventh exercise of mindful breathing proposed by the Buddha is concentrating our mind: "Concentrating on my mental formations, I breathe in." This is the art of taking care of negative mental formations. If we embrace them mindfully with our joy, peace, and happiness, we will cultivate more positive seeds. That was the practice of the tenth exercise: gladdening our mind. Now we are dealing with our negative seeds, like pain, suffering, grief, and sorrow. We try to ignore them, because when they surface and manifest themselves, we suffer. We wish these blocks of pain, sorrow, and fear would lie still, deep down in the bottom of our consciousness, so that we can be at peace. But they won't always stay down there; they emerge in our dreams or when we are not busy with the television, magazines, conversations, and so on.

We are partly responsible for these blocks of suffering because we have lived in a way that enabled them to form. The people who live around us and with us are co-responsible for the formation of these internal knots. Unless we know how to untie them, these knots will continue to make us suffer.

The Sanskrit word for these internal formations is *samyojana.* The samyojana can be sweet or bitter. For instance, when you drink alcohol or take drugs, you may become addicted to the samyojana. The samyojana of the drug is in your body and in your consciousness. To satisfy its need, you might steal or kill to get money to buy more drugs. That fatal need makes you lose your freedom. That is an internal knot, a samyojana. Sometimes we don't have the courage to let the internal formation go, and we cling to our suffering. Twelve-Step programs are one way of untying the internal knot of alcoholism. Another example of a samyojana is the kind of binding love that deprives you of your freedom and joy. At first, it seems sweet and pleasant, but if you become addicted to it, it turns into an obstacle in your path.

Looking deeply into our body and consciousness, we recognize our internal knots. True happiness is not possible unless we know how to untie these knots and become free. When the person you love says something unmindful or unkind, you might get an internal knot — it may be a small knot, but it is a knot. It can become harmful if you don't untie it, and the next time your beloved makes the same mistake, the knot will grow. Out of forgetfulness, we create internal knots in each other and don't realize it, until one day we can no longer look each other in the eye, and we watch television instead. To untie the knot, we have to begin anew with our beloved. Say, "Darling, why did you say such a thing to me? Why did you do such a thing to me?" If we are skilled practitioners, we do not allow the knot to become stronger.

Mindful living helps us know when an internal knot is being formed. If you are a good practitioner, you don't let it go unnoticed. You are aware that you must untie the knot right away to ensure your long-lasting happiness. Young couples need to practice looking deeply every day to see whether their situation is safe.

You do not have to sit quietly by yourself to practice this. You can sit with your beloved and practice directing your deep looking in the same direction. If the internal knots are already very strong, you have to learn how to untie them. Most of us don't do this because we don't know how. We are afraid of going back to our true home and encountering these blocks of suffering. That is why we run away and escape. We do not behave responsibly. Television and shopping provide us with countless ways to escape.

Mindful Consumption

A Vietnamese refugee who immigrated to the United States told me that he bought a statue of a Buddha and placed it on his TV. Since his house was small, he did not have an altar. I told him, "The TV is not an appropriate place for the Buddha. The two things don't go together. The television lets you escape from yourself, and the Buddha calls you back to yourself."

The Buddha calls you back to yourself to take care of your internal situation. The mind consciousness is like the living room, and the store consciousness is like the basement — we put the things we don't like down there. But internal formations always try to emerge. They don't need to be invited into the living room; they just push the door open, come in, and settle down. When our living room does not look tidy and beautiful, we suffer. We lock the door. We practice suppression. We do not want these knots to emerge. We invite other guests into the living room so that every minute of our life is filled with newspapers, magazines, novels, television, conversations, and the telephone. We do everything to keep the living room busy, so that the unpleasant things don't surface. Most of us do this because we are afraid of ourselves. There are many disadvantages to this behavior.

The first disadvantage is that the guests we invite in cause more damage to the base of our being. We consume toxins daily. If we entertain toxins in our mind consciousness for an hour, then we are also nourishing our internal formations down in our store consciousness. One hour of television feeds the seeds of fear, craving, and despair in our consciousness. This is the process of self-intoxication. We also allow our children to become intoxicated with television for several hours a day. We must practice mindful consumption of television.

In detective films, someone always gets killed. If this doesn't happen, it's not a detective film. Every time you see a detective film, you witness someone's death. The characters use guns to eliminate the character they don't like. Later, when there is something we don't like in our life, we want to get rid of it by eliminating it. Through films, we allow our children to be penetrated by tendencies of violence, anger, and despair. I don't understand why legislators in the U.S. do not stem this self-destruction of our consciousness. We know there is an epidemic of children shooting each other, yet there is no law forbidding the use of guns. In the name of freedom and self-defense, we allow people to buy and sell guns. Where is our enlightenment? Mindfulness is the capacity of knowing what is going on. Teachers, educators, journalists, and filmmakers have to create awareness and enlightenment. You have to remind the Congress and Senate to act. We cannot allow things to go on like this.

At the age of twelve or thirteen, some children are beginning to have sex. They don't even know what love is. It is empty sex. If young people become used to empty sex, they lose their innocence. There is no more innocence or meaningful love. There is also violence — even among children — coupled with sex. We have to act. We have to wake ourselves and others up. We have to ask people to think and move in the direction of self-protection and protection of the whole nation. We cannot practice solely as individuals, but as a Sangha. The city should practice as a city Sangha, and the country should practice as a country Sangha.

The second disadvantage of keeping our mind consciousness occupied by unwholesome things is that we create bad circulation in our psyche. Like our blood, our psyche should circulate properly. If our blood circulation is poor, then symptoms of disease appear. If we massage ourselves, our blood flows better. The most painful spot in our body needs to be massaged more, because it holds more toxins. Likewise, we need to massage the spots of pain and suffering in our psyche. By seeking distraction, we do the opposite and prevent the blood of the psyche from circulating. We don't want our blocks of suffering to surface. When the psyche is blocked and has bad circulation, symptoms of mental illness appear. We have to do something to restore good circulation in our psyche. We need to unlock the door so that the pain and sorrow we fear can circulate. That is why the Buddha teaches us to cultivate the energy of mindfulness so that we are ready to embrace our pain when it comes up.

[BELL]

Embracing Our Negative Seeds

When the seeds of hatred, anger, or violence emerge, they manifest as mental formations. Mind consciousness is the home of mental formations. When we allow our negative energy to surface, we are ready to touch our seeds of understanding, awakening, and mindfulness. We invite them to the surface so they can help us take care of our pain. This is why the daily practice of mindfulness is so important. We need this positive energy to help us embrace our pain.

If your energy of mindfulness is not strong enough to embrace your negative energy, ask someone to sit close to you and lend you his mindfulness, so that together you are strong enough to embrace the feelings. Take your friend, your son, your daughter, or your partner's hand. Breathe with her, generating the energy of mindfulness. Help her to embrace her anger or despair. During this process of embracing and recognizing, the energy of mindfulness will begin to penetrate the negative energy. This is a beautiful practice. You take care of your suffering and help your beloved take care of her suffering. Families should do this often. This is meditation. Meditation is not just sitting quietly in the meditation hall.

Mindfulness is like the sunlight. In the morning, the tulip is not yet open. The sun rises and begins to shine on the tulip. Light is made of tiny particles called photons. When the sunlight embraces the flower, the photons try to penetrate into the flower. If the sun continues to shine for a few hours, there will be enough energy for the flower to open her heart to the sun. We let our mindfulness tenderly embrace our anger, like a mother embraces her suffering baby. We say, "I'm here. Don't worry, I'll take care of you." This is our first mantra. As we continue to hold the suffering baby in our arms of tender mindfulness, the energy of mindfulness begins to penetrate our affliction. It is like when a mother suddenly hears her baby crying. She stops what she is doing, picks up her baby, and holds him tenderly in her arms, without even knowing what is wrong with him. The baby may find some relief and stop crying just through being held tenderly.

When you generate the energy of mindfulness and embrace

your anger, even though the anger is still present, you find some relief. The second form of energy has begun to penetrate into the first. If the mother continues to hold her child for a while, she is able to see what is wrong with him. A mother is very skilled in this practice. With insight, the mother can easily remedy the situation. If the baby is hungry, she gives him some milk. If his diaper is too tight, she loosens it. If he is sick, she nurses him back to health. Happiness and well-being are the results.

While holding our block of pain, we find some relief. Looking deeply into it, we get some insight into the nature of our anger and affliction. This insight liberates us. Sometimes, we don't succeed one hundred percent in the practice, but we always succeed to some extent. After holding the baby of suffering for a while and finding some relief, our suffering will go back to our store consciousness in the form of a seed. It will come up again at some time in the future. When it surfaces, we practice in the same way — holding it tenderly with mindfulness. Every time we do this, our pain and sorrow weaken a little more before they return to the base. We gain some confidence, knowing we have the capacity of holding and taking care of our sorrow. This is wonderful.

[BELL]

The Five Remembrances

There are many ways for us to confront our fear. The practice of the Five Remembrances helps us to cultivate non-fear. The First Remembrance is to breathe mindfully and say, "I will grow old. Breathing in, I know I will grow old. Breathing out, I know I cannot escape old age." We are afraid of growing old. We think, "Old age is for other people, but I am still young. I don't want to think about it." But the fear lingers. The Second Remembrance is, "I will die. I cannot escape death. Breathing in, I know that I will die. Breathing out, I know that I cannot escape dying." The Third Remembrance is, "I will get sick. I cannot escape the sickness that accompanies old age and dying." The Fourth Remembrance is, "One day I will have to leave everything I cherish today and the people I love. I will have to let them go. This means I cannot take them with me when I die. I have come empty-handed, and I will also leave empty-handed." The Fifth Remembrance is, "I am the sole inheritor of my actions. I only take the fruit of my actions with me." Action here means *karma.* We reap what we have sown. We take only the outcome of our actions with us.

These are hard facts to confront: sickness, old age, death, the abandonment of loved ones and what we cherish, and the fact that we cannot take anything with us except the fruit of our actions. These are the bare facts. This is reality. Intellectually, we know this, but emotionally, we don't want to think about it. The seed of fear is always there at the base of our consciousness. The Buddha said, "Allow those seeds to surface." He urged his monks and nuns to practice the Five Remembrances. Each morning, we breathe in and out and confront our fear. Even if fear does not surface, we invite it to come up. We think, "I will die. I cannot escape dying. Good morning, my fear. I know you are there." After having been invited, your fear will return to its original place. This is good circulation for the psyche. During that time, your fear takes a bath in the ocean of mindfulness. You offer a swimming pool to your internal formations. You embrace your afflictions for a few minutes, they are weakened, and then they return to the store consciousness.

If you do this every day, your fear will lessen. This is the Buddha's prescription. We deal not only with fear in this way, but with whatever afflictions we have in the depth of our consciousness. When the psyche has good circulation, our symptoms of mental illness soon disappear.

I would like to say a bit more about anger. Some therapists say that you have to get in touch with your anger, recognize it, then get it out of your system by venting it. I think that they are right to say that you have to touch your anger and recognize it;

you cannot suppress your anger. But the important point is that we touch and recognize our anger with the energy of mindfulness. I'm not so sure about venting. Some therapists advise their clients to vent their anger by expressing it. Expressing anger is not a safe thing to do. Some therapists advise their clients to go into their room, lock the door, and pound on a pillow. They say, "Get a big, solid pillow and use your whole strength to beat it." This is called venting.

Of course, you may get some relief from beating a pillow for half an hour; you become exhausted. Then you get hungry, eat something, and are recharged. If someone then waters the seed of your anger, you might get as angry as you were before — maybe even angrier. While you were expressing your anger, you were actually rehearsing your anger and making the seed of anger grow bigger. That is dangerous.

I don't believe in venting. A number of therapists, after advising their clients to do it, have told me that it is dangerous. The person becomes used to venting his or her anger. Maybe he sees someone in the street and vents right there. He may land in jail because of his habit of venting. He is no longer locked in a room with his pillow; the object of his anger is a person. I do not see how beating a pillow means you are getting in touch with your anger. If you are not mindful, how can you get in touch with your anger? You are just allowing your anger to overwhelm and dominate you, and that is not getting in touch. You aren't even in touch with the pillow. If you were really in touch with it, you would know that it is only a pillow and wouldn't hit it so hard. That is why we practice embracing our anger, recognizing it, talking to it, and looking deeply into it.

The Buddha said, "When you get angry, refrain from talking or acting. Talking and acting while you are angry can be very dangerous. Don't say or do anything. Just go back to your in-breath and your out-breath and take good care of your anger." When you are angry, you usually pay careful attention to what the other person is saying and doing, but you do not pay enough attention to your own suffering. The more you listen to the other person, the angrier you become. That is why it is better not to do anything. Go back and take good care of your anger. When your house is on fire, the first thing you do is try to put the fire out — not to run after the person you think started the fire.

You may like to practice walking meditation to calm your anger while you continue looking into it. Practicing in this way, you may get the insight you need. Your first insight may be this: "The main cause of my suffering is not really that person. It is because my seed of anger, my internal knot, has grown too big. As soon as someone touches it, it becomes very powerful, and I suffer. Other people have weaker seeds of anger, and they don't get as angry as I do when they hear or see the same things." Your first insight may be that you have a huge internal formation of anger, and that that is the main cause of your suffering. The other person is only a secondary cause.

As you continue to walk calmly, you may have other insights — like how much better you feel now. You know how to embrace your anger and bring yourself some relief. But the other person may still be in hell. He does not know how to take good care of his anger. When a person suffers so much, his suffering spills over, and the people around him also experience it. If your husband or wife, or your son or daughter suffers a lot, you must help him or her. If you don't help, who will?

By this time, your anger has been transformed into compassion. Your garbage is transformed into flowers by the practice of breathing, walking, and embracing your afflictions. We can train ourselves to do this. First, we do it with a brother or sister in the practice, and later, we do it alone. We set an example for the members of our family. We inspire respect. When people see us dealing with our anger like this, they truly respect us and want to learn how to do it themselves.

[BELL]

CHAPTER EIGHT

Transformation at the Base

My dear Sangha, today is the second of June, 1998. Our breathing should be pleasant and joyful. If you are ever unsure about what to do, go back and enjoy your breathing.

I believe you already know this exercise: "In/out. Deep/slow. Calm/ease. Smile/release. Present moment/wonderful moment." It is a very pleasant practice. You can practice mindful breathing while driving, on the bus or train, or even while washing the dishes. Smile to yourself and your dish washing. "Breathing in, I know that I am breathing in. Breathing out, I know that I am breathing out." "In/out." Enjoy your in-breath and your out-breath. If you do this very simple exercise correctly, it yields miracles. Be at one with your in-breath and your out-breath. Be fully alive — fully present in the here and the now. This is a miracle that you can perform at any time. When you breathe with mindfulness and concentration, life becomes present. You stop thinking about everything else and become one with your breathing. It's wonderful. After a few minutes doing this practice, the quality of your breathing automatically improves.

Now let's try the second line: "Deep/slow." It means, "Breathing in, I know that my in-breath has become deep." It has deepened naturally, not because we make it deeper. "Breathing out, I know that my out-breath has become slow." It has become slower by itself, not because we make it slower. Whenever mindfulness touches something, it improves the quality of that thing. With mindfulness, our breathing becomes more harmonious and calmer, and we feel a growing sense of pleasure in our body and consciousness.

[BELL]

Then we practice the third line of the gatha: "Calm/ease." "Breathing in, I calm the formation called body. Breathing out, I calm the formation called feeling. Experiencing the feeling, I breathe in and out. Calming the feeling, I breathe in and out."

This exercise is very rewarding and pleasant. To calm means, "Breathing in, I feel calm within my body and my feelings." We experience our body and feelings, breathing in and out to calm first one, then the other. "Ease" means, "Breathing out, I feel at ease with myself, and I do everything with ease." We take our time; we do not hurry, and we feel wonderful in the present moment. We feel light; we aren't burdened by our worries and afflictions, and we have freedom within. We feel that we are really being ourselves, not the victim of our regrets about the past or worries about the future.

The next line is: "Smile/release." "Breathing in, I smile. Breathing out, I let go." We let go of our projects, worries, and regrets. Because the present moment is so wonderful, and we are capable of touching the wonders of life in the present moment, we smile while we breathe in. Our smile releases all the tension left in our face and body. It is a smile of victory, a smile of loving kindness directed toward our body and feelings. When we breathe out, we release and become free.

There is nothing more precious than our peace, stability, and freedom. We cannot exchange these for anything else. "Release" means we have become ourselves. We are capable of releasing all of our cows and our ideas — even our ideas of happiness. Each of us is caught in an idea of happiness. We believe that we will be truly happy when certain conditions are fulfilled. We don't realize that this idea is an obstacle to our true happiness. If we can release our idea of happiness, true happiness is born in us right away. I know some young people who think that they can only be happy if they earn a degree, get a certain job, or marry a certain person. We set up conditions for our happiness and become trapped. Happiness can come to us at any time if we are free. Why do we commit ourselves to only one idea of happiness? When we do this, we limit our happiness. If we let go of that idea, happiness will come to us from every direction.

A whole country may be under the spell of an idea of happiness for many years. A whole nation may think that unless it carries out a certain five-year program, or embraces and realizes a particular ideology, there will be no future for its citizens. Unless the nation realizes that this idea is an obstacle to its happiness, it might experience tragedy. If we are lucky, we can release such false ideas. "Breathing in, I smile. Breathing out, I release."

[BELL]

We can be extremely happy just sitting and breathing in and out. We don't have to do or achieve anything. We enjoy the miracle of life, the miracle of simply being here. "Smile/release" can bring us a lot of much-needed happiness. That nourishing joy and happiness will help heal the wounds within our body and soul.

Present Moment/Wonderful Moment

The last line of the gatha is: "Present moment/wonderful moment." "Breathing in, I establish myself in the present moment. Breathing out, I know that this is a wonderful moment." Someone may ask you, "Has the most wonderful moment of your life arrived?" You may feel embarrassed to say, "I don't think so. But I believe it will arrive soon. Otherwise, my life will have had no meaning." Using our intelligence to look deeply, we know that if we continue to live in the way we may have lived for the past twenty years — not mindfully, always running, always trying to escape — then the most wonderful moment of our life will not arrive soon. In this teaching, we learn that we have to make the present moment the most wonderful moment of our life, because the present moment is the only moment available to us. If we know how to go back to the present moment and be fully alive, to touch the wonders of life in that moment, it is the most wonderful moment of our life. We have the capacity to do this. Through simple practices like walking, breathing, smiling, or touching the beauty of life with mindfulness, we can make paradise — the Kingdom of God — available to us in the here and the now.

I always tell my friends that they don't have to die to enter the Kingdom of God — in fact, they have to be alive to do so. We know how to be alive. Breathing in and out mindfully, becoming fully present, with body and mind united — these are the conditions for entering the Kingdom of God. You need only take one step, and you are there.

This practice is not difficult; we can all do it. But as I have already mentioned, we have a strong habitual energy that prevents us from doing it. This habitual energy is always pushing us ahead, telling us that happiness is not possible in the present moment, but in the future. We follow that belief and are pushed by that energy. We run all our lives searching for the most wonderful moment. First we have to practice stopping — *shamatha.* To meditate is, foremost, to master the art of stopping and to not allow the horse of habitual energy to carry us away from the here and the now. While we breathe in, we ground ourselves in the here and the now. We united our body and mind and establish ourselves in the present moment. Breathing out, we know that this is a wonderful moment. "Present moment/only moment."

As you walk from your room to the cafeteria, enjoy this practice. You don't need to practice all five exercises: "In/out, deep/

slow, calm/ease, smile/release, present moment/wonderful moment." You can practice just one or two. Coordinate your steps with your breath. Enjoy walking and stepping into freedom. Every step you take helps you to arrive in the here and the now. Every step helps you make the most wonderful moment of your life happen. Deep down, you know you can do it. And remember that the Sangha is here to support you. You can transform the land of suffering into a land of bliss — the Pure Land or the Kingdom of God. Everything depends on you and your mind.

If your habitual energy is very strong, you can try this exercise: sign a treaty with a portion of a path, or with a set of stairs, agreeing that every time you walk on this path or go up and down these stairs, you will practice mindful breathing and walking. If you forget to take mindful steps, stop and begin again. You will see a difference if you practice like this for a few weeks. I have signed such a treaty with the stairs in my hermitage. In the last twenty years, I have never taken one forgetful step there; I have honored my treaty with the stairs. That is why I walk mindfully everywhere. Climbing into an airplane, I walk as if I am climbing the Gridhrakuta Mountain where the Buddha used to sit. Peace is always available. If there is a set of stairs in your house, sign an agreement with it. Commit yourself to going up and down those stairs in mindfulness, and train yourself to enjoy every step. If you take the bus to work, sign a treaty with the road leading from your house to the bus stop. Vow to walk to the bus stop with mindful steps. It doesn't have to be a long path; forty or fifty steps is enough. Walking meditation is a wonderful way to learn how to live each moment of our daily life deeply. Please try it.

In Plum Village, we support each other in our practice, so it is easier for transformation and healing to take place. It would be wonderful if you could arrange for your whole family to take part in the practice. Use loving speech, and don't focus too much on the form of the practice. Let it be natural and pleasant, and set an example. If your smile — your loving kindness, your freshness — is real, you will persuade your family to join you in the practice.

Transformation at the Base

Today we will continue with the eleventh and twelfth exercises of mindful breathing proposed by the Buddha in the *Discourse on the Full Awareness of Breathing*. The eleventh is: "Concentrating the mind, I breathe in and I breathe out." The twelfth is: "Liberating the mind, I breathe in and I breathe out." Please remember that the mind means the mental formation that is present in our mind consciousness. If it is a wholesome mental formation, then by concentrating on it, we can develop it for our greater joy and happiness. If it is a negative mental formation — fear, anger, or doubt — concentrating on and embracing it will bring us some relief and help us look deeply into it. Looking deeply can bring us liberating insight.

Transformation means transformation at the base *(ashraya-paravritti)*, which is true transformation and not just momentary relief. For transformation at the base to take place, you have to practice looking deeply. Only by looking deeply into the nature of our suffering can we discover its causes and identify the sources of the nutriments that have brought it into being. After we have practiced for some time, we will see that transformation always takes place at the bottom of our consciousness. Our store consciousness is like the support, the base, or the foundation for our consciousness — in the same way that these table legs are a support for the table. *Ashraya* means support, or base, and *paravritti* means transformation — transformation at the base.

Looking deeply, we gain insights that can liberate us and transform our afflictions in their form as seeds. The mental formation is manifested on the level of mind, but the seed of the mental formation always stays in the store consciousness. If we know how to acknowledge and recognize the presence of the mental formation, embrace it, calm it, and look deeply into it, we will gain insight. If a seed of anger manifests and a seed of mindfulness also manifests, the energy of mindfulness embraces the energy of anger. It recognizes, embraces, calms, and looks deeply.

Transformation and emancipation can only take place when insight is attained. Insight is attained through the practices of stopping and looking deeply. Meditation is made up of two elements. The first is shamatha — stopping, concentrating, and calming. If you go to China, you will see this sign 止 on the roads. It means "Stop." I suggest you display this sign somewhere in your home. Facing it, you may like to practice mindful breathing for five or ten minutes so that you can realize stopping. The second element of meditation is vipashyana. It means deep looking, inquiry, and observation. It is difficult to look deeply without stopping. If you are capable of looking deeply, it means you are able to stop.

As we already know, we have to deal with the energy that is always pushing us and not allowing us to stop. I have described our habitual energy as a runaway horse. The Buddha proposed stopping habitual energy with mindfulness. Every time we are restless — no matter what time of day it is or what we are doing — we practice mindful breathing to recognize our habitual energy. We say, "Hello, habitual energy. I know you are there." We smile at it. *Vasana* is the name of that energy. As I have already mentioned, we have all received this habitual energy from our parents and ancestors, who were unable to transform it. This is why it was transmitted to us. We have to learn how to deal with it. If we don't learn how to transform it, we will transmit it to our children.

Every summer at Plum Village, we celebrate Thanksgiving Day in our own way. Groups of students from different countries come together, cook their own national dish, and place it on their ancestors' altar. If there are people from twenty-five different countries practicing, we make twenty-five different dishes. Each group comes together and discusses what kind of dish it will offer. The students prepare their dishes mindfully, touching their ancestors and their nation's culture.

Transmission

One time, a young American man went to buy provisions for the meal in Ste. Foy la Grande. He had been at Plum Village for three weeks, and he felt wonderful — very peaceful and joyful. Surrounded by a practicing Sangha, he had been practicing walking and sitting meditation and mindful work. Alone in Ste. Foy la Grande, he suddenly felt in a rush. Relying on his three-week practice of mindful breathing and walking, he was able to identify it as the negative energies of restlessness and haste. His mindfulness was sufficient for him to go back to his breathing. He breathed in and out, smiling, and said, "Hello, Mommy. I know you are there." He realized that this restless energy came from his mother. Always restless and in a hurry, she had transmitted that energy to him. During the three weeks of practice in the Upper Hamlet, he had been surrounded by a powerful Sangha, and the seed of restlessness had not had the chance to surface. Only when he ventured to the market alone could the environment touch that seed in him and allow it to manifest. After he recognized this energy with mindful breathing, his restlessness disappeared and returned to its seed form. From then on, he continued the practice of mindful breathing, maintaining his peace and joyfulness.

Watering Our Positive Seeds

As I have mentioned before, we have all received both positive and negative seeds from our parents and ancestors. Some of us were abused as children — treated violently by our parents — and we suffered a lot. We have sincerely vowed never to behave like our parents when we grow up. But if we don't know how to transform our negative energy, we will treat our children exactly as our parents treated us.

I have seen this happen many times. As a child, you suffered because your parents let you down and abandoned you. The wounded child in you is still alive. You are vulnerable and afraid that your friends, partner, and other people will also let you down. You know the pain of being abandoned, and you don't want other people to suffer as you did. Yet if you don't know how to heal the wounded child within or to transform your negative seeds, you will make your children and friends suffer as you were made to suffer. You will blame people for having made you suffer. You know that it is not good to abuse people, let them down, exclude them, and hurt the already wounded child in them, yet you still do it. If your children do not have the chance to be with a Sangha and meet a good teacher, they may not be able to transform this seed in themselves, and they will transmit it to their children. This is the vicious cycle called *samsara.* To practice means to cut through this cycle and end it. We should recognize our negative afflictions — our negative elements — and realize that they are present at the base of our consciousness. We have to intervene and practice so that there is true transformation, not just temporary relief. This is transformation at the base; it can be achieved in two ways.

The first way is direct contemplation of the nature of a seed. We invite the seed of suffering to surface. If we have already cultivated the energy of mindfulness, it will not be difficult to invite the seed up, embrace it, and look deeply into its nature. This is the direct way to disintegrate it. Only the light of insight and understanding can transform our seeds of affliction. The second way is indirect and equally effective. We sow and water our positive seeds. Instead of inviting the seed up to embrace it and look deeply into it, we leave it where it is and do other things to aid its transformation. We can do this individually or as a Sangha. Touching the positive, refreshing, and healing elements of life every day is a pleasant practice that can lead to healing and transformation.

I left Vietnam in 1966 to come to the West and call for peace. I was not allowed to return home. The two warring parties were angry with me for daring to speak the truth about the nature of the war. Most of us in Vietnam were not in favor of the war, and wanted it to end. We were its victims. We didn't want the people in our country to kill each other. But our voice was lost amidst the bombs and mortars. Sometimes we burned ourselves alive in the hope that our voice would be heard abroad. We were suppressed and desperate and wanted people to listen to us; we had no means to make our suffering understood or our voice heard. So we converted our bodies into torches to capture people's attention and let them know what we really wanted — not victory, but a quick cessation to the killing. I left Vietnam so I could speak for the majority of my people who did not support the war and wanted to stop the killing. Because of this, I could not return home.

I became an exile at the beginning of June, 1966. At that time, all my friends, my work, everything was in Vietnam — the School of Youth for Social Service, the *Buddhist Weekly* magazine, Van Hanh Buddhist University. It was very hard for me to be away. There were times when I woke up at night and did not know where I was, because I was traveling to so many speaking engagements. I often dreamed of going home to my monastery to see my friends, my brothers, sisters, and coworkers. In a recurring dream, I saw a beautiful green hill with many lovely trees. After climbing halfway up the hill, I would always wake up and find myself in exile. It was a hard time for me, and I had this dream over and over again.

I adopted Europe as my home. At that time, America was at war with Vietnam, so there was no option of staying in America. Everything in Europe was different — the trees, the fruit, the birds, and the people. I practiced walking, breathing, and touching the wonders of life that surrounded me. I played with the French and German children. I made friends with Catholic priests and Protestant ministers. I learned to eat Western food — bread instead of rice. I realized that the mountains, rivers, people, and children in Europe were beautiful. I survived because of this practice. Gradually, I watered my seeds of happiness. One day I realized that my recurring dream had stopped. I was no longer bitter about my exile and did not suffer because of it.

Now I can say that I no longer miss my home, because I can see my country and my people within my body and consciousness. I am practically there at the same time that I am here. Friends who have gone to Vietnam tell me that I am present in Vietnam; my teachings and my books have found their way back to Vietnam. My books are published underground, and my tapes — even videotapes — I don't know how — are there. Many of the younger generations of monks and nuns listen to my teachings through reading my books. The suffering and bitterness of 1966 is no longer with me. This is not because I have invited the seed of suffering and exile up and looked directly into it, but because I have practiced watering the seeds of happiness. I continue to recognize what is beautiful, refreshing, and healing around me.

When you help your positive, wholesome seeds to grow, they will modify and transform your other seeds. They are like antibodies surrounding a foreign body. They take care of, surround, and transform the negative seed. Our seeds are impermanent and can change at any moment. If we know how to plant seeds of the opposite nature, we can help our wholesome, refreshing seeds to grow. They will embrace our negative seeds and help transform them. This explains why my unpleasant dream stopped of its own accord.

[BELL]

Looking Deeply

We know that the transformation and healing we seek is attained through our insight and understanding. Thanks to understanding and compassion, release becomes possible. The Buddha said that our afflictions — fear, sorrow, and pain — are born from a lack of understanding. That is why the practice of looking deeply is so important for gaining insight. In Buddhism, salvation and emancipation are realized through understanding. Looking deeply helps us to understand the nature of our suffering, and also the nature of the suffering of the person whom we believe to be the cause of our misery.

About fifteen years ago, a fourteen-year-old Swiss boy used to come and stay at Plum Village. Every summer, he came with his younger sister and practiced with us. This boy did not like his father at all. He was very angry with him because his father did not speak kindly. If the boy fell down and hurt himself while playing, instead of helping and comforting him, his father would always shout, "You're stupid! Why did you do such a thing?" The boy thought his father should help him and comfort him with kind words. He had difficulty understanding his father and vowed that he would behave differently as an adult; if ever his son should fall and hurt himself, he would help him up and comfort him.

One day, this boy was sitting in the Lower Hamlet watching his sister play on a hammock with another girl. They were swinging back and forth. Suddenly, the hammock turned over and both girls fell to the ground. His sister cut her forehead. When the boy saw his sister bleeding, he became furious and was about to shout at her, "You're stupid! Why did you hurt yourself like that?" But because he knew of the practice, he went back to his breathing and decided to do walking meditation instead. During his walking meditation, he discovered something wonderful: that he was exactly like his father. He had the same kind of energy and, as he called it, stupidity. When your loved ones are suffering, you should be loving, tender, and helpful, and not shout at them out of anger. He saw that he was behaving exactly like his father. That was his insight. Imagine a fourteen-year-old boy practicing like that. He realized he was the continuation of his father and had the same kind of energy, the same negative seed.

Continuing to walk mindfully, he discovered that he could not transform his anger without practice, and that if he did not practice, he would transmit the same habitual energy to his children. I think it is remarkable for a fourteen-year-old boy to succeed like this in meditation. He gained these two insights in less than fifteen minutes of walking meditation.

His third and final insight was that he should go back to Switzerland and discuss his discoveries with his father. He decided to invite his father to practice with him so that both of them could transform their energy. With this third insight, his anger at his father vanished because he understood that his father was also the victim of the transmission of a negative seed. His father might have gotten it from his own father. I was astonished by this third insight because it meant the young boy was able to understand that his father was a victim of transmission.

Many of us have suffered because of our parents. As I have mentioned before, many of us know we have a wounded child within. Some of us say, "I don't want to have anything to do with my parents." This is not possible, because we are the continuation of our parents; we are our parents. There is no way to escape this. The only way is to have some reconciliation with ourselves and with our internal parents. There is no other way. The path is clear. We have been victims of negative behavior, negative seeds, but by practicing deeply, we realize that the other person may also be the victim of the transmission of that seed. He or she never met a teacher and a Sangha, and the seed was not transformed. Later, it was transmitted to us. When you see your parents as victims of transmission, your anger will vanish. This practice of looking deeply to gain understanding and freedom from your anger is very important.

One time, everyone staying in the Upper Hamlet in Plum Village was asked to write a love letter to their father. One young practitioner from North America said that he would never be able to write this letter; just thinking about his father made him angry and caused him a lot of suffering. His father had, in fact, passed away, and yet there was no reconciliation between them. I proposed he do the following exercise for one week: "Breathing in, I see myself as a five-year-old boy. Breathing out, I smile to myself as a five-year-old boy." Breathing in, I asked him to visualize himself as a very vulnerable five-year-old boy. When he saw how vulnerable he was, it was easy for him to have compassion for the child he had been. Breathing out, he smiled to himself as a five-year-old boy. At five years old, he had already experienced problems and suffering with his father. Maybe he had tried to tell his father something but could not find the words. While he was searching, his father, who may have been in a bad mood, may have shouted, "Shut up!" That would have created a wound in the boy's tender heart and made him afraid to try again. He was never able to tell his father of his suffering and difficulties because he wasn't encouraged to do so; his father did not have the patience to listen. When he breathed out, he used the compassion that was born in him to embrace his wounded child within. "Breathing in, I see myself as a five-year-old boy. Breathing out, I smile to myself as a five-year-old boy."

The following week, I gave him another exercise: "Breathing in, I see my father as a five-year-old boy. Breathing out, I smile to my father as a five-year-old boy." Maybe you have never thought of your father as a vulnerable five-year-old. If you can see him like that, you will understand him. Like you, he may have been a victim and carried a wounded child within him.

You can ask for a picture of your father as a little boy. The young man asked for one and put the picture on his desk. Every time he left or entered his room, he would stop, look his father in the eyes, and practice breathing in and out mindfully three times. At the same time, he practiced visualizing his father as a five-year-old boy. Finally, he discovered that his father was also a victim and had not had the chance to practice and realize transformation. When he was able to see his father as a victim, his anger began to dissolve. One night, he sat down and wrote a love letter to his father: "Daddy, I know that you also suffered a lot as a child, and that you did not know how to transform your suffering, so you transmitted it to me." After writing the letter, he was transformed, and knew that reconciliation was possible.

When we take a shower or a bath, we have the chance to practice looking deeply into our body. The Buddha invites us to look into the nature of each element and find its emptiness of transmission or its interbeing nature. The three elements are one and interdependent and cannot exist as separate entities in themselves. The three elements in the transmission are: the one who transmits, the object transmitted, and the recipient of the transmission. The Buddha invites us to look into the nature of each thing and find its emptiness of transmission. We ask the question: What did my father transmit to me? The answer is: He transmitted himself to me. The object transmitted is no less than himself, and I really am the continuation of my father. I am my father. The object of transmission is one with the transmitter. Then we ask: Who is the recipient of the transmission? Is he a separate entity? No. The recipient of the transmission is both the object of transmission and the transmitter.

When you penetrate this truth, the reality of the emptiness of transmission, you can no longer say, "I don't want to have anything to do with my father; I'm too angry." In fact, you realize that you are your father. You are the continuation of your father, and the only thing you can do is to reconcile yourself with him. He is not out there; he is in you. Peace is possible only with this knowledge and reconciliation.

If we recognize something as positive, healthy, and beautiful, then we will develop and preserve it. If we recognize something as negative and destructive, then we will embrace and transform it. When we are able to achieve transformation, we do it not only for ourselves, but for our fathers, our mothers, and our ancestors. That is why when I practice breathing in and calming, and breathing out and smiling, I am liberating my father, my mother, and my ancestors. I am also liberating my children and their children. Every time I take a peaceful, happy step, I take it for all my ancestors. This practice helps us to transform and heal. We do it for everyone at the same time. Only through such practice is true reconciliation possible.

Reconciliation takes place inside us; we do not need to sit down with the other person to achieve reconciliation. Someone once wrote to me, "Thây, I know I have made mistakes in the past, and now I want to have some reconciliation with my daughter. But every time I write to ask her to meet with me, she refuses. What can I do?" You may believe that reconciliation is only possible by meeting and talking with the other person. This is because you have not achieved reconciliation within yourself, and it is difficult to visualize it with the other person. True reconciliation is made through insight and compassion. When you have insight and compassion, helping another person becomes easier. When reconciliation is internal, peace and love become possible. If you embody peace and love, you can change a situation more easily.

CHAPTER NINE

Questions and Answers Session Two

Dear Sangha, today is the third of June, 1998. We are in the meditation hall for questions and answers. Please read a question.

Question: I am wondering whether you have any observations on practicing with loyalty for spouses and partners, including gay and lesbian partners. How can our mindfulness practice help us live with our sexual energy?

Thây: Sexual energy is only one kind of energy. If we go back to its source, we cannot name it. At the source, this energy can be channeled in other directions. If you are interested in doing and realizing other things, then that energy will be channeled in those directions, and you will not have a lot of time to think about sex. We monastics recognize that sexual energy is there, but with the support of the Sangha, we learn to invest our energy in other directions, towards our highest aspirations. The Sangha needs our time and energy for many other things. We devote time to studying and learning the Dharma, and we discuss how to put it into practice. We devote time to take care of our second body, which is another member of the Sangha that every monastic has to take care of. Each monk is responsible for the well-being and practice of another monk. The same is true with the nuns. We also devote time to help the people who come to us to practice. We can be very happy devoting our energy in these directions. We can say from our experience that if you organize your life intelligently and direct all of your energy skillfully, and if you are capable of helping other people suffer less, then sexual energy will no longer be a major problem in your life.

Question: This is from the Bluebonnet Dharma discussion group.

Dear Thây, our group is very healthy. There is a lot of circulation, insight, and practice, and also space in it. It seems, though, that we need to learn more about watering our wholesome seeds. We also need to learn about conflict resolution and beginning anew. A question we have is how to practice when someone continually waters your negative seeds.

Thây: How to practice when someone continually waters your negative seeds? I would like to speak a little about this question. When someone waters your negative seeds, it is an opportunity for you to practice. Some of us think it would be easier to practice if we went on a solo retreat in the mountains, but if you do so, you will not have the opportunity to be challenged. To live with a person and the difficulties presented by that person is also an opportunity for practice. Please use your private time, when you are sitting or walking alone, to practice and prepare yourself so that when someone comes and waters a negative seed in you, you will be able to respond in a most positive and beautiful way. If we do not prepare ourselves, then when a negative seed is watered, we suffer and react in a way that is not wise. We bring the suffering into ourselves and into the other person as well. But, if we are mindful and follow our breathing while doing our work, we are practicing and preparing ourselves so that our mindfulness will become stronger. We are working out a strategy, so that when a negative seed is watered, we will breathe, smile, keep calm, and look at the other person with a smile. If we succeed once, we will have tremendous confidence in the Dharma and in our practice, and I am sure we will do even better the next time. We will also make a good impression on the person who waters the negative seed in us. If we do well, then in maybe one or two months, he will ask us admiringly, "How can you do that?" Then it will be time for us to share our practice.

There is the question of how to continue the practice if the other person — the partner or the family — doesn't accept it. My answer is always this: Practice naturally. Don't get caught up in the forms of practice. Don't show that you are practicing. It is possible. For example, when you practice walking meditation, you can practice in a very natural way so that nobody knows you are practicing walking meditation, and yet you can cultivate your peace, mindfulness, and joy. We call it practicing the non-practice. And don't be too eager to share your practice with — or impose your practice on — the other person. Don't talk a lot about it, either. Just practice so that you become more capable of listening, smiling, acting, and reacting in a refreshing way. If you succeed once in responding beautifully to your negative seeds being watered, then that success will continue and help you and the other person at the same time.

Question: I don't understand how my practice in the present — my becoming more peaceful, calmer, and living with more loving kindness and compassion — can help my ancestors, my grandmother, grandfather, and uncle — how it can make their lives more beautiful — when they were killed in concentration camps. I don't understand how our practice applies to mass horrors like genocide.

Thây: There is affliction and suffering within us. Our suffering represents both our individual suffering and the suffering of our ancestors, parents, and society. Every time we practice mindful breathing and take good care of our bodies and feelings, we relieve some of our suffering. We get the benefit of the transformation and healing, and our ancestors and society also get the benefit. Any smile that we produce will affect society. We can touch society within ourselves. Any step we take in mindfulness that brings us a little more solidity, freedom, and joy, also benefits society and our ancestors. Do not think that what you do to yourself does not affect the rest of society and the world. Peace and freedom always begin with our own practice. We know that the one contains the all. The emancipation of the individual is also the emancipation of society, of the collective element in us. The victory of Siddhartha at the foot of the Bodhi Tree was not for one individual alone. It was for the peace, joy, and emancipation of many, many living beings. If transformation takes place in us, at the same time, it takes place in the world. Even if you don't see it, a transformation has taken place. If peace is in you, peace becomes possible everywhere in the cosmos. When you have peace inside, you look at the world, and it is different. I think many of us have had this experience.

[BELL]

Question: Thây, there are many questions about cows. One such question was whether our discriminating mind, our tendency to form judgments, is a cow that we should consider releasing.

Thây: When I use the word "cow," its first meaning is something that you think is essential for your happiness. It is something you have never questioned: a position in society, a business, a diploma, an ideology. But when you get it, it seems you do not have the happiness you wanted, and you continue to suffer, even if you actually have your cows. We are invited to practice looking deeply into the nature of our cows to see whether they are really necessary for our well-being and happiness. If we find out that it is only a cow that creates more anxiety and fear, then we will be able to let it go. That is why I have asked all of you to practice looking deeply and to call your cows by their true names.

The other day, I spoke about a friend in Germany who was able to release many of his cows. Among his cows were some that looked very spiritual. He was the chairman of many Buddhist organizations. He attended a lot of meetings and did a lot of work. It took a lot of his time and energy and caused him a lot of stress. He could not enjoy his breathing, walking, or sitting. He didn't feel happy. To be happy, he had to release some of his cows. The more cows we release, the greater our freedom and happiness. This is what I mean by cows.

Maybe you have a job, but you think it is not enough, so you get a second job. You work overtime, thinking you need to create more opportunities to increase your wealth or fame. You get sucked into that way of thinking for a long time. But one day you find out that you are not really happy, and you really want happiness. You do not want to waste your energy in worries, anger, and so on; you are determined to let go of your cows. Each of us can look deeply, identify our cows, and release them. A cow can also be an ideology or an idea that we take great pride in. We think that we are someone very special if we follow that idea or ideology. But if it hasn't really given us any true happiness, it is a cow that we need to release.

I spoke before about a monk who was very busy building a temple. You may ask, "What is wrong with a monk building a temple?" When he was building it, he worried so much about the temple that he didn't have time to practice walking meditation, mindful breathing, or to enjoy touching the present moment. He was sacrificing his own happiness. He sacrificed the most important thing and focused on the less important things. When the monk complained to a friend, his friend said, "Why don't you become a real monk? A real monk is free from cows." So even a temple can be a cow. It does not mean he should not build the temple, but there are ways to build temples without making them into cows, and where you still remain a free person. Whether something is a cow or not depends on your behavior. Releasing cows does not mean releasing responsibilities.

Question: My question is how to be completely free at any moment and all the time, even when you think you're keeping cows or doing things that you don't think are right.

Thầy: To be perfectly free, we need to practice every day. Freedom is rare. Most of us are not free. We may have the feeling that freedom is there, but we often act under the direction of our karma — our habitual energy — and are dictated to by society and our collective consciousness. We are very seldom free. When we drive our cars, clean our toilets, wash our dishes, we may have the feeling that it is we who want to do these things. But if we look deeply, we may find that, in fact, we do not have any freedom while doing these things. Even when we walk, we do not have freedom; something is pushing us to go ahead. To me, freedom is being mindful of what we are doing and what we are not doing in the present moment. When we scrub the floor, clean the toilet, or breathe in and out, if we are aware of what we are doing, we begin to have freedom. In order to have greater freedom, we have to begin with this kind of freedom. Otherwise, we live in an unfree way. We are governed by powerful habitual energy and conventional forces.

I like to describe the practice of mindfulness in our daily lives as the practice of reclaiming our liberty as human beings. By practicing mindfulness in our daily lives, we can recognize our afflictions and suffering and transform them. This can be described as the practice of freedom. I am not speaking of political freedom, but freedom from forgetfulness and afflictions. The first freedom we get is the freedom from forgetfulness. We live and yet we do not live. We live like dead people. That is how the French writer Albert Camus described it. We seem to be alive, but we are not truly alive. We carry about our own dead bodies on our shoulders. If we look around, we will see that people live like this, unaware that they are alive. Mindfulness is the practice of reclaiming our freedom to be. Slowly, with this practice, we recognize that we are governed by our forgetfulness. We recognize our afflictions and cultivate our freedom little by little. Happiness is born from that true freedom.

[BELL]

Question: Thây, the guided meditations have resonated deeply with many participants. One member of the Sangha describes his experience in this way and asks a question: "Through participation in my Dharma discussion group and the practices, I have made contact with my wounded child. But now I need help in finding my lost child. By using meditation and mindfulness practices, and trying to look deeply within myself, how can I find myself if the self doesn't really exist?"

Thây: "How can I find myself if the self doesn't really exist?" It sounds like a philosophical question. We are going to examine the practice of mindful breathing that proposes looking deeply into the true nature of reality, impermanence, and nonself. There is a lot of misunderstanding concerning self and nonself. We should not get caught up in words. The practice of looking deeply helps us to see the nature of reality. The nature of reality can be labeled with words like "self" and "nonself." But, if you are capable of seeing reality in itself, you will no longer be caught up in the words "self" and "nonself." The other day, when I spoke about the emptiness of transmission, I said that every time we look at our bodies when we take a shower, we see that our bodies are objects of transmission. We are the receivers of the transmission, and our parents have transmitted our bodies to us. I invited you to look deeply into the nature of the transmission: the transmitter, the object transmitted, and the receiver are all empty. This doesn't mean that they don't exist, but they don't exist as separate entities. You cannot divide the three. You cannot divide the transmitter, the transmitted, and the receiver, because the transmitter transmitted himself or herself to you. You, the receiver, are also one with the object of transmission and, therefore, you are also one with the transmitter.

When you look into the true nature of transmission, you touch the reality of nonself. When you look into what you call "yourself," you see that you are a continuation of your parents and ancestors. You may touch the fact that all your ancestors are alive and present in you. That is why I say that every time we smile, that smile is being smiled by all our ancestors. That is really the teaching of nonself. Nonself does not mean that you are not here. The self is made only of nonself elements — like a flower. You cannot say that the flower is not here; the flower is here. But a flower is made only of non-flower elements, like the rain, the sunshine, the earth, minerals, compost, etc. The wounded child within us is also a co-product of everything. If we have been attentive during the last week, we will have already seen that the wounded child within can also be the wounded child of our father or mother. There may be a multitude of wounded children within our wounded child. If we know how to embrace and heal our wounded child, we will also heal the multitude of wounded children that have been transmitted to us by generations of our ancestors.

We should not get caught up in the idea or notion called nonself. Nonself does not mean not existing. Nonself means there are no separate entities. When you touch yourself, you touch your father, your child, your ancestors, the sunshine, clouds, and the earth, because everything in the cosmos has come together in order for you to manifest. You are made of non-you elements, which does not mean that you are not here. The self that we speak of as a separate entity is just a notion, a concept, and that concept exists. With the practice of looking deeply, we are able to make that concept evaporate, and then we are free. Freedom also means freedom from all concepts and ideas. That is the meaning of the word "nirvana." Nirvana means extinction, and it is firstly the extinction of all ideas, like the idea of self. If you think that nonself is an idea that opposes self, then nirvana is also the extinction of the idea of nonself. In nirvana, the ideas of self and nonself do not exist.

Question: Dear Thây, dear Sangha, this question is about watering negative seeds and about cows. I had my seeds watered a little earlier this evening. The first question referred to lesbians and gays, and I didn't hear the question answered. Rather I heard it somehow not being addressed. So I said to myself, "OK, my seeds got watered again. What do I do with that? Do I just sit with it?" Then I realized that that's what I've done my whole life. Lesbians and gays have their seeds watered their whole lives, because they are constantly being told that they are invisible. For many years, I followed the Sufi path and studied with a very esteemed teacher. One of the seeds I had to deal with was once hearing him refer to homosexuality as disgusting. I had to sit there and ask myself if I should leave. It was a real struggle.

I am a newcomer to this community, looking for refreshment and learning from the Sangha, and my seeds have been watered as they are everywhere else in my life. I see no visibly lesbian or gay speaker here on the stage. I wonder about that. In the week and a half that I've been here, I've never heard lesbians and gays mentioned. I live with that. Now I come to my cow. I am a therapist and workshop leader. I travel the world and am always up on stage. My cow is speaking up like this. I was at a conference for therapists this year, and when I perceived homophobia in the community, I spontaneously stood up in front of everyone and said what I'm saying now about that community. So I sat here and I wondered: "Do I do that again? Is this a cow?"

We had a gay and lesbian meeting earlier today and very few people showed up. I respect the people who didn't come because they were in silence or in another space, but I also got feedback that some people didn't come because they were concerned about visibility. When I never hear it mentioned on stage and in the

Sangha, I think it feeds that fear. I'm very concerned about the young people here because I fear that I, being older, endorse that. Then, again, is that my cow, and what do I do with it if it is? I would like to hear your views on homosexuality, including sex in appropriate relationship.

Thây: A cloud is a cloud. Looking deeply into the nature of a cloud, we see the cosmos. A flower is a flower, and if we look deeply into it, we see the cosmos. Everything has its own place. The base — the foundation of everything — is the same. When you look into the ocean, you see different kinds of waves, different sizes and shapes, but all the waves have the water as their foundation, base, and substance. If you are born gay or lesbian, your ground of being is the same as mine. We are different, but we share the same ground of being. The Protestant theologian Paul Tillich said that God is the ground of being. You should be yourself. If God has created me as a rose, then I should accept myself as a rose, and my relationship with God will be with a rose God. If you are born a lesbian, then be a lesbian, and your relationship with God will be with a lesbian God. Looking deeply, you see that if you touch the ground of your being, then you will find peace.

If you are a victim of discrimination, then your way to emancipation is not only to cry out about injustice, for injustice cannot be repaired by people's recognition alone, but by your capacity to touch the ground of your being. I have a very deep experience of this. Discrimination, intolerance, and suppression stem from lack of understanding, lack of tolerance, and lack of knowledge. If you are capable of touching your ground of being, you can be released from the suffering that has been created in you through discrimination and suppression. You may be suppressed due to your color or your race because the person who discriminates against you is ignorant. He does not know his own ground of being and does not realize that we all share the same ground of being; that is why he or she can discriminate against you. People who are ignorant, who discriminate and drive other people to suffer because of their ignorance, are not happy within themselves; they suffer. Even if you are the victim of discrimination, if you can touch the ground of your being, then you can see and express yourself in the way the wise have expressed God: "Forgive them because they do not know what they are doing. They are committing atrocities and discrimination out of ignorance. So forgive them."

Once you get deep into the nature and ground of your being, you will be equipped with the kind of understanding that makes compassion and tolerance possible, and you can forgive even the people who suppress you or discriminate against you. If you are discriminated against or wronged, don't believe that relief or justice will come through society alone. True emancipation lies in your capacity to look deeply. Once you've touched the depth of the ground of your being, you will be emancipated, and will even be able to embrace and help the person or groups of people who have wronged you and discriminated against you. Of course, when you suffer because of discrimination, there's always an urge to speak out. But even if you spend one thousand years speaking out, your suffering will not be relieved. Only by deep understanding, by true liberation from ignorance can your suffering be liberated.

You know, during the Vietnam War, we suffered a lot. If you look a bit more deeply into the nature of the war, you will see that the value of life of the Vietnamese civilian was nothing compared to the life of the American soldier. When an American pilot received orders to drop bombs on a specific area, he didn't know what would happen after he dropped them. He didn't have to know. The lives of the people below meant nothing. When you suffer like this, what kind of shouting can relieve your suffering? When you see the truth, when you break through to the truth, compassion springs up like a stream of water. With that compassion, you can embrace even the people who wronged you, discriminated against you, and persecuted you. When you are motivated by the desire to help those who are victims of ignorance only then are you free from your suffering and feelings of violation. That is my recommendation. Don't wait for things to change around you. Don't believe that shouting for one thousand years will bring you relief. You have to practice liberating yourself. Then you will be equipped with the power of compassion and understanding, the only kind of power that can help transform an environment full of injustice and discrimination. You have to become such a person — one who can embody tolerance, understanding, and compassion. You transform yourself into an instrument for social change and change in the collective consciousness of mankind.

[BELL]

Question: Dear Thây, how can I give up my achievement addiction? I know that achievement is an illusion, is the ego, is impermanent. But every time I finish a project, my mind says, "What's next?" I know that I contain seeds of generations who believed in the work ethic and thought idle hands were the devil's playground. Giving this up is a daily struggle. Is there some understanding that would make it easier?

Thây: I recommend not stopping doing the things you like to do, but doing them mindfully. When you do things mindfully, you know whether what you are doing is the best thing you can do for yourself and for the world; mindfulness helps you to know the nature and purpose of your work. If it is only for fame, to show off, or something like that, you will know it is not worth doing. But if, working mindfully, you realize that your work is an expression of loving kindness and compassion, then your work will cultivate more compassion and joy in you and, at the same time, bring smiles, happiness, and joy to other people. Working mindfully like that will bring about a lot of benefits.

Question: Thây, there's a lot of discussion among Sangha members and practitioners about how to deepen our practice. One person has put the question this way: How can we deepen our practice and nourish our *bodhichitta?*

Thây: To me, deepening our practice means having a genuine practice, practicing not in form only. When your practice is genuine, it will bring joy, peace, and stability to yourself and to the people around you. I think I prefer the phrase "true practice." To me, the practice should be pleasant. True practice can bring life to us right away. As you practice mindful breathing, you become alive, you become real. It is not only when you sit or walk but, for instance, when you are making breakfast for your beloved. If you know how to breathe in and out mindfully while making breakfast with a smile, you will cultivate freedom — freedom from thinking about the past or worrying about the future — aliveness, joy, and compassion. While making breakfast, you can make joy, peace, compassion, and aliveness real. That is true practice, and its effect can be seen right away.

The second part of the question was how to nourish our bodhichitta. To nourish our mind of love is the third kind of nutriment — our deepest desire. We are all sustained by desires. There are desires that can take us to the realm of suffering and desires that can take us to the realm of happiness. The desire to be alive and to bring relief and joy to people is the kind of desire we call bodhichitta, the mind of love. That desire is a tremendous source of energy and can make us more alive. It can make our eyes bright and our steps more firm. When we study the Five Mindfulness Trainings deeply, we realize that it is energizing to live according to them. Looking deeply into the Five Mindfulness

Trainings, we know that they can help protect us, our families, and society, prevent suffering from taking place, and allow peace, joy, and happiness to occur. A deep understanding of the Five Mindfulness Trainings can bring you a tremendous desire to live according to them, so that you become an instrument of love and peace.

To me, the Five Mindfulness Trainings are the substance of a bodhisattva. Bodhisattva means a living being animated by the strong desire to help awaken other people, relieve their suffering, and bring them a lot of happiness. I think that by receiving the Five Mindfulness Trainings, being determined to train ourselves to live our lives accordingly, we become bodhisattvas and live not only for ourselves, but for the well-being of many people in society; our life serves as a source of energy for their happiness. Studying and looking deeply into the Five Mindfulness Trainings, we will gain insights. We may be motivated by the bodhisattva vow of receiving the Five Mindfulness Trainings and making them the substance of our lives.

When you study the Fourteen Mindfulness Trainings, you touch the same source of strength. Our daily practice can be motivated by the desire to help people. The Buddha was motivated by such a desire; that is why he spent a lot of time practicing, and, after he was enlightened, he spent forty-five years helping people. His life and what he achieved sprang from the strength of that deep desire. I am sure that if you have that kind of desire, it will be reflected in your way of doing and looking at things — in your smile and your walk — because you will have a lot of energy. You will no longer be afraid of hardships and suffering. With such a tremendous amount of energy, you can easily overcome suffering, because your heart will be big enough to embrace it. You will no longer have the tendency to exclude. You will only want to embrace the whole world. And every daily practice — walking, sitting, smiling, and breathing — will tend toward that direction.

Question: Dear Thây, you always say that it's very important to practice with a Sangha. And I must say I have been nourished a lot by the Sanghas I have belonged to. My situation now is that I am going to work in West Africa for one or two years, in a country where it is not very likely that I will be able to build a Sangha around me. I really do not want my practice to suffer, and I wonder how I can do a Dharma discussion just sitting by myself. It will be a bit one-sided. My question is: Do you have any special advice for lone practitioners who want to deepen their practice?

Thây: I think it is possible to build a Sangha wherever you are. People everywhere need stability, calm, and mindfulness. The obstacle may be that we want to use Buddhist terms. When I was forty years old, I succeeded in writing a book on Buddhism without using any Buddhist terms. When the president of South Africa came to France for a visit, he was interviewed by the press. They asked him what he would most like to do. He said, "What I want most is just to sit down. Since I was released from prison, I have been so busy. Sitting down and doing nothing is what I want the most." I used to tell that story to my monks and nuns. In our community in France, there was a young monk from South Africa to whom I said, "Sit for your president." So, the needs of people everywhere are the same.

There are many people who just want to sit and do nothing, become peaceful and calm, be mindful of every moment of their daily lives. My recommendation is that you refrain from using Buddhist terms; just embody the Dharma in your mindful living and be fresh and communicative. Listen to people deeply, using loving speech. Then you will make friends. You can also have trees, rivers, and rocks as members of your Sangha. The air you breathe is one element of your Sangha. The path you use for walking meditation is part of your Sangha. The child that you talk to, that you make friends with, can be a member of your Sangha. Don't use the word "Sangha." If you invite some people over for tea, don't say, "Let's have tea meditation." Say, "Let's have tea peacefully and be aware that we have some time to spend together, enjoying our tea and our togetherness." I think if you learn to use this kind of language, you'll soon be able to build a Sangha. If you use Buddhist language in the beginning, you will turn people off and you will not be successful. Maybe you can use Buddhist terms later. I wish you a lot of success. I know that you can do it. All of us can build Sanghas wherever we are.

— ∞ —

Dear friends, next Saturday will be a Day of Mindfulness. There will be bus meditation. We will sit on buses and enjoy breathing, smiling, and the beautiful landscape of Vermont. When we arrive at Green Mountain Dharma Center, we will practice walking together in that beautiful place. We shall gather after walking meditation for a short Dharma talk, and we will tell you about Green Mountain Dharma Center, Maple Forest Monastery for monks and nuns, and the Mindfulness Practice Center, which is a new Dharma door to welcome those who are not used to Buddhist language and the religious aspects of Buddhism. We have found that it is perfectly possible to practice mindfulness as a nonsectarian, nonreligious practice, without sacrificing anything.

We are contemplating serving the twenty-first century with the formation of mindfulness practice groups and mindfulness practice centers without Buddhist liturgy, rituals, and terminology. We have tried it and seen that it can be very successful.

In Green Mountain Dharma Center, we have a training program for mindfulness practice. This can consist of two-week training sessions, and we will ask for your ideas on how to help with those. You don't need to be a Dharma teacher to start a mindfulness practice group. As I have said before, we would like to see students in schools and universities start mindfulness practice groups to improve their quality of life. Teachers can form mindfulness practice groups to support each other and enjoy a deeper, more relaxed life. Also, people who live in correctional houses can start mindfulness practice groups, so they can suffer less and enjoy the practice in prison; many groups have already begun in prisons and report that the practice of mindfulness makes life much more pleasant. All of us can begin mindfulness practice groups in our own homes. You don't have to be trained for years before you can do this. We will try to provide people with the means to be trained, and offer financial assistance to those who need it in order to have the training. We need our collective wisdom and insight to make this project our offering to the beginning of the twenty-first century.

The first Mindfulness Practice Center — nonreligious and nonsectarian — has been operating in Woodstock for the last six months. As a Sangha, we may offer our insights on how to do certain things better. Sister Annabel, who gave the lecture this morning about the *Discourse on the Full Awareness of Breathing,* is in charge of Maple Forest Monastery. There are fourteen monks and nuns practicing there. Some friends are building it. We hope that American monks and nuns, like Sister Fern, will live and be trained there and in Plum Village, so they can serve in North America.

It is also my deep desire to have, in the future, one Mindfulness Practice Center in every city for people to enjoy. We have to help train facilitators for these centers, and we should organize a body to help set up the centers. The Order of Interbeing will be instrumental in that work. Please join us in making mindfulness practice available to people in North America. We trust that you can help us with this project.*

[BELL]

* See back of book for contact information.

CHAPTER TEN

Learning True Love

[LED BY A SANGHA MEMBER]

"Body, speech, and mind in perfect oneness — I send my heart along with the sound of the bell. May the hearers awaken from forgetfulness and transcend the path of anxiety and sorrow."

[SINGING]

"Listen, listen. This wonderful sound brings me back to my true self.

"May the sound of this bell penetrate deeply into the cosmos. In even the darkest places, may living beings hear it clearly so that without any hardship, understanding comes to their hearts, and they transcend the realm of birth and death.

"Listening to the sound of the bell, I feel the afflictions in me begin to dissolve. My mind becomes calm, my body relaxed, and a smile is born on my lips. Following the sound of the bell, my breathing guides me back to the safe island of mindfulness. In the garden of my heart, the flower of peace blooms beautifully.

"The universal Dharma door is already open. The sound of the rising tide is clear. The miracle happens. A beautiful child appears in the heart of a lotus flower. A single drop of the compassionate water is enough to bring back the refreshing spring to the mountains and rivers."

Mindful Looking and Listening

Dear Sangha, today is the fourth of June, 1998, and we are in the second week of our twenty-one-day retreat. Paying attention to our in-breath and our out-breath affects our breathing. It is like projecting light onto an object. Even if the object is as small as an elementary particle, the light we shine on it changes it. When the object of observation is touched by the subject of observation, there is a transformation. When we light up our mindfulness and begin to touch our in-breath and out-breath, we might think that our breathing has changed and that we are working our breath instead of letting it flow naturally. But if we observe more carefully, we will see that we are not really intervening. We are simply becoming more aware of our breath and letting it flow more naturally.

As long as our breathing feels pleasant, we know that we are not working or manipulating it. Please pay attention to the effect of your in-breath and out-breath on your body. If your breathing continues to give you pleasure, then you are doing it correctly. Sometimes your in-breath becomes longer and deeper. Just allow that to happen. You do not have to make an effort. If you make an effort, you might disrupt your feeling of well-being. Just allow your breathing to bring more well-being and pleasure to your body and consciousness.

We don't need to practice all the sixteen exercises proposed by the Buddha at once or in consecutive order. If we understand the deeper nature of the sixteen exercises and why they have been proposed, we will know which ones we need to do. When we begin our sitting meditation, we practice the first few exercises to bring stability and well-being into our body and mind. Then we select an exercise appropriate to our state of being. If we need to go to a different exercise, we can stop the one we are doing and begin another. This is intelligent practice.

We know how to take care of and attend to our body's needs, our feelings, and our mental formations. The Chinese character for mindfulness 念 is made up of the characters "now" and "mind." We bring our mind into the now, the present moment. The upper part of the character means "present moment," and the lower part means "mind." By bringing them together, we create mindfulness. The mind goes back to the present moment to be aware of what is happening in that moment. When the mind goes back to the present moment, it also goes back to the body; body and mind are united. We only need to practice breathing in and breathing out once to reach that oneness of body and mind. Then we are well-established in the present moment. We become more real and alive because we are fully present. That is why mindful breathing is so wonderful. It is not the only way, but it is a wonderful way. Breathing is the bridge between body and mind.

Mindfulness can be cultivated by our ears, eyes, feet, and breath. When we practice walking meditation, we see the person in front of us walking mindfully and beautifully. If we are not mindful and have gotten lost in our thinking, the sight of our co-practitioner walking peacefully and happily reminds us to go back and produce mindfulness in ourselves. We need to know how to use our eyes to nourish our mindfulness. When we enter a temple, the objects, the architecture, and the garden are all arranged to help us return to our mindfulness. The real artist creates opportunities for one to go back and give birth to mindfulness within. Also, sounds — like the sound of a bell or chanting — can revive our energy of mindfulness.

We can also strengthen our eyes and use them to look mindfully. Looking mindfully, we will see more deeply. I can look at my hand with or without mindfulness. The best way is mindful looking; it brings concentration and helps me to break through and see the object more deeply. What we see can strengthen our mindfulness, and mindfulness also helps us to see more mindfully. Our eyes and mindfulness help each other.

The same is true with sound. When we hear chanting, it helps us go back to ourselves and cultivate the energy of mindfulness within. When we have mindfulness within, we begin to listen more mindfully. When we listen more mindfully, we understand better and more deeply. Those of us who practice mindfulness should cultivate the art of looking and listening deeply. Mindful listening is an important practice that can relieve a lot of suffering. Psychotherapists should acquire the art of deep listening. Without good listening, you cannot be a good therapist. To listen deeply, you have to bring your mind back to your body and realize the oneness of body and mind. Mindful breathing is one of the means through which you can be fully present for your client, with body and mind united.

If you are mindful and present, the quality of your listening will be good. We call this empathetic, mindful, deep, or compassionate listening. You are willing to help the other person. You know that he or she suffers deeply, and has no one who will listen. You may be the first person who has been willing to listen to him or her. If you are obsessed with your own problems, pulled into the past or sucked into the future, you cannot really be there for the person who needs your help. Therapists can carry much suffering within them. If the therapist does not cultivate compassion, concentration, and mindfulness within herself, then the client may touch the seed of suffering in the therapist and make her suffer more. Then the quality of her listening will be poor. A therapist has to practice being fully present and has to cultivate the energy of compassion in order to be helpful. It is absolutely necessary to have the energy of compassion so that we can listen with empathy.

Listening deeply can help the other person suffer less. Let's think of a woman whose family was unable to listen to her. Everyone in her family was filled with suffering and did not have enough patience or compassion to listen to her. Maybe she also did not know how to speak calmly, and touched the seeds of suffering in them. Her family avoided her; they did not want to punish or shun her, but because they were absorbed in their own suffering, they could not bear to listen to her. She wanted to speak kindly to them because she knew that they did not want to listen to her. But despite her good intentions, she could not do it, because her suffering was too great. She would begin with a few kind sentences, and then once she touched her suffering, her voice would vibrate with bitterness and pain. Other people avoided her because her speech touched the seeds of suffering in them.

Many people in our society have lost the capacity of listening and using loving speech. In many families, no one can listen to anyone else. Communication has become impossible. This is the biggest problem of our time. We have invented sophisticated technological means for communication that enable us to instantly send messages halfway across the globe. But communication between father and child and between whole nations has become very difficult.

Look at someone who is full of suffering and does not have an opportunity to speak of it to anyone. He looks like a bomb ready to explode. There is a lot of tension and pain, and, in fact, that person explodes many times a day. That is why the people in his family are afraid of him. They try to keep away from him, and he feels isolated. We have to learn the art of defusing the bomb. We have to become skilled in the art of compassionate listening and the use of kind, loving speech.

Compassionate listening has one purpose: to help the other person suffer less. You have to nourish the awareness that no matter what the other person says, you will keep calm and continue to listen. You do not judge while listening. You keep your compassion alive. The other person may be unjust, may say inaccurate things, or blame, attack, and judge. Yet you maintain your energy of compassion so that your seed of suffering is not touched. Practicing mindful breathing while listening is very helpful. "Breathing in, I know that I am listening in order to make this person suffer less. Breathing out, I remember the person in front of me suffers very much." We have to train ourselves to be able to sit and listen for forty-five minutes or one hour without becoming irritated. Avalokiteshvara is a person who has that capacity and practices the art of deep listening.

We all have relatives who suffer. We are eager to help them suffer less, but we are not therapists. We have to practice like therapists. We don't want our seeds of suffering to be watered while we are listening. This is why we have to practice. The amount of time we spend practicing mindful walking, breathing, and sitting is important. We have to help ourselves before we can help anyone else. The first time we try compassionate listening, we may realize that our limit is only fifteen minutes. After that point, we may feel too weak to continue. Then we have to say, "Darling, shall we continue later? Now I need to do some walking meditation." We have to renew ourselves before continuing. It is important to know our limit. If we don't know our limit, we will fail in our attempt to help other people.

I have attended meetings where a person, whom no one had listened to, was unable to talk. We had to practice mindful breathing for a long time. We sat attentively, and he tried again and again until finally he could tell us of his pain. Patience is the mark of true love. If you truly love someone, you will be more patient with him or her.

[BELL]

Loving Speech

The other aspect of the practice is learning how to speak with loving kindness. When you attend a retreat or spend time at a practice center, you have the opportunity to cultivate compassionate listening and loving speech. They are crucial to restoring peace and harmony in your environment. You have to practice so that you can restore your solidity and freedom. You need to tell the other person about your suffering and pain, especially if you consider him or her to be the person you love the most. But please use only loving speech. Only loving speech will enable him or her to listen.

The basis of all these things is mindfulness. Mindful speech nourishes our mindfulness and produces mindfulness in the other person. In Buddhism, the Bodhisattva Avalokiteshvara, or Kwan Yin, is skilled in the art of deep listening. There is also the Bodhisattva Manjushri, who has the capacity of looking deeply. The bodhisattvas of deep listening and deep looking are inside us. When we practice looking deeply to understand someone's suffering, the Bodhisattva Manjushri is alive in us. We cultivate that capacity through our practice. The Bodhisattva Avalokiteshvara is in us when we listen with compassion to understand the suffering and pain of another person. It is not a question of believing in the existence of a god. It is the capacity of touching the energy of compassion and expressing it in our manner of looking and listening.

Great Action

The bodhisattva of great action, Samantabhadra, is also within us. The symbol for this bodhisattva is a hand. When we are motivated by compassion and want to do something, we can use our eyes, like Manjushri, our ears, like Avalokiteshvara, and our hands, like Samantabhadra. Love and compassion always express themselves by looking, listening, and acting deeply. In Buddhist temples, there is often a statue of a bodhisattva with one thousand arms. We may ask, why so many arms? Because the energy of love and compassion is so great and helps many beings simultaneously. Many of us actually have more than two arms. There are so many things that we want to do: take care of the ecosystem, relieve the suffering of the homeless, help the hungry in the Third World. Looking deeply, we realize that bodhisattvas are all around us. They live a simple life, and yet their presence is everywhere. They support many projects and act in many ways that alleviate people's suffering. Bodhisattvas with one thousand arms aren't just statues; they exist.

I know a woman who lives in Holland. During the Second World War, she helped save tens of thousands of Jews from the Holocaust. If you see her on the street, you might not recognize her as a bodhisattva, because she looks like everybody else. You can only recognize the bodhisattva if you know her personally. Although bodhisattvas look like they only have two eyes, they may have eyes in the backs of their heads. They see many things and can see for great distances. In fact, the bodhisattva of compassion has more than one thousand arms, and each of its hands has an eye in it. When we act out of compassion, we need to understand and see deeply. If understanding is not present, our actions will not be authentic.

Sometimes we are motivated by the desire to help, but we do not understand the situation. Then, we will do more harm than good. We want to make someone happy, but we push him into doing things that make him suffer. Maybe you are concerned about your son's happiness. You may think your actions are making him happy. But if you look deeply, you might see that you are creating suffering in him because you don't understand him. We have to reconsider the nature of our love. In the Buddha's teaching, true love comes from understanding. The secret is to put an eye in your hand. Before doing something, look at your hand to see whether there is an eye in it or not. If an eye is there, then whatever you do will make him or her happy. If it is not there, don't do anything yet, because it might cause suffering.

In Vietnam, there is an expensive fruit called durian. I cannot bear the smell of that fruit. One day, there was a durian on the altar in the temple. I was chanting the *Lotus Sutra,* and I could not concentrate because of the smell. Halfway through the chant, I stopped, went to the altar, and used the bell to imprison the fruit. Then I continued chanting. Afterwards, I liberated the fruit. You might think, "Poor Thây, he practices so hard, I will offer him some durian," and ask me to eat it. If you do, I will suffer a lot. If you don't understand the needs of the person you love — if you don't know her difficulties and aspirations — you cannot love her; your love is not made of understanding. To understand, you have to use the eyes of Bodhisattva Manjushri to look deeply. Ask the person you love, "Darling, do I understand you? Please help me understand you. Otherwise, I will do things that will make you unhappy. I really want to understand your pain, suffering, and difficulties. I want to know your deepest aspirations, because I want to love you and make you happy." Have you ever asked your beloved that question? That is the language of someone who cares and loves.

If two people know how to use their eyes, ears, and speech to help and understand each other, communication can be restored and happiness becomes possible. The three bodhisattvas that we invoke each morning are not gods that exist somewhere in the sky; they exist in our hearts. We can cultivate their presence so that we become capable of looking, listening, and speaking with kindness.

True love is made of understanding — *prajña.* We cannot achieve prajña unless we practice deep looking and deep listening. Afterwards, we can use our hands. Our actions will bring relief and happiness to the person we love. Bring the bodhisattvas within you to life. By becoming the bodhisattva of deep listening, deep looking, and great action, you can truly be there for the person you love.

The Four Brahmaviharas

The Buddha's teaching on love can be seen in the four *brahmaviharas,* the four elements of true love. We use these elements to improve the quality of our love. We look into the nature of our love to see whether these elements are present. The first element is maitri. As I have mentioned before, maitri can be translated as "loving kindness." The word "maitri" has roots in the word *mitra,* which means friend. The object of your love is a friend. When it is yourself, you are your own friend. Friends always benefit from each other's presence. Maitri is the capacity to offer joy and happiness. It is a practice, not a feeling. When you know how to breathe in and calm your body, you bring peace and stability into your body. That is friendliness or maitri. When you smile your lovely smile, that is maitri. The willingness to love is not love. You might have a lot of goodwill, but without understanding or skill, you might hurt the person you love. Your hand doesn't have an eye in it yet. That is why maitri, loving kindness, is the capacity of bringing joy and happiness to the person you love. You can only do this through understanding.

Look into your love to see whether you are capable of understanding your beloved and bringing him or her joy every day. Asking questions is important. "Darling, do I understand you well enough? Please help me understand you. Please tell me of your pain, sorrow, and suffering." This kind of request should be made regularly. You are speaking the language of love and understanding.

The second aspect of true love is karuna. As I said before, karuna can be translated as "compassion." Compassion means shared suffering. Compassion is composed of *com* (together with) and *passion* (to suffer). "Compassion" is not the truest translation of karuna. Karuna is the capacity of removing your beloved's pain and transforming it. You are like a physician. To remove a patient's pain, the physician needs to understand the patient's body. He has to practice looking and listening deeply to see what is wrong with the patient. He has to be really present to understand the patient's situation. A lover has to do the same thing. A lover has to be present to look and listen deeply to identify the pain in his or her beloved. When you understand the nature of your beloved's pain, you know what to do and what not to do to relieve it and make him or her suffer less every day. That is the practice of true love. Look deeply into the nature of your love to see whether there is karuna in it. It may be there, but in small amounts. We have to learn how to love. Learning to love means increasing our maitri and karuna every day.

The third aspect of true love is *mudita,* joy. If two people create misery and suffering for each other every day, that is not true love. We have to transform this misery. We look into the nature of our love to see whether it creates joy. If mudita is not present, it is not true love.

The fourth aspect of true love is *upeksha,* which means equanimity, nondiscrimination, freedom, or space. When you love someone, you don't impose your ideas on her and deprive her of her freedom. You offer her space both inside and outside. Often, we make our love a prison. We lock up our beloved, and she can no longer be herself. This is a kind of dictatorship, where upeksha is not present. We have to go to him or her and say, "Darling, have I deprived you of your freedom? Do you still feel that you can be yourself? Do you have enough space inside you and around you? Have I deprived you of that space?" If you ask sincerely, she will tell you. If she still feels free, you know that upeksha is present in your love.

Upeksha also means equanimity. You love someone unconditionally, because he or she needs your love. If you set conditions, it is no longer true love. We love our children without conditions. We do not say that they have to do this or that if they want to be our children. True love means looking deeply into the person and seeing their suffering, their difficulties and needs, and acting out of that insight. We act so that our beloved suffers less, becomes more comfortable and joyful. In a flower arrangement, each flower needs space so that its beauty can radiate. Each person is a flower. We need space inside and around us so that we can radiate our beauty and happiness. Upeksha means offering space.

If we cultivate these four aspects of true love every day, suffering is reduced, and joy and happiness are increased.

[BELL]

I would like to invite you to try four exercises concerning perception. The thirteenth exercise of mindfulness breathing is: "Contemplating impermanence, I breathe in. Contemplating impermanence, I breathe out." Impermanence is the key to unlock the door of reality. Most of our suffering is created by our wrong perceptions. Unless we understand the next four exercises deeply, we cannot understand the other exercises, so they are important. Liberation is not possible if we are not capable of correcting our perceptions. Insight on impermanence is the beginning. Intellectually, we know that things are impermanent, but we behave as if they were permanent. We suffer when someone we love passes away. We regret that we did not spend more time with our father when he was still alive. Insight on impermanence is helpful and can prevent us from suffering. It can bring us happiness in the here and the now.

Here is an exercise that you can try when you get angry at your beloved. You may be about to punish each other with strong words. When you are angry, you want some relief. You think that if you can make him suffer, you will feel better. You behave like a child. You know that if the other person suffers, you will suffer, too. Happiness is not an individual matter. We escalate our anger and suffering through mutual punishment. We behave like this as individuals, groups, and nations. The exercise is this: Close your eyes, take a deep breath, and visualize yourselves and your beloved three hundred years from now. Once you have gained some insight, open your eyes, and you will find your anger and ignorance are gone. We know that the only meaningful thing to do is to open our arms, hug the other person, and enjoy the fact that we are both alive. This is an insight into impermanence. It may seem like you and your beloved will live for an eternity. But the facts are plain: Just fifty years from now, things will be very different.

Once you have touched the nature of impermanence, you will do what you can to make your beloved happy. If you live like this, you will not have any regrets. To avoid regret, all you have to do is take care of the present moment. Whatever you can do for your beloved today, please do it. Whatever you can say, please say it. If you can smile right now, don't wait. If you live in this way, you will enjoy and enrich your friendship.

There was a practitioner in England who spoke to his daughter about impermanence in a pessimistic way. He used notions and concepts. His daughter's reaction was this: "Daddy, why do you complain about impermanence? If things were not impermanent, how could I grow up?" This is an intelligent question. It is because of impermanence that we change and grow. When you sow seeds in the field, you hope that things are impermanent so that the seeds will sprout.

[BELL]

Using our intelligence and insight, we recognize how crucial impermanence is to life. Impermanence allows us to transform and move in a better direction. Without impermanence, dictatorships or illnesses would last forever. Impermanence is not a pessimistic note in the music of reality; in fact, it is vital for life to be. Instead of complaining about impermanence, we should say, "Long live impermanence."

Impermanence is not an intellectual concept. Our practice is to nourish the insight of impermanence in every moment of our daily life. It is the starting point, the first door that helps us enter reality as it is. If we know how to touch the nature of impermanence, we can discover many insights, like interbeing, nonself, and nirvana, which bring us deep into the heart of reality. The Buddha proposed the teaching of the Three Dharma Seals. If a teaching doesn't have the seals of impermanence, nonself, and nirvana, it is not the Buddha's authentic teaching. These three insights are wonderful keys to unlock the door of reality. When we are capable of touching reality, all our wrong perceptions will vanish. When those perceptions are replaced by true understanding, our suffering will be removed.

[BELL]

CHAPTER ELEVEN

Practicing the Three Dharma Seals

Dear Sangha, today is the fifth of June, 1998. It is the second week of our twenty-one-day retreat.

Fasting

Many of you have asked how to practice fasting and resting. Fasting is an opportunity to rest and to heal. Fasting is a part of all spiritual traditions. It is beneficial because it lets our body and consciousness begin anew. We need to learn about the art of fasting by talking to friends who have practiced it for several years. In Germany, there are clinics where people can fast under the supervision of doctors. If you are healthy, fasting for ten to fourteen days, drinking only water, is fine. But if your body is weak, your capacity for eliminating toxins will also be weak, and you should have a doctor's supervision during the fast, because many toxins will be eliminated. Sometimes you will feel tired, exhausted, or paralyzed by all the toxins. If you feel tired — especially on the third or fifth day — it is not due to lack of food (you have a two- to three-week reserve of food stored in your body) but due to the toxins entering your bloodstream.

During the fast you need to drink at least three liters of warm water every day to cleanse your body. You can drink herbal tea instead, but you must vary the type of tea. You should practice total relaxation, do physical exercise, and have massages, so that the toxins in the muscles are released into the bloodstream. By drinking only water during the fast, we help the masses of toxins in various parts of our digestive tract to disintegrate. Some of these toxins will be eliminated, but many of them will enter our bloodstream, so we have to help these toxins leave the body.

During a fast, our organs work extra hard to eliminate toxins. There are tonics available to aid your organs during this process of elimination. If your kidneys are weak, you may have problems with fasting, so it is wise to have a kidney test before your fast to see whether they are functioning normally and can effectively eliminate toxins. Also, toxins are eliminated through the lungs, so deep breathing is important. Toxins are also eliminated in the form of gas, through the skin and intestines. That is why taking a shower daily and drinking liquids are recommended.

After two or three weeks, you will look like a new person because you have eliminated many toxins from your digestive system and many other places in your body. I usually fast for two or three weeks, during which time I continue my normal activities.*

[BELL]

The Inner Teacher

Yesterday I spoke about our capacity for understanding our beloved. "Darling, do you think I understand you well enough? Please help me to understand you better because I really love you and want to make you happy. I don't want to make you unhappy. If I make you unhappy, it is unintentional and entirely due to my

* If you are pregnant or have any special medical conditions (such as heart, liver, or kidney problems, diabetes, or an eating disorder), make sure your doctor or health professional knows this before you begin a fast. If you have any unusual or disturbing symptoms while engaged in a fast, contact your doctor right away. Remember that you need to make your own educated decision, with your doctor's guidance, as to whether to fast at all, and for how long to fast.

ignorance." If we really love each other, we can speak the language of trust. If your beloved is not present, you can write to her or call her. If she is here, you can ask her directly. Or you can talk to her inside yourself, because she is inside you. Talking to her like that and asking this question will make you feel better.

I always feel love and gratitude for my students who practice according to the teachings. I am grateful that they have listened, understood the teachings, and put them into practice. Herein lies the relationship between teacher and student. The connection and deep love between us is there. I remember when I was about to marry a couple in Plum Village and they asked me, "Thây, we have twenty-four hours before our wedding ceremony. What should we do to prepare ourselves?" I told them that if there was anyone they were still angry with, they should try to reach some kind of reconciliation with that person.

When I saw them trying their best to do this, my love and trust for them grew. For me, a good teacher is someone who helps give birth to the student's inner teacher. The relationship between you and your teacher will continue to improve when it has freedom, respect, and nonattachment. It will be deep, authentic, and good, and will help many people around you. You shouldn't rely on your outer teacher all the time. You have an inner teacher, as well, who will develop and grow and upon whom you should ultimately rely. In this retreat, I am not offering you theories or ideas but practical suggestions. I hope you can apply them to your daily life.

[BELL]

Contemplating Impermanence

There are many teachers and psychotherapists at this retreat who, with love and compassion, help people suffer less. The quality of our work and action depends on our capacity for healing and transforming ourselves. That is why we need to apply the teachings to our daily lives. We mindfully recognize and embrace our suffering and afflictions, and transform them with mindful breathing, walking, sitting, deep listening, and loving speech.

I always tell my Dharma teachers that they should be happy and know how to relieve and transform their own suffering so they can help other people. If they are unhappy, I ask them not to teach, because they won't have a lot to share. They should stay at home and practice. First, apply the teachings to your own life. Embrace your pain and sorrow, relieve your suffering, practice transforming yourself until you have enough freedom, stability, and solidity to go out and try to help others. I advise school teachers and psychotherapists to do the same, and I follow this rule myself. Everything I share with you comes from my personal practice.

This retreat is a place where we can act. Among us, there are those who suffer very deeply. You don't have to go to a hospital to find people who suffer; they are right here. We must do our best to help relieve the suffering of our fellow practitioners. One stable step taken in mindfulness can contribute much to relieving their suffering. A smile of understanding, connection, and compassion can be very healing.

We have to take good care of ourselves. We have to bring all of our energy, time, and heart to the practice. Together, we produce the collective energy of mindfulness, embracing, and healing that will benefit all of us. At the beginning of the retreat, I promised that I would do my best to infuse my every step, word, and breath with that spirit. Let us act as a Sangha. Our work is right here in the retreat. By practicing self-transformation, we will also transform the suffering of our Dharma brothers and sisters.

Yesterday I spoke about the insight of impermanence. Many teachers, including those of ancient Greece and China — Heraclitus and Confucius — gave teachings on impermanence. In the Buddhist tradition, impermanence is not just a description of reality but also an instrument for understanding. You cannot understand impermanence without understanding the teaching of interbeing or emptiness. Yesterday I spoke of impermanence as the first key to unlocking the door of reality. I spoke about impermanence as *samadhi,* a form of concentration. Intellectually, you may agree that things are impermanent, but you might behave as if reality were permanent. We have to train ourselves to maintain the insight of impermanence every minute of our lives. Then we will always have wisdom and happiness.

We all feel insecure. We don't know what the future holds. Accidents happen. A loved one may suddenly be struck by an incurable disease and die. We are not sure if we'll be alive tomorrow. This is all part of impermanence. This feeling of insecurity makes us suffer. How can we deal with it?

When the French poet Victor Hugo lost his beloved daughter, Léopoldine, he suffered greatly. He asked God, "Why? Why have you broken my heart?" He was drowning in an ocean of suffering and spent many weeks in that state. Afterwards he wrote the poem *"A Villequiers."* He said, "God, I am bringing you the pieces of my broken heart. You have broken my heart. You have taken my daughter away. Man is like a reed that trembles every time the wind passes by. Things are so impermanent. We are so vulnerable. We don't really see reality. We see only one end of reality. The other end of reality is plunged into a night of terrifying mystery. God, you are the only one who knows. We humans don't know. When we suffer, we don't know why we suffer. The only thing to do is to surrender to you because you are the only one who knows."

How can we face this feeling? What is our practice? Because life and reality are impermanent, we feel insecure. I think the teaching on living deeply in the present moment is what we have to learn and practice to face this feeling of insecurity. We have to handle the present moment well. We live deeply in the present moment so that in the future we will have no regrets. We are aware that we and the person in front of us are both alive. We cherish the moment and do whatever we can to make life meaningful and to make him or her happy in this moment.

Yesterday I proposed hugging meditation for when we are angry with each other. We close our eyes, take a deep breath, and visualize ourselves and our beloved three hundred years from now. Then, the only meaningful thing to do is to open our arms and hug him or her. I haven't yet given you instructions on how to hug someone. When you hug someone, first practice breathing in and breathing out to bring your insight of impermanence to life. "Breathing in, I know that life is precious in this moment. Breathing out, I cherish this moment of life." You smile at the person in front of you, expressing your desire to hold him or her in your arms. This is a practice and a ritual. When you bring your body and mind together to produce your total presence, to become full of life, it is a ritual.

When I drink a glass of water, I invest one hundred percent of myself in drinking it. You should train yourself to live every moment of your daily life like that. Hugging is a deep practice. You need to be totally present to do it correctly. When you open your arms and hold the other person, you practice three mindful breaths. "Breathing in, I know that he is still alive in my arms. Breathing out, I feel so happy."

Life becomes real at that moment. Architects need to build airports and railway stations so that there is enough room to practice hugging. You can also practice it in the following way: during the first in-breath and out-breath, you become aware that you and your beloved are both alive; for the second in-breath and out-breath, you think of where you will both be three hundred years from now; and for the third in-breath and out-breath, you go back to the insight that you are both alive. Your hugging will be deeper, and so will your happiness.

Happiness and Suffering

Happiness cannot be separated from suffering. Happiness is clear and strong only against the backdrop of suffering. If we have not known hunger, we cannot fully realize the happiness of having something to eat. Those of us who are from the Third World know what hunger is. Hunger is not being served lunch two hours late; that is appetite. If you have suffered, you have the conditions to be happy. If you do not know anything about suffering, you cannot be happy. Impermanence should be practiced in this spirit. When we know how to practice dwelling fully in the present moment, happiness is born against the backdrop of impermanence and suffering.

After her first year of practice, a young nun in our community told me that she saw how happiness and suffering were entwined. She wasn't merely repeating something I had said in a Dharma talk; this was her true insight. As a young person, she had suffered, and only recently had she discovered happiness. She knew that if she had not suffered, the happiness she was now enjoying would not be possible. Sometimes, all of our conditions for happiness are fulfilled, but we are not happy. This is the case for many of us. Others might envy our situation, but we are not happy because we are unable to see the contrast between happiness and unhappiness.

Happiness and unhappiness inter-are. Happiness can be present only if unhappiness is present, and vice versa. It is like the rose and the garbage. Without the garbage, there can be no rose. If there is no rose, there can be no garbage. We have to see the nature of interbeing in the rose and the garbage. If you know how, you can transform garbage into roses. If you don't know how, the rose quickly turns into garbage. It is a matter of skill. Skill is connected to mindfulness. By speaking, listening, communicating, observing, and acting mindfully, you become skilled at mindful living.

Sometimes, if we are not skillful enough, despite our goodwill, we create suffering. We should learn to see things not as good and evil, right or wrong, but as more or less skillful, more or less artful. In Plum Village, we call anger and craving unskillful states of mind. If I make you suffer, it is not because I am evil or wrong, but because I am unskillful. Forgive me and teach me, so that I can be more skillful next time.

If we look at things in this way, we will not be judgmental or motivated by the desire to punish and blame. We don't want to make each other suffer. We can say, "Darling, if you really love me, please help me to be more skillful so that I will not make a mistake that causes you a lot of suffering."

[BELL]

Interbeing

Yesterday we spoke about the Three Dharma Seals: impermanence, nonself, and nirvana. Nirvana is the subject of contemplation in the fifteenth exercise of mindfulness breathing proposed by the Buddha, "Contemplating nirvana, I breathe in. Contemplating nirvana, I breathe out." Many of us do not know what contemplating nirvana means. It is as simple as contemplating impermanence. If you contemplate impermanence well, you touch nirvana at the same time. We say that impermanence is the mark of reality, the expression of reality from the viewpoint of time. Everything, from form to feelings to mental formations, is impermanent. Touching impermanence during our in-breath, we touch the nature of impermanence in the whole cosmos. Touching one thing, we touch everything.

"Experiencing my body, I breathe in." Our body is also impermanent. Birth and death take place in every moment in our body. Not a single cell is permanent. When you review all your bodily and mental formations, you see that everything is impermanent, especially what we call the "self." We know this, yet we fear that we are nothing without a permanent self, and we still believe that we have one. We are not satisfied with being form, feelings, formations, and consciousness. We want more. We want to live forever.

Scientifically, we can't find anything permanent. Everything is always changing. There is no permanent entity anywhere. My body of this moment is no longer my body of the previous moment. We have to confront the fact that everything is impermanent. Even the blocks of pain, sorrow, and despair hidden in the depths of our consciousness are impermanent. If we know how to practice, we can bring about deep self-transformation. We have learned that there are two ways to transform our pain. The first way is to invite it up and look deeply into its nature. The second way is to water the seeds of the opposite nature, and know that they will bring about transformation down in the bottom of our consciousness.

In Buddhist literature, the shortest unit of time is called *ksana.* If you divide one second into one thousand parts, and divide this one thousand times again until you cannot divide it any more, that is a ksana. Impermanence is the manifestation of reality from the side of time. Time is not a separate entity. It inter-is with something else in order to be possible: space, consciousness, and so on. Einstein showed that time is not possible without space. Time is space. It is like the wave and the particle in physics. Sometimes reality manifests itself as a wave, and sometimes as a particle. Sometimes reality manifests itself as time, and sometimes as space. It looks like two things, but it is not. It is not one thing, either. The notions of one and two are not applicable to reality.

Let us visualize the aspect of reality called space. Impermanence is called nonself from the perspective of space. Nonself means impermanence. Nothing stays the same in two consecutive moments. There is no permanent entity and, therefore, no self. Self is defined as a permanent entity, something that lasts forever. If you acknowledge that things are impermanent, you have to acknowledge that things are without a permanent entity, without self. Nonself does not mean nonexisting. The Bodhisattva Avalokiteshvara said that everything is empty. What does this mean?

To be empty is to be empty of a separate self. Let us look again at the example of a flower. It is a manifestation of reality. If we look deeply into the flower and touch it deeply, we touch everything in the cosmos: the sunshine, a cloud, the earth, time, space, everything. We can say that the flower is full of everything, is full of the cosmos. Why do we call it empty? Because the flower is full of everything except one thing: a separate existence, a separate self. This means the flower cannot exist by itself alone. The flower inter-is with a cloud, the sunshine, and the earth. If you remove the cloud, the sunshine, and the earth from the flower, it will collapse. Our true nature is interbeing. Interbeing is a very important word. We hope that it will soon appear in the dictionary.

Interbeing applies to everything. Look into your body. Your body cannot exist alone by itself. It has to inter-be with the trees, the earth, your parents, and your ancestors. There is nothing in the cosmos that is not present in your body. When you touch your body deeply, you touch the whole cosmos. You touch not only your ancestors, but all the future generations that are already present in it.

My body is like a flower. There are many clouds in me. If you remove the clouds from me, I will collapse. That is how I inter-am with the clouds. Not only was I a cloud in my past life, but I continue to be a cloud in this moment. You cannot take the cloud out of me. I inter-am with the cloud, the sunshine, and the forest.

When I breathe in and out, I feel happy. Touching my in-breath and out-breath deeply, I know that my in-breath is not possible without all of the vegetation in nature. As I have mentioned before, the mountain and its vegetation are lungs outside of my body. I have two lungs in my body and many lungs outside of it. If you are from New York, you know that Central Park is also your lungs. You have to take care of it. Without lungs outside, you cannot survive. I have a heart inside my body, and I will die if it stops functioning. Looking deeply at the sun, I see that the sun is my second heart. If it collapses, I will die. We have more than one heart. This insight made me write my book *The Sun My Heart.*

This is the fruit of looking deeply. When you look at a tree and practice breathing "In/out," you know that you inter-are with the tree. The Buddha said several times, "This is because that is." It is very simple. If someone asks about the Buddhist teaching on Genesis and how the world came to be, you only have to repeat that simple sentence. It is so simple and so deep. It means interbeing. I will add something myself, "This is like this because that is like that." If your beloved suffers, somehow it is because of you. You are co-responsible for her happiness or unhappiness. "This is because that is. This is not because that is not. This is like this because that is like that."

We share everything. We cannot reduce something into nothing. If we could reduce a speck of dust into nothingness, we could reduce the whole cosmos into nothingness. There are people who think that they can reduce things to nothing, that they can eliminate or kill people, make someone into no one. John F. Kennedy, Dr. Martin Luther King, Jr., Mahatma Gandhi, and so many others were killed so that they would forever disappear. But in fact when you kill someone, he or she becomes stronger than before. Looking deeply, we discover the nature of no-birth and no-death. First, we touch deeply the nature of impermanence. If we continue, we will touch the nature of interbeing. Interbeing is another name for nonself. Nonself means that we are made of nonself elements.

Let us look at our body again. It was transmitted to us by our ancestors. This transmission is empty. If we look deeply, we can see that when our ancestors transmitted our body to us, they transmitted the whole of themselves. There is no distinction between the transmitter and the transmitted. Every cell of our body contains everything we need to know about our ancestors. That is why there is an emptiness of self between the transmitter and the transmitted. We are the receiver of the transmission, and not a separate entity. We are at once the receiver, the object of transmission, and the transmitter.

When we touch our body and consciousness, we touch the body and consciousness of all the generations of our ancestors. With this insight, we touch the reality of nonself and of interbeing. It is no longer a word or concept. If we live by this insight, we will not create any suffering for ourselves or the people around us. That is why interbeing and impermanence should become a living insight and not a system of thought, a doctrine, or a dogma.

[BELL]

If we practice looking deeply and touching reality deeply, we understand what is meant by emptiness or nonself. These terms no longer frighten us. We abandon the illusion that we have carried for so long of a separate self, of reality as unchanging and permanent. If this insight is alive for us, we know that the wisdom of the Buddha is within us. If we speak, listen, and act on the basis of that wisdom, we can only create happiness and communication, not suffering and misunderstanding.

Each step we take and each breath we draw can cultivate this insight. We have to live deeply and in a concentrated way for this insight to become real and alive, not merely an idea. When I look at my students during a Dharma talk, I see them as myself. I try to transmit to them the nourishment that I am giving myself. The distinction between student and teacher vanishes. Let us live our daily lives so that we touch the nature of interbeing in every moment. Then we will avoid making mistakes and creating suffering. That is the meaning of "Breathing in, I experience impermanence. Breathing out, I experience interbeing." This is a very deep practice, the cream of the Buddha's teachings.

Touching Nirvana

Yesterday I said that impermanence, nonself, and nirvana constitute the Three Dharma Seals. Why "Seals"? Because they testify that a teaching is an authentic teaching of the Buddha. Any teaching that does not bear the seals of impermanence, nonself, and nirvana is not an authentic teaching of the Buddha. This coin represents the Three Dharma Seals. The head and tail represent impermanence and nonself, and the metal represents nirvana. You cannot take nirvana out of impermanence and nonself. Impermanence is nonself; they are two sides of the same reality. If you touch impermanence deeply, you touch nonself, interbeing, and emptiness. These terms all mean the same thing. Empty means empty of a separate existence. Interbeing means you cannot exist by yourself alone, you have to inter-be; this is nonself. Touching one side of reality deeply, you also touch the other side. You can only understand the meaning of impermanence when you have understood the meaning of nonself or interbeing.

You may ask, what does nirvana mean? When you touch the reality of impermanence and nonself, you are touching nirvana. Why? I have already mentioned the image of an ocean with a multitude of waves. The waves are all different — some are small and others are large. You may say some waves are more beautiful than others. You can describe the waves in many ways. Each wave has a beginning and an end. But when you touch a wave, you are also touching something else — the water.

A wave may not be aware that she is water. That is the origin of all of her suffering. We don't know our ground of being. We don't know that the Kingdom of God is within us. We are not able to touch nirvana inside us, and that is why we suffer so much. Our greatest relief should be to touch nirvana. This is not an idea. We can do it in this very moment. When you touch the wave deeply, you are also touching the water. We can touch a cloud, a flower, or our own body, but we may not touch them deeply enough to touch their ground of being. Deep touching, with mindfulness, concentration, and insight, will allow us to touch the ground of our being.

I have not yet explained the last line of the gatha I gave you on the first day of our retreat. "I have arrived. I am home. In the here and in the now. I am solid. I am free. In the ultimate I dwell. In the ultimate I dwell." We cannot understand the last line unless we learn how to touch the ground of our being. There are two dimensions of reality — the historical dimension and the ultimate dimension. We live in history. In this dimension, there are birth and death, a beginning and an end, being and nonbeing, high and low, success and failure. We are used to dwelling in this dimension. We have not had the chance to touch this dimension deeply in order to dwell in the ultimate dimension. But the two dimensions belong to each other. You cannot take the historical dimension out of the ultimate dimension, or the ultimate dimension out of the historical dimension. It is like the wave and the water. You cannot take the wave out of the water, nor the water out of the wave.

Do not throw away impermanence and nonself in order to touch nirvana. If you throw away impermanence and nonself, there will be no nirvana left. It is like if you throw the water away, there will be no waves left, and if you throw all the waves away, there will be no water left. That is why when we touch the historical dimension deeply, we also touch nirvana. This is a very deep Buddhist teaching. We find relief from our suffering by embracing our despair, fear, and sorrow, but the greatest relief comes through touching nirvana.

[BELL]

Waves and Water

Let us visualize ourselves as a wave on the surface of the ocean. We are subject to fear, jealousy, despair, and anger because we have not been able to touch the ground of our being — water. We are caught in concepts of permanence and self, being and nonbeing, beginning and end, beautiful and ugly, high and low, and we discriminate against the other waves. We see that we have been created, have a beginning, rise up a little, stay up for a while, then descend. We know that we are going to end at some point. We don't see that we inter-are with the other waves, that we share a common ground of being. We are locked into our idea of a separate self when, in fact, we are here because all the other waves are here, and our shape is created by the other waves. If we know how to bend down and touch our ground of being — water — all our fears, discrimination, and suffering will vanish, because we will see the nature of our interbeing with every other wave.

The notions that we apply to waves cannot be applied to water. As a wave, we share the life of the water. If we only live the life of a wave, and are not capable of living the life of water, we suffer a lot. It is so important for the wave to touch the water within her. When she has touched the water, she knows that she is not subject to birth, death, being, and nonbeing. Her fear vanishes.

Continuation

We don't have to throw away the phenomenal world to touch the ground of our being. In fact, we have to touch the phenomenal world deeply. This sheet of paper belongs to the historical dimension. We believe there was a time when it was created and that there will be a time when it will cease to exist. It is conditioned by being and nonbeing. Let's practice looking deeply together into this sheet of paper so that we may touch the ultimate dimension — the ground of being — of the piece of paper. If you can touch the ground of being of this sheet of paper, you can touch your own ground of being, because you are also a sheet of paper.

Looking deeply into this sheet of paper, you can see a cloud floating in it. Even if you are not a poet, you can still see the cloud. If you remove the cloud from the paper, the paper will collapse. Without the cloud, there can be no rain, the trees can't grow, and there will be no paper. The nature of paper is interbeing. The paper inter-is with the sunshine, the minerals, the earth, the paper factory, the workers in the factory, and the food that the workers eat every day. If you touch the paper deeply, you touch everything in the cosmos.

You may think that this paper did not exist before it was created. You may think that to be born means you suddenly become something from nothing, someone from no one, that your identity starts at the date specified on your birth certificate. Did this paper exist before it was created, or has it come from nothing? No, something never comes from nothing, and someone never comes from no one. Did you come from nothingness? No. The moment of our birth was actually a moment of continuation, because we had already existed in our mother for months. The date on our birth certificate is not correct and should be pushed back nine months to the moment of our conception, the moment when we began to exist.

But we continue to ask, "Before that moment, were we nothing, no one?" No. Before that moment, you existed in your father and mother in another form. Even the moment of conception is a moment of continuation. Like the sheet of paper, we have been here for a long time in other forms. Before its creation in the factory, the paper was sunshine and a tree. The reality is that we have never been born. Every moment is a moment of continuation. We just continue living in new forms. Shall we see whether we can reduce this piece of paper to nonbeing? Does anyone have a match?

When a cloud is about to become rain, it is not scared, because it knows that even though it was wonderful to be a cloud floating in the sky, it will be just as wonderful to be rain falling down on fields, oceans, and vegetation. When a cloud becomes rain, it is not a moment of death, but a moment of continuation. That is why I suggest that my friends sing "Happy Continuation Day" instead of "Happy Birthday." The day of our so-called death or passing away is also a continuation day. Every day is a continuation day. We should celebrate our continuation every day, in every moment.

[BELL]

CHAPTER TWELVE

Transforming Our Suffering

[THREE BELLS]

Today is the seventh of June, 1998, and we are beginning the third week of our twenty-one-day retreat. We have learned the gathas "In/out, deep/slow" and "I have arrived, I am home." Now we will learn the wonderful gatha, "Being an Island Unto Myself."

Being an Island Unto Myself

Being an island unto myself.
As an island unto myself.
Buddha is my mindfulness.
Shining far, shining near.
Dharma is my breathing, guarding body and mind.
I am free.

Being an island unto myself.
As an island unto myself.
Sangha is my skandhas, working in harmony.
Taking refuge in myself.
Coming back to myself.
I am free.

This practice brings us home. The Buddha said that there is an island in each of us, and when we go home to ourselves, we are on that safe island. There, we touch the energy of the Buddha, which sheds its light on any situation, enabling us to see near and far and to know what to do. We touch the living Dharma on that island by practicing mindful breathing. Mindful breathing and mindfulness practice are the living Dharma. They generate energy and protect our body and mind.

You can touch the energy of the Sangha within yourself in your five skandhas: body, feelings, perceptions, mental formations, and consciousness. Through mindful breathing, these elements come together to work in harmony. Unhappiness, sorrow, fear, and conflict are transformed into harmony. When we touch the energy of the Buddha, the Dharma, and the Sangha, we are safe, and not overwhelmed by the negative energy of confusion, despair, and panic. Returning to our island and practicing mindful breathing helps tremendously.

I always practice this gatha at the most difficult times. If I were in an airplane and thought it was going to crash, I would practice breathing in and out. It is the best thing to do. Please cherish this practice. It has saved many lives. It is a Dharma treasure. You can memorize this gatha and practice it while driving, making breakfast, or having lunch. Dwelling in the island of self, you chew each morsel of food with this gatha in mind. You can practice arriving, being at home, and being in a pure land. You will feel as though you are surrounded by the Sangha and are absorbing its energy. You are also producing energy and offering it to the Sangha at the same time.

When was I in China, I translated this gatha into Chinese. In Taiwan, we taught the children to sing it. I also shared mantras with children in Japan. The Chinese children wrote mantras in Chinese and put them on the wall. The mantras were, "Darling, I am here for you"; "Darling, I know you are there, and I am very happy"; "Darling, I know you are suffering. That is why I am here for you"; and "Darling, I am suffering, please help." You may like to write these mantras in beautiful script and put them on your door so that you remember to practice them every day.

We have been learning about impermanence, interbeing, and nirvana. Touching nirvana is not a vague or abstract notion. It is something we can do in the present moment. The Buddha said that we can touch nirvana with our own body. We can all breathe in and experience impermanence. We can also breathe in and touch the reality of nirvana; it is no more difficult than experiencing impermanence. It is just like touching water or a wave. When I ask you to breathe in and touch a wave, you are confident that you can do it. But when I ask you to breathe in and touch the water, you might feel like you can't. The water and waves are one. Impermanence and nirvana are one. The nature of everything is impermanence, interbeing, nonself. If you touch the phenomenal world deeply, you will touch the ground of being at the same time.

In many Mahayana sutras, it says that everything has always been in the state of nirvana. We are dwelling in nirvana. Our true nature is no-birth, no-death, and no-being, and no-nonbeing, because nirvana means the extinction of all ideas and notions. Everything shares the nature of no-birth and no-death. Birth and death are perceptions, not reality. We know that something cannot come from nothing, and someone cannot come from no one. Something cannot be reduced to nothing; being cannot be reduced to nonbeing. As I have said before, "To be or not to be" is not really the question; the question is whether we can touch the nature of interbeing so that we are free from birth and death, being and nonbeing.

We have the notions of coming and going. Where do I come from and where am I going? This is a difficult question. According to the teaching of nirvana, we come from nowhere and we go nowhere. We manifest when conditions are sufficient. When conditions are no longer sufficient, we no longer have the perception that we exist. We may think that we actually no longer exist. In many of the Buddha's discourses, he says that when conditions are sufficient, things reveal themselves. We think this means that they exist, that they are. When one of the conditions is lacking and things do not manifest themselves to our perception, then we incorrectly think that they do not exist and that there is nonbeing. This meditation hall is filled with signals: television programs, colors, images, and sounds. Because we don't have the machines to capture these signals, we think that there is nothing here. If we had a television, we would see colors and forms and hear sounds. We cannot describe the signals as nonexistent or nonbeing just because they are not manifesting. Our perception is like that. The terms being and nonbeing, birth and death are just notions. They cannot be ascribed to reality.

Another pair of opposites is one and many, unity and plurality. We know that reality, being both one and many, is free from these concepts. Consciousness is both individual and collective. We may think that collective consciousness is independent from individual consciousness, but the two are intertwined. We may wonder whether transformation at the base refers to the base of our individual consciousness or collective consciousness when, in fact, they are one and cannot be separated.

[BELL]

Non-Dual Looking

Let us look again at the notions of left and right. We cannot conceive that right is also left; right must be the opposite of left. We even use the expressions "extreme right" and "extreme left." Politicians who belong to the left would like to see the right vanish. But if the right vanished, the left would also vanish. When you cut into a cake, either side of that point immediately becomes the left and right. Where are the real left and the real right? We imagine that there is a straight line that divides left from right. But left and right meet all the time. If we look deeply, we see that a straight line doesn't exist, and that if it continues moving to the left or to the right, the two sides will join at one point in space. It is more real to look at every point of the line and see both left and right in it. In fact, there is no left or right. It is more real to look deeply into the right and see the left in it, because the left is made of the right.

Every point of the road in between Boston and New York contains both Boston and New York. If we look in the direction of Boston, the spot where we are standing contains Boston. If we then turn toward New York, New York is also contained in that spot. It is like birth and death. If we look deeply into death, we see birth. Birth and death make each other possible. Our tendency to divide reality into pairs of opposites leads to misunderstanding and wrong action. We need to learn another way of looking that transcends opposites — non-dual looking. This wise way of looking helps us allow reality to reveal itself.

Sangha Eyes

Here are some real, practical questions that I have received that can be used to illustrate the role of the Sangha:

1. "Dear Thây, this is a question about the role of upeksha in daily life. Spiritually, our love should be unconditional, but are there times when right action needs to end a relationship? Does the Dharma offer teachings to guide us in lovingly stopping a harmful relationship? When the relationship is harmful, is it possible for us to get a divorce? Is divorce compatible with the Dharma?"
2. "A person who has been beaten repeatedly by a partner has grown to be afraid of him, and fears for her life. The partner denies the problem and does not seek to address it. Should the abused person leave?"
3. "An adult son does not work. He uses drugs and will not seek help. There are young children in the house. Is it best to ask him to leave?"

4. "An employee at a small company has become totally nonfunctional. His failure to work may cause the company to fail. All possible remedial steps have been taken, but to no avail. Is it right to fire the employee?"

— ∞ —

My answers to these questions come from my experience of practicing with the Sangha. I suggest that the Sangha decide such questions. According to tradition, everything needs to be solved in the context of a Sangha. The Sangha is like a big family. Today, the nuclear family is small, and we decide matters individually. We try to solve our problems alone. Our families do not "interfere." They do not offer insight and support. In the past, when two people got married, the wedding was organized by both families. It was not just up to the young couple. They were supported by their large, extended families. We need this support and the support of the Sangha.

During the time of the Buddha, a skilled horse tamer once came to hear the teachings. The Buddha met with him and asked him how he tamed horses. He explained that there were some horses that responded well to gentle treatment, others that responded well to harsh treatment — such as the whip — and yet others who required alternately gentle and harsh treatment.

The Buddha asked, "What if none of these three methods works?"

The horse tamer said, "In that case, my lord, I have to kill the horse, because if I leave him with the others, they will all become impossible to train." The horse tamer then asked the Buddha, "Lord, I would like to know how you deal with your students. How do you treat them?"

The Buddha looked at his guest, smiled, and said, "Well, I deal with them in a similar way to yours." He explained that there were some students who responded well to gentle treatment, others that responded well to harsh treatment, and yet others who required alternately gentle and harsh treatment.

The horse tamer asked, "What if none of these three methods works?"

The Buddha answered, "Then I would do something similar to how you treat the horses."

"You mean you would kill your student?"

The Buddha said, "Yes."

"But, my lord, you are a teacher of nonviolence. How can you kill your student?"

The Buddha replied that when a student causes trouble in the community and prevents the Sangha from continuing its practice, the Sangha decides whether or not that person can stay in the community. If they decide he cannot stay, it is — for the student — a kind of death. If he does not have the chance to be in the community and receive its support and guidance, he has ruined his spiritual life.

Sometimes the Sangha does this for the sake of its practice. During the time of the Buddha, one of the monks was not permitted to continue with the Sangha because he prevented the Sangha from practicing and set a bad example for the young monks. Not allowing him to stay did not mean that he was totally excluded and received no compassion. The Sangha explained to the monk, "We are sorry, but if you don't follow our precepts, if you don't practice in the same mindful way as us, there is no reason for you to stay with us. We are here to practice the precepts and mindful manners so that we can reach enlightenment and transformation. By not doing that, you have excluded yourself. We welcome you back any time you are ready to accept the practice of the precepts of concentration, mindfulness, and mindful manners. We will always remain open to you, should you like to join us."

One of the discourses states that there was a monk who asked to disrobe, and his request was accepted. Six months later he asked for readmission into the Sangha of monks, and the Buddha allowed him back. This happened seven times. Each time that he wanted to return, his request was granted. This proves that the compassion of the Buddha and the Sangha was large. If you have good intentions, you are allowed to try again and again.

Sangha eyes are much better than individual eyes. In Plum Village, if you want to become a permanent resident or want to be ordained as a novice monk or nun, it is the Sangha and not the teacher that decides. The teacher takes refuge in the Sangha and trusts its insight. If you have a Sangha where you can rely on the insight of its members, you can reach decisions based on compassion, not anger or exclusion.

[BELL]

We celebrate weddings at Plum Village with the Sangha present as a witness to the ceremony. The collective energy of the Sangha supports the couple. The couple vows to practice the Five Awarenesses and recite them every month on the full moon so that they will remember that their practice and lives should serve not only their individual well-being, but also the larger community of their families, society, ancestors, and future generations. If they have difficulties, the Sangha will support them. They are committed to making decisions not just for themselves alone.

As a Sangha, let us look at the question I received concerning the young man who is not working, is using drugs, and setting a bad example for the younger children. If you have a big family with a circle of uncles, aunts, and grandparents, it is much easier. Love requires patience and insight, and we should help the young man through many means — beyond reasons or principles. We should use loving kindness and loving speech to encourage him to stop using drugs, find work, and become a good example for his younger siblings. We have to do everything we can to help. The final decision is made on the basis of these efforts, with the collective insight of the whole family or Sangha. If he isn't allowed to stay in the family, he needs to be told that he is always welcome to return if he agrees to live like the other members of the family.

We can solve these problems with insight, compassion, and in the spirit of inclusiveness.

Exclusion and elimination never work. Many people think that you can eliminate someone by killing them, but, like Gandhi or Dr. Martin Luther King, Jr., they return in strength. The idea of elimination is not valid. But what about Hitler? Should we have killed him or not? I think the same principle applies. If you kill Hitler and people like him, they will appear in other forms. In Germany, there are many young people who follow the new Nazism. Our practice of inclusiveness and compassion is important. We must do our best to help those who do not have enough insight and compassion and are creating disruption and harm. If necessary, we can lock them up, but neither punishment nor elimination is the solution.

There are two ways to lock somebody up. One is out of fear, anger, and the will to punish; the other is out of compassion. Punishment alone never helps anyone. There must be compassion. Those who are behind bars should be taken care of and loved more than those who lead normal, pleasant lives. We try to touch the people in prisons, help them to suffer less, and show them a way out of their suffering. Many books about the practice of mindfulness have been sent to prisons. Many prisoners have begun to practice and have found it possible to live in peace in prison. Some of them have written about their experiences. We show compassion so that transformation can take place. Prison guards know that punishment is not enough. Prisoners tend to quickly return to prison. The policy of punishment means we will need a lot more jails, now and in the future. We have to be willing to help prisoners by using loving kindness, compassion, and inclusiveness. We have to include Hitler, too. If we need to lock him up, we do it out of compassion and in the effort to help him. If we are motivated by the desire to eliminate him, he will be reborn in many different forms.

Inclusiveness

Inclusiveness is very important. When we have difficulty in our relationships, it is tempting to think that things might be easier without the other person. We think divorce may be the solution. But to divorce or not to divorce is not the question; the question is transformation. Many of us who get divorced continue to suffer because no transformation has occurred. In fact, our habitual energy might cause our new partner to suffer, too. A temporary separation might be a better solution, so that each person can practice and try again on the basis of compassion and inclusiveness. We have to include difficult people and difficult elements because only this attitude and practice can change our situation. It is best if we make these decisions as a Sangha. Without a Sangha, we are weak. Whether or not we consider ourselves Buddhists, we always need a Sangha. That is why Sangha-building is important. Make use of your Sangha. Using your Sangha eyes, practice inclusiveness and open your heart.

One day the Buddha gave Rahula, a young novice, a Dharma talk about the earth's capacity to receive, embrace, and transform all kinds of elements. There are four great elements: earth, water, fire, and air (mahabhuta). The four great elements all have the capacity to receive, embrace, and transform. "Rahula," the Buddha said, "learn to be like the earth. Whether people pour milk or fragrant liquids, deposit flowers or jewels, or pour urine, excrement, and mucus on the earth, the earth receives them without discrimination." Why? Because the earth has the capacity to receive, embrace, and transform. The earth can receive excrement and urine because it is immense. It transforms them into flowers, grass, and trees. If you cultivate your heart so that it is open, you become immense like the earth and can embrace anyone or anything without suffering.

If you put a handful of salt in a bowl and stir it, the water becomes so salty that it is undrinkable. If you put that water in a river, the river is not affected because it is immense. If your heart is like the river, you won't suffer because of small problems. We suffer because our hearts are too small and not inclusive. Our hearts have a tendency to exclude and eliminate. The four unlimited minds* are the real elements of true love. They have the capacity to receive, embrace, and transform everything. I don't know how much of the Buddha's teaching the novice Rahula was able to absorb. But standing behind him was an older monk, the Venerable Shariputra, and he was delighted with this teaching and put it into practice. He became a great monk and helped many of his younger brothers in the community.

The First Prostration

The Three Prostrations were created at Plum Village to help you practice this kind of embracing. If you practice the Three Prostrations deeply, you can heal yourself quickly. Your physical ailments and mental suffering will disappear. Your heart will grow as big as the earth's, and you will be able to embrace, accept, and transform everything. The Three Prostrations also help us understand the Three Dharma Seals. Perhaps you remember the coin. The head represents impermanence, the tail, nonself, and the metal, nirvana. The Three Prostrations also represent these three things.

The First Prostration represents the dimension of time, impermanence. We stand and breathe mindfully in the present moment. We visualize our parents, grandparents, and ancestors above us. We are aware that all of them are alive within us. We exclude no one. Although our children and their children may not yet be visible, they are also within us. Even if you hate your father and won't have anything to do with him, your father is alive within you. As I have said before, you are a continuation of him; you are your father. When we recognize and accept this fact, we transform our sorrow, anger, resentment, and suffering. The cause of

* See chap. 10 for more information on the four brahmaviharas.

our suffering is alienation — being uprooted from the ground of our being. If we have become hungry ghosts with nowhere to call our true home, it is because we have become alienated from the ground of our being.

The First Prostration can be described as a vertical line. In the First Prostration, we reenter the stream of life as the continuation of our ancestors. We bow. We touch our forehead — representing our wisdom and insight — with our hands. We bring all our intelligence and wisdom to the practice. With our two palms, we touch our heart. We use all our heart to practice touching the earth. We visualize the presence of all our ancestors (both blood and spiritual ancestors) within us. We may be angry with some of our ancestors or be running away from them, but they remain our spiritual and blood ancestors. We cannot remove them from ourselves. We know that some were almost perfect and some were nowhere near it, but they are all our ancestors, and it is important to accept them.

Next we look at our blood family — our father, mother, brothers, and sisters — the youngest generation of our ancestors. Some of them are almost perfect and others are not, but they are all our ancestors. There are aspects within us that are close to perfection and others that are far from it. Who are we to not accept our ancestors? We have to look deeply. We may have intentionally not recognized one of our ancestors because he or she caused us a lot of suffering. He or she was not perfect. That is why we feel uprooted from our ground of being. We are excluded from the stream of life and have become wanderers, hungry ghosts looking for something to believe in and trust. We need to be mindful and realize that all our ancestors — the near-perfect and the very imperfect — are present in us.

Then we look at our children or, in my case, my students. We have children whom we like very much, who are close to being perfect, and others who may have caused us much suffering. But no matter what, they are all our children. Who are we to not accept them as they are? If we practice in this way, we will be able to accept all our ancestors and children.

We bring all of our intelligence, insight, and heart to bend down and touch the earth. Allow all of your sorrow, suffering, and despair to pour down onto the earth. The earth is there to receive everything. When you touch the earth you become one with it, so that your heart opens. We receive, include, and embrace everything so that we can transform it. We might cry the first time that we bend down and touch the earth. We may not have been able to cry before. We may have been lonely, unable to touch and embrace our ancestors and children. We may have been running away. Now it is time to go home, to recognize and accept them. When we touch the earth, we surrender our body and consciousness to it. There is no more resistance; we become one with the stream of life. Then healing can take place. I know some practitioners who suffer much less after just one hour of practice. A lot of sorrow, loneliness, and bitterness are sent into the earth, and transformation occurs.

You stay touching the earth as long as you need to — until every bit of sorrow, bitterness, and despair in you is poured into the earth. Then your ancestors and children within you will smile, because you are capable of connecting, forgiving, and understanding. We are humans. We make mistakes and are, at times, unskillful. We make each other suffer. When we know how to breathe deeply, concentrate, and touch reality, understanding is born. This understanding liberates us. It brings tears of happiness and forgiveness to our eyes. We also feel better physically. Our suffering may have created an illness that we thought was incurable. But if we allow our body to touch the earth and connect with our ancestors, and allow our spirit and consciousness to be open and welcoming, the illness may disappear.

[BELL]

The Second Prostration

The Second Prostration represents the dimension of space. We breathe in and out mindfully and look deeply into ourselves. We realize the nature of interbeing with all living beings around us. We become one with the living bodhisattvas around us. Their presence in the world is so refreshing and encouraging. When we watch them sitting, walking, and smiling, we see solidity, freshness, love, and understanding. We don't need to go to heaven to see bodhisattvas; they are here among us. They may exist in the form of a doctor, a social worker in South Africa, or an unknown Mother Teresa working in the Third World. They are not abstract ideals. It is a great support to know that they are here among us. We breathe in and out, knowing that they are here, and that we can receive their energy. If we ever get discouraged, we can practice mindful breathing and touch the presence of the bodhisattvas. They beautify our world, emanating loving kindness, mindfulness, solidity, and joy. We should vow to be one of them. It is a pity if we are not open to their energy. If we are embedded in sorrow or despair, we do not receive it. That is why we perform the Second Prostration. The Second Prostration is represented by a horizontal line, the here and the now. When we touch the earth in this position, we touch all living beings who are with us in this moment.

During the Second Prostration, we breathe mindfully, feeling the presence of the bodhisattvas, and becoming one with them. We inter-are with them. The tree in the backyard is also a bodhisattva. She stands strong for the whole winter. Her capacity for enduring the coldness and harshness of life is huge. She sheds all her leaves to be strong enough to survive the winter. When spring comes, she manifests all her beauty. When you look at such a tree, you see a real bodhisattva. Her presence supports you. How many bodhisattvas can you identify around you — human and non-human? Why are you pessimistic or overwhelmed by despair? We get tremendous energy from bodhisattvas if we allow them to enter us and be with us. With this power, we can touch other beings who are oppressed, who suffer from poverty and sickness, who are in some kind of hell, and who are unable to speak out about the injustices they have suffered.

There is a lot of suffering in the human, animal, and vegetable worlds. Who is suffering? We are, because we inter-are with everyone. We are the person who manufactures weapons to sell to underdeveloped countries. We are the child in Rwanda who is only skin and bones. We are the little girl who is raped on the ocean by a sea pirate. If we do not receive the power and strength of the bodhisattvas, how can we bear this? How can we rescue these beings who are suffering deeply in the present moment? We identify ourselves with the great beings in the world and also with those who suffer terribly. We bend down, touch the earth, and stay there until we feel we have become one with it. Only when we become one with the earth and experience its power of embracing and healing can we do the work of transformation. We will discuss the Third Prostration tomorrow.

[BELL]

CHAPTER THIRTEEN

Throwing Away Our Wrong Perceptions

Dear Sangha, today is the ninth of June, 1998. It is the third week of our twenty-one-day retreat. We have been studying the thirteenth exercise, "Experiencing impermanence, I breathe in and out," and the fifteenth, "Experiencing nirvana, I breathe in and out." Today we will study the sixteenth, "Experiencing letting go, I breathe in and I breathe out." We will study the fourteenth exercise tomorrow.

Touching Our Ancestors

The practice of letting go of our wrong perceptions is very important. We have learned that the Three Dharma Seals and the Three Prostrations are concrete ways of practicing the thirteenth, fifteenth, and sixteenth exercises proposed by the Buddha. In the First Prostration, we surrender our so-called separate self and embrace the stream of life. We touch our ancestors, our children, and future generations, becoming one with all of them. In the Second Prostration, we connect with every living being in the present moment. First, we connect with the great beings, benefiting from their solidity, freedom, joy, and compassion, and gathering enough strength to embrace the suffering of the world and our own suffering, which reflect each other.

When you practice the First Prostration, remember the emptiness of the transmission of your body. Observing your body deeply, you touch your ancestors. They have transmitted themselves to you. You are their continuation and are one with them. As I have mentioned before, the receiver of the transmission is one with the object of transmission and the transmitters. Emptiness of transmission means the three elements of transmission — transmitter, transmitted, and receiver — are empty of a separate self; they are all one. When monks and nuns ask for food, they practice the emptiness of giving. The one who gives, the object being given, and the one who receives are one. There is perfect equanimity in this practice, and it is the best way of giving and receiving. You have to practice the same thing with love, so that the lover becomes one with the beloved.

When a father loves his son or daughter, he should not say, "I have given you everything, yet you don't respond. You behave badly." That is not equanimity. When you give in the spirit of equanimity, you give something of the greatest value. When you love in the spirit of equanimity — upeksha — that is the greatest love. You do not expect love in return. That would not be true love. We don't know much about how to love and have a lot to learn. That is why love can make us suffer.

When you practice the Three Prostrations, please remember the five-year-old child, the wounded little girl or boy, within you. He or she may also be your mother or father's wounded inner child who was never healed, but was transmitted to you so you could take care of him or her. Now that you have touched the Dharma, you know how to take care of your wounded child within. You do it not only for yourself, but for all of your ancestors. As I have mentioned before, many of our ancestors didn't know how to take care of their wounded child and that is why they have transmitted him or her to us. We can talk to our child within, smile at her, and embrace her every day.

If you are judgmental towards yourself and others, practice

looking deeply and touching your ancestors. This seed of judgment is not yours alone. It comes from many generations of your ancestors. If you are unskillful and create suffering, it is not just you who are responsible. Your ancestors are also responsible. Unskillfulness is an object of transmission. When you can see the collective responsibility for an unskillful act, you will not be so hard on yourself. You can say, "I know I have done this together with my ancestors. Now that I have touched the Dharma and know how to embrace and heal, I will do my best to transform this habitual energy and emancipate us all." We promise that we will do better in the future. Using mindful breathing, walking, smiling, and embracing, we transform our habitual energy for ourselves and our ancestors.

We transform mistakes through our mind, spirit, and consciousness. Everything comes from the mind. The mind is the painter that paints everything in the world. This is the teaching of the Buddha in the *Avatamsaka Sutra.* During the First Prostration, use the insight of emptiness of transmission. If you have an illness, touch one of your ancestors who had a healthy body and lived a long life and ask for his or her help: "Please help me. I know that your cells are healthy." Breathe in and out and allow your cells to become strong and take care of the weaker cells. Lie down on the earth for a long time, and allow your strong cells to heal the weaker ones.

If you feel that you have become one with your stream of ancestors and future generations, then your practice is successful. Your loneliness and feelings of being cut off will soon disappear. They will be absorbed by the earth, because you have become one with the earth. Who among us is not a child of the earth? We are one with her and possess her strength. When we touch the earth in the Second Prostration, we look into the nature of interbeing and see that we are one with the tree in the backyard, the cloud floating in the sky, the sunshine penetrating the apple, with our ancestors, and the great bodhisattvas who are present in this moment. It is important to touch the healthy and solid elements in and around you. Too many of us allow ourselves to be overwhelmed by despair. Despair can lead to suicide. We have to touch our seeds of hope, strength, and love. Then we will be strong. Let us touch the bodhisattvas around us and not allow ourselves to be touched only by negative elements. As I have said before, there may be a few trees in the garden that are dying, but that is not the whole picture. There are still many healthy, vigorous, beautiful trees, and we have to touch them every day. Many people are caught up in drugs, sex, and violence. They are drowning in the ocean of suffering. But there are others who are still healthy, loving, solid, and ready to help. Every time we take a peaceful, solid step, or draw a mindful breath, we are changing things for the better.

[BELL]

Awakening

Thirty years ago, the Fellowship of Reconciliation organized a meeting with a small group of scientists on a mountain in the south of France. Sister Chân Không, who is a biologist, was one of them. They practiced walking and sitting meditation and discussed the environment. At that time, no one was talking about ecosystems. Trying to create awareness about our dangerous situation, they sent a statement about the environment to thousands of scientists all over the world. After a few months, they had collected over four thousand signatures from them and submitted these to the Secretary General of the United Nations. The United Nations and the Fellowship of Reconciliation set up an organization called Dai Dung, which means "Great Togetherness," and began working on raising awareness about the environment. Two years later, the United Nations organized the first international conference on the environment in Stockholm.

Thirty years ago, we could not imagine that there would one

day be nonsmoking flights. I suffered when I sat amongst the smokers. Yet awakening was possible: So many of us demanded nonsmoking flights that they now exist. Awakening is possible if we are determined to practice. We practice to awaken ourselves and others. This is the only way to address a difficult situation. Now, we are much more aware of the foods we eat. Cigarette packages contain health warnings. This is the fruit of awakening. We should wake up as individuals and as nations. Now we can go on to make laws protecting us from other harmful things, like weapons, and films full of sex and violence.

The Sanskrit word for awakening is *bodhi.* The Buddha is the one who is awake. Every one of us has the seed of awakening, insight, compassion, and loving kindness. In the Second Prostration, we get in touch with these positive elements. Once in touch with these, we inspire confidence in the people around us. We have to help each other practice as a Sangha. When we see a group of people living mindfully, we have confidence in the future. We cannot let the younger generation lose hope. That would be the end. We have to live our daily lives in a way that makes the future possible.

[BELL]

As I have mentioned previously, some of our children spend many hours a day watching television and touching violence, fear, craving, anger, and despair. The job of educators is to create a situation that helps them touch the healthy, healing elements inside and around them. Many of us here are teachers. We should use our intelligence and creativity to do this work. This is also a way of practicing the Second Prostration. We have to ask our representative in Congress to practice with us and make the kinds of laws that we need for our protection and the protection of our children. Now is not the time for us to meditate as sole practitioners; we have to practice meditation as groups, cities, and nations. Our collective insight comes from individual insight, and vice versa. We practice on both levels so that we will know what to do and what not to do on the individual, familial, and national levels. Mindfulness is our instrument. Without mindfulness, negative things will continue to take place everywhere. Awareness helps us know which actions to stop and which to continue. Practicing the First and Second Prostrations, we represent our whole society and are no longer separate entities. Now it is easy for us to practice the Third Prostration.

The Third Prostration

The Third Prostration helps us touch nirvana. If you have practiced the First and Second Prostrations well, you have already touched nirvana. If you haven't succeeded in the First and Second, you will not be able to do the Third. When you surrender your separate self and become one with the stream of being, you touch nirvana. This is connected to the sixteenth exercise on contemplating letting go. To let go means to throw away one's wrong perceptions, to not cling to them anymore. The Vietnamese meditation teacher of the first half of the third century, Master Tang Hoi, taught that first, we throw away our wrong perception that we are only our body. We have had the opportunity to look deeply and see that we are much more than our body. We know that we are also the cloud floating in the sky.

Do you remember the discourse for the dying that Venerable Shariputra practiced with Anathapindika? "Dear Anathapindika, let us practice together. Breathing in, I know this body is not me. Breathing out, I know that I am more than this physical body. I am not caught in thinking of this body as myself. I am life without boundaries. I have never been born and I will never die." When you practice like this, you touch nirvana. You see your nature of no-birth and no-death. The body is like everything else. When certain conditions are present, it manifests as an object of perception and we believe it exists. If one condition is lacking and does not manifest, we think it is nonexistent. The true nature of reality is free from both notions: existence and nonexistence, being and nonbeing. When we examine reality and touch the nature of impermanence, interbeing, and nonself, we are emancipated. When you look at the cloud and the tree, look in a way that helps you see that you cannot be cut off from them. You are one with them. This is what the Buddha meant when he said, "This is because that is." Look at everything and realize this truth.

I am standing on U.S. soil, Vermont soil, and North American soil. Without moving, I see that I am standing on the whole continent of America — North, Central, and South America are linked. From where I stand, I perceive that I am standing on the whole planet. It is my perception that has changed. If you are caught up in the idea of nationalism or chauvinism, you are touching only one part of reality. The Israelis and Palestinians each think that the same piece of land belongs to them. The land belongs to everyone. This insight will bring about more peace, reconciliation, understanding, and love. We cannot touch nirvana if we practice exclusion. It is only through inclusiveness that we can touch nirvana. Looking deeply, we see that everything inter-is with everything else. You cannot take the Palestinians out of the Israelis, and vice versa. The insight of interbeing is crucial for our well-being. True peace is not possible without this insight.

Nirvana is the ground of our being, the ground of togetherness. In Christianity, there is the trinity: God the Father, God the Son, and God the Holy Spirit. These three are actually one. That is the emptiness of the trinity. One cannot exist without the other two. Jesus is both the son of God and the son of man. We can look deeply into the nature of emptiness of everything. We cannot have true peace, true understanding, or true love if we are not touched by the nature of interbeing, the nature of nirvana. What is nirvana? It is the nature of interbeing, impermanence, and nonself. It is defined as the extinction of all notions, including notions of self. When we use the word "self," it is with the insight that the self is made only of nonself elements, just as development is made of nondevelopment, and the Third World is made of the First World. We inter-are. Nothing exists by itself alone. The first step in the training is to throw away the idea that our body is our self.

Lokadhatu and Dharmadhatu

As I have said before, happiness is not an individual matter. If our beloved isn't happy, we cannot be happy either. Everything is made of the collective and the individual. The words *lokadhatu* and *dharmadhatu* describe reality. Lokadhatu describes a realm of separations and limitations, of differences; and dharmadhatu, a realm of the ultimate reality, of suchness and unity, of interbeing. If we are caught in discrimination, lokadhatu reveals itself to us. In the lokadhatu, everything exists outside of everything else; the cloud exists outside of the flower, you exist outside of me. This is the world we live in when we are ignorant. We cut reality into small pieces and identify ourselves with only one piece. There is a lot of darkness in the lokadhatu.

We suffer because we discriminate and are caught up in our perception of opposites: being and nonbeing, birth and death, self and nonself, Black and White, Muslim and Hindu, and so on. The nuclear scientist David Bohm has come up with two terms very similar to lokadhatu and dharmadhatu, through which he tries to illustrate the nature of interbeing of electrons. He says that there are two orders of being — the explicate order, where each electron seems to exist outside of the other electrons, and the implicate order, where each electron contains all the other electrons. Recently, a group of scientists discovered that the subatomic particle, the neutrino, has mass. For a long time it was thought that the neutrino had no electric charge or mass. But experiments showed that the neutrino can change and release energy and therefore has mass. The scientists are very excited about this discovery. I think this insight could have come sooner. If you know that the one contains the all, then how could the neutrino not contain mass and other elements? In the Buddhist concept of mahabhuta, each of the great elements of fire, water, air, earth, space, and consciousness contains all the others.

When we have the insight of interbeing, of nonself, then the world of the dharmadhatu, full of light, love, and wisdom, manifests itself to us. It is the equivalent of the Kingdom of God. The dharmadhatu is a world in which everything contains everything else. The flower contains the sunshine; the sunshine contains the flower; the father contains the son; the son contains the father. This insight is very clear, and that is why there is a lot of light in the dharmadhatu.

When we practice walking in the dharmadhatu, every step brings us a lot of joy. We have released the idea that our body is our self and that another body can be our enemy. We can walk in the dharmadhatu right now if we have the insight of interbeing. When we touch the nature of interbeing in each person, we release our suffering and stop feeling lonely. We only need to look deeply to see this. It would be a shame to lock ourselves away in the lokadhatu, where everything is separate from everything else, and never live in the dharmadhatu.

[BELL]

Upeksha

Look at my hands. My right hand, which has written hundreds of poems, can also write calligraphy and ring the bell. Yet it is not proud of itself. It never tells my left hand, "You are good for nothing. You don't write poems or practice calligraphy." Why? Because my right hand has the wisdom of equanimity, upeksha. It knows that it is also my left hand, and it acts according to that wisdom. One day, as I held a nail in place with my left hand, my right hand, holding the hammer, missed the nail and pounded my finger instead. The moment my right hand made the mistake and caused me pain, it put down the hammer and started taking care of my left hand. It did not say, "I'm sorry." This way of behaving is perfect. My right hand considered itself one with my left hand and made no distinction such as, "I am the right hand. I am taking care of you, the left hand. You should remember that." My right hand practiced the emptiness of loving perfectly. Our body and consciousness have this wisdom of nondiscrimination — in Sanskrit *nirvikalpajñana.*

We can develop this wisdom and use its guidance in our daily life. We need to look at each other in the same way as the right and left hands. We should look upon our fellow brothers and sisters, our partners, parents, and children in this way. Hindus and Muslims, Whites and Blacks, Israelis and Palestinians should treat each other like this. Only the wisdom of nondiscrimination can bring about true peace and true love and remove fear. Our right and left hands are not afraid of each other. With the wisdom of nondiscrimination, they know that they belong to and contain each other. Everything that happens to the right hand happens to the left. Mindfulness, looking deeply, is the only way to touch the nature of interbeing, which allows the wisdom of nondiscrimination to manifest. If we act according to the spirit of nondiscrimination, we create happiness and well-being.

When I first tasted a peanut butter cookie at the Tassajara Zen Center fifteen years ago, I liked it so much that I learned how to make them. I found that when the cookies were in the oven, they began to discriminate against each other and push each other around, as if to say, "Let me be in the center. You don't deserve that place." They didn't know that they were one. This is how we deal with each other, because we don't know how to touch our ground of being. We have lost the wisdom of nondiscrimination.

As I have mentioned, there are four elements of true love. The first element of true love is maitri, the capacity of offering joy and happiness. Karuna is the capacity of removing and transforming pain and sorrow. Mudita is joy. True love should give us joy. If we cry all day and night, we know it is not true love. The fourth element is upeksha, equanimity, the wisdom of nondiscrimination. When you truly love someone, you don't discriminate between yourself and your beloved; you become one with your beloved. Only with the wisdom of equanimity can you perfect your love and cleanse it of suffering and discrimination. If you don't see equanimity when you look into the nature of your love, you need to practice. Love that is based on notions of self and other, inside and outside, is not deep enough.

No-Birth, No-Death, and Throwing Away the Notion of Self

Psychotherapists can learn a lot from this teaching. The aim of psychotherapy is to regain a healthy self. Even if you have a so-called healthy self, you will continue to suffer if you are trapped in the idea of a self. True relief comes when you are free from the notion of self. If your notion of self is strong and you are in a relationship, you know what will happen: There will be a clash between self and self. When we give ourselves up and become one with our beloved, we are practicing nonself. Our degree of happiness, understanding, and love increases a thousandfold. We look deeply to realize the nature of interbeing and to know that the self is made only of nonself elements. This insight greatly enhances the quality of our healing.

Master Tang Hoi taught that we have to release a second notion: the notion of life span. We believe that we begin to exist and cease to exist at certain moments in time. We have to throw away the concept that our life lasts for seventy or eighty years, or that, according to the doctor, we only have two more years to live, and after that we will be nothing, no one. We have to throw away the notion that from nothing or no one, we have become something or someone, and that at some point we will again revert to being nothing and no one. These ideas do not correspond with reality.

We have practiced looking into the nature of a sheet of paper. We have seen that the sheet of paper does not come from nothing. Before being paper, it was many other things: a tree, sunshine, a cloud. We burned the paper, thinking we could reduce it to nothing, but we did not succeed. The sheet of paper transformed itself into several things at once: smoke rising, heat penetrating the cosmos, and ash that might become a tiny flower in the grass tomorrow. Our ideas of being and nonbeing, birth and death, are just ideas, which we have to throw away. They cannot be applied to reality. Master Tang Hoi said that we have never been born and we will never die. There is only manifestation and continuation.

We know that heat and water form clouds; clouds do not come from nothing. If we look deeply at a cloud floating happily in the sky, we can see its previous life. When cold air touches the cloud, the cloud continues in the form of rain. This is not the death of the cloud but a transformation and continuation. The new form the cloud takes on is no less beautiful than its previous form. The cloud does not panic, rather, it sings aloud while transforming itself into rain. It is wonderful to be a cloud floating in the sky, but it is also wonderful to be rain falling on the ground and becoming part of a river or a rice field. Nothing is created; nothing is destroyed. There is no birth or death. This is what we recite in the *Heart Sutra.* The ideas of creation and annihilation are discarded. It is not only Avalokiteshvara who uses this language, scientists also use it. The French scientist Lavoisier said of matter and energy: "Nothing is born, nothing dies." He uses the same language as the *Heart Sutra.* There is only transformation. Sometimes we call this reincarnation or rebirth, but transformation is a better word.

We are free from birth and death. Our true nature is no-birth and no-death. We realize the ground of our being by looking deeply and touching reality deeply. This is the only way to dissipate our fears. If we have this deep insight, we will be liberated from our anguish and fear of being and nonbeing. The Buddha said that all fears and cravings are born from ignorance. Through knowledge and insight, we gain emancipation. We cannot have insight if we don't practice looking deeply. Looking deeply is the practice of meditation; we stop and gaze into the nature of reality. It is a shame if we are too busy in our daily lives to live mindfully and with concentration, to touch reality deeply.

Master Tang Hoi said, "Throw it away." Throw away the idea that you are only this body. Throw away the idea that your life span is only fifty years. Be a cloud. Be the rain. Be the sunshine and touch your own immortality, your nature of no-birth and no-death. Use your intelligence, your daily life, the Sangha, and your practice of looking deeply. I know people who contemplate their passing away in a joyful, wise, and calm way.

When I was a young monk in Vietnam, I discovered something very interesting while meditating on a banana leaf. Visualize, if you will, a young banana tree with three leaves. I looked deeply into the first leaf and saw myself. The second leaf was still unfurling and not yet fully open. The third leaf was the younger sister of the other two leaves. The oldest leaf was exposed to the sun and rain and enjoyed her life as a leaf. While she unfolded, she was doing something meaningful — helping her younger sister to grow. She saw that she and her younger sister were one. They belonged to the same reality of the banana tree. The other sister did the same thing. She unfolded, enjoying the sunshine and the rain. She sang every time the wind blew. She also helped her younger sister to grow. With the wisdom of nondiscrimination, the first and second leaves saw themselves in the third leaf. When the time came for the first leaf to wither and dry up, she did not cry, because she now lived on in the third leaf. She went back to the soil and served as nourishment for the banana tree and the other leaves.

Our lives have meaning. We are here to do something. While I enjoy my life as a leaf, I nourish my sister and transmit joy, hope, and the best of myself to her. She helps me to nourish our brother, the third leaf. Thanks to the wisdom of nondiscrimination, we do not fight. We are not caught in the notion of a self; that is why we are in harmony with each other. When I teach my sister how to practice, I don't call myself "teacher," and her "student." I can transmit something to her because I am capable of practicing equanimity, the emptiness of transmission. There is no transmitter and no receiver. The transmission takes place in a natural way because it is done in the spirit of equanimity, upeksha, or the wisdom of nondiscrimination.

As I have mentioned before, we are aware that every cell in our body contains all the information we need to understand the cosmos. Every cell contains information about all of our ancestors — both human and non-human — and future generations. The one contains the all. We throw away our notions of one and many. This is the practice of the sixteenth exercise of mindful breathing proposed by the Buddha. Throw away your ideas, notions, and perceptions so that reality has a chance to manifest itself. As we already know, nirvana is defined as the extinction of all notions. A lot of our suffering is born from our wrong perceptions. We feel anger and despair because we are ignorant. We don't understand ourselves or other people. We discriminate. One meaning of meditation is to sit down on the bank of the river of perceptions and observe them. If you know the nature of your perceptions, you will be free from them. You can throw them away so that reality will reveal itself fully to you.

We will continue with the fourteenth exercise, experiencing non-craving within. This is an important practice. When we know the true nature of the object of our craving, we will stop craving it, and freedom and happiness will be ours.

[BELL]

CHAPTER FOURTEEN

Questions and Answers Session Three

Dear Sangha, today is the tenth of June, 1998. We are having questions and answers.

Question: Dear Thây, if you have been suffering with cancer for a long time and the pain is great, is it OK to end your life — assuming that you have discussed this with your family and Sangha? What kind of fruit will be born of that action?

Thây: This is a very difficult question. During the time of the Buddha, there were monks who suffered from diseases. The Buddha gave many discourses on how to practice during the last days of our lives. We can study these discourses to learn how to help people who are suffering or dying. We can also learn to apply these discourses to ourselves if we experience a death-threatening illness. As I have mentioned before, the Buddha helps us to practice feeling less pain in our bodies. There are ways to lessen our physical pain. We recognize the existence of our physical pain but we do not exaggerate it through fear or despair. The Buddha said that when we are struck by an arrow, we suffer. But if another arrow strikes us in exactly the same spot, the pain will not only be double, it will be ten, twenty, or thirty times more intense. This is like when a person magnifies his or her physical pain through fear, anger, or imagination. That is why it is helpful to practice breathing in and out and recognize physical pain for what it is, and not to exaggerate it.

If you have a doctor or a friend who knows about pain, you can ask him or her to tell you that this is only a physical pain. She can tell you exactly what it is, so you will not exaggerate it with strong emotions like fear, anger, or despair. There are also other ways of practicing with pain. You can restore your inner balance so the pain will be bearable. When you water your positive seeds, you will suffer less and feel that you can continue. When you suffer a lot, you feel like you don't have enough strength to be on your own. When a friend comes and holds your hand, you feel as if you can bear your pain and continue. There is strength and happiness within you. It is the same when you touch these elements, they will manifest and help restore your balance. And you will be able to bear your physical pain more easily.

I remember when one of Sister Chân Không's sisters was dying in a hospital in North America. She had had a liver transplant that began to disintegrate after three or four years. When she was about to die, she suffered so much. She was in a coma, and her husband and children, and even the doctors did not know how to help her suffer less. She twisted, moaned, and cried all the time. Then Sister Chân Không arrived. She knew that she could not talk to her sister, whose coma was impenetrable. So she played her a tape of the monks and nuns from Plum Village chanting "Avalokiteshvara" in Vietnamese. She put earphones on her sister and turned up the volume quite high. Then, after only half a minute, a miracle happened. Her sister became very quiet, and from that moment until she passed away, she no longer cried or twisted.

You can see that her sister had the seed of the practice. She had heard the chanting before and knew it belonged to her spiritual tradition. It became the source of her peace and well-being during the last months and weeks of her life, when the people around her did not know how to help her get in touch with her seeds of well-being. Those seeds had become weakened, and she had become overwhelmed by pain and despair. The chanting that penetrated her was able to touch the source of spiritual energy in her. Suddenly she was able to get in touch with that source. That source of energy gave her enough strength to reestablish the balance she needed. That is why she was able to lie quietly until she passed away.

We have to realize that while we are suffering physical pain, there are many elements in us of solidity, well-being, and trust. For our balance to be restored, we need to touch those seeds. If we are practicing the teachings of the Buddha, we know what to do in the moment for people who are dying or suffering. We know what to do for those who have lost their balance. We have listened to the *Discourse to Be Given to the Dying Person* in the chanting book. That discourse provides us with many practices with which to help dying people and also ourselves in difficult moments.

When the Buddha or his senior disciples visited a dying person, they always knew what to do to help restore the person's balance so that he or she would suffer less. The practice is to water the seeds of happiness and well-being in the person, and it always helps. I myself have practiced that several times, and it has been effective each time. When you ask whether it is all right to end our lives if our lives have become unbearable, I say we should first try to get help.

One day, after helping a dying man, the Buddha went back to the mountains. Later he learned that the man he had tried to help had used a knife to take his life the very next day. In fact, the man had suffered less when he was with the Buddha and practicing according to the Buddha's suggestions. Of course, in the presence of someone like the Buddha, he felt greatly supported and was able to establish some balance. But after the Buddha left, he could not maintain it by himself, so he took his life. When the

Buddha heard about the suicide, he did not blame or condemn the man. He sent his disciples to take care of the situation. That is all I can tell you at this moment: The Buddha's actions were full of compassion both before and after the death of that man.

Question: Dear Thây, during this retreat you have given great teachings on forgiveness. They have been very helpful to me and I thank you for them. I find that many times the most difficult person for me to forgive is myself. Do you have additional suggestions that would be especially helpful for self-forgiveness?

Thây: I think most of us — probably all of us — have done something unmindful during our lifetime that has damaged or created suffering for our loved ones and others. We may hate ourselves, or not be able to forgive ourselves. But we don't know or don't remember that we have also done a lot of damage to ourselves. In fact, we have damaged ourselves most of all. Please reflect, look deeply, and you will see that the person who has made you suffer the most is yourself, and no one else. This is something we do not see very clearly. We have made mistakes out of ignorance, anger, hatred, discrimination, and unskillfulness. We know that our habitual energy is responsible for that. Sometimes we are intuitive enough to know that our words or actions can cause suffering. But our habitual energy is stronger than we are, and we do or say things that we later regret. We promise ourselves that next time we won't do or say those things again, yet we do. We think it is stronger than we are.

The Buddha advised us to recognize the presence of our habitual energy so that we can control it better and minimize its strength. As I have mentioned before, if we are mindful and know how to cultivate mindfulness, we can recognize our habitual energy: "Hello, my old habitual energy. I know you are there. This time you cannot run away with me." That is mindfulness, that is the Buddha, that is the Holy Spirit. We are protected. Each time we practice that recognition, our habitual energy loses some of its strength. If we continue like this, one day it won't be able to push us anymore toward doing or saying harmful things. Maybe our habitual energy has been transmitted to us by many generations of ancestors. That is why we should not feel guilty about it; we are a victim of transmission. If we have not learned how to recognize and transform that habitual energy, we will continue to be its victim, and we will transmit it to our children and their children for many generations to come. We are not the only ones responsible for that habitual energy; it is a collective thing. If we can recognize our habitual energy as having been transmitted to us by our parents and our ancestors, we won't feel guilty about it anymore.

When you encounter the Dharma and learn how to practice mindfulness, you know you have an instrument with which to transform that habitual energy — transforming it not only for your own sake, but for the sake of your ancestors and children. This alone can remove feelings of guilt and self-hatred because you come to know your nature as the nature of interbeing, the nature of happiness. With the energy of happiness and joy, you will have enough strength to do the work of transformation. You know that your energy of self-hatred was transmitted to you by your mother or father, your grandfather or grandmother. When you recognize this energy as also belonging to them, you say, "Hello, Grandma, I know you are there," and you help both yourself and your grandmother. You are doing the work of transformation for all of them.

Question: Dear Thây, I can touch the earth for all my ancestors and reenter the stream of life. When I want to do the same for my mother-in-law, it doesn't work for very long. Do you have any suggestions? [laughter]

Thây: Yes, I do. I think that feeling comes from the fact that you look at your mother-in-law not as a brother or a sister. It is more difficult for you to embrace her as you do the people in your own lineage. But she is the mother of your partner, and that is very important. Your partner is a part of her and her lineage. You have made a commitment to share all your partner's happiness and suffering, and your mother-in-law is a part of that. Your mother-in-law can be both a source of happiness and sorrow for you and your partner. That is why your practice has to embrace her — your partner's happiness depends very much on your in-laws' happiness. If your partner is not happy, it will be difficult for you to be happy. Taking care of your in-laws is taking care of yourself and your partner.

When a Buddhist has a friend who is not Buddhist — a Christian, for instance — he needs to learn about Jesus Christ and learn how to pay respect to his friend's teacher. Because our friendship is so precious and crucial to our happiness, we want to treasure it. Everything that belongs to our friends belongs to us. This is very natural.

As partners, your love and commitment is very important. You have to learn to take care of whatever belongs to your partner because you care about his or her well-being and happiness. That is why you have to look far and wide and recognize everything and everyone that is linked to her, so that you can really make her happy — your happiness depends on her happiness.

First of all, we must be polite. When you go to your in-laws' house, you greet them politely, because they are your wife's parents. Whether or not your mother-in-law is lovely, your behavior and your capacity to respect, embrace, and help her is related to your own and your partner's happiness. That is why, looking more deeply, the boundaries will be removed and you will be able to accept her as an important ancestor of your partner. Good luck! [laughter]

[BELL]

Question: My question has to do with the First Mindfulness Training and, specifically, with the reference to killing — the killing of animals for human benefit in research laboratories. I have felt compassion for animals and have been a vegetarian since age eighteen. I don't buy leather products and do whatever I can in my daily life to show compassion for animals. But I became a research scientist in the hope of helping human beings with diseases like leprosy and tuberculosis. Because these are diseases that don't make money for pharmaceutical companies, I find myself, as a government scientist, in the position of heading the largest program to find new drugs for tuberculosis, a disease that kills three million people every year. At some point in the search for new drugs, we have to give these drugs to animals to determine if they are safe enough to give to human beings. I think this is different from what Sister Val shared with us in the first week about the unnecessary suffering animals are put through in cosmetic and shampoo testing. These drugs for tuberculosis will be given to people. I would take the drug first, but I am just one person, and that would not give me enough information. We have tested certain drugs to the point where they might be considered safe for human beings, but in order to get high-quality data and feel confident that we can safely give people the drug, I now have to design experiments to give them to animals. For me, this feels like a conflict between compassion for animals and compassion for humans. I would like to ask for a different perspective, another way of viewing this while remembering that we don't want to kill any species.

Thây: The first thing I would advise is that you continue what you are doing but do it mindfully. I trust that some insight will come to you later, and this insight will help you to improve your work in such a way that the animals will benefit, too. Fifteen years ago, a visitor came to Plum Village. He told me that he was responsible for designing atomic bombs and that he did not have a tranquil, clear conscience about doing such a disruptive and disturbing thing. He also told me that if he quit his job, it would not help, because someone else would take over and continue doing the same thing. After a long pause, I told him to continue — but mindfully. It's better to do things mindfully because then you will have the chance to gain some insight that will lead you to finding a better way. If you just do something mechanically, you will continue in that vein for a long time.

Killing animals is the same. Man is in a stronger position. If animals could organize a protest, they certainly would organize one around laboratory testing. But because we are in a stronger position, we are using them to discover ways to better the human condition. My advice is that you continue, but be aware of all this. You are using animals for research for the benefit of human beings. You represent all of us and are doing it in our name. We are all responsible with you in this act. We also suffer with you in this act. And we are anxious to find a way to reduce the suffering of animals, vegetables, and minerals.

One more thing you can do is to help us know what is going on, because many of us are very ignorant. We don't pay enough attention. We do not know how much animals suffer. You are on the spot; you are the flame at the tip of the candle. You suffer for all of us. You should wake us up and tell us what you are doing. We will help you live more deeply and mindfully, and we will participate in your deep looking so that you might gain some insight sooner, so we can significantly reduce the suffering of animals.

This answer comes from my suffering and from insight. There is no "yes or no" answer, but what I can say is, please do it in mindfulness and please share with us the reality of the suffering of animals so that we can feel co-responsible with you. We may be able to help you gain that much-needed insight. The seed of compassion may be getting smaller and smaller as we are caught up in our daily problems. We cannot have a happy life without compassion. So notice your compassion and do not become a machine. Remain a human being, and keep your compassion alive. Be mindful and help us to be mindful, too. You are doing it for all of us, and we are co-responsible for everything you are doing.

[BELL]

Question: Dear Thây, with all due respect to your privacy, what is it like for you when so many people stare at you, film or photograph you, flash bulbs in your face? Some people idolize you. What is it like? Does your mind get fettered? Do you ever feel anger, aversion, loneliness in response to this? How do you work with fame in your practice? How do you stay steady and calm? Do you ever get the opportunity to practice hugging meditation with the people you are closest to?

Thây: Yes! [much laughter] If you took ordination, you might find the attention difficult at first. But my country is a Buddhist country, and people are used to seeing monks and nuns in their brown robes. When they see the brown robe, they think of Buddhism and the Buddha and they always want to pay respect. They want to touch the earth in front of a monk or a nun. If you have just been ordained, it can be difficult for you. You can't say, "Don't do that to me. I'm a very new monk." You have no right to do so. You have to sit very still and follow your in-breath and out-breath. You have to visualize the person in front of you paying his or her respects to the Buddha, the Dharma, and the Sangha through you as a symbol. You have to learn to do this right away, on the day of your ordination. In fact, right after their ordination, I tell my student monks and nuns about this practice. We already know that people need to feel peaceful and happy while touching the Three Jewels. They are not paying respect to your ego; they are paying respect to the Buddha, the Dharma, and the Sangha. If you think they are paying respect to your ego, you are wrong. You can ruin your life as a monk or a nun with that kind of illusion. The moment you become a monk or a nun, you have to learn how to sit quietly, calmly, and at your best, allowing people to touch the Three Jewels through you. It's like saluting the American flag; you don't salute the cloth itself but the country, the people, and the history, right? So the brown robe is only a symbol. If you get caught up in it, you lose yourself.

I practice in a way so that fame cannot touch me. It's only when you are not mindful that you can lose yourself. If you are mindful, you can preserve yourself, and fame and fortune will not be able to touch you. Not every monk and nun can do it. Many of them get caught up and fall prey to celebrity, wealth, and so on. They become victims and are destroyed. In my case, I have not been affected by these kinds of things. My happiness is made of other elements — among them, freedom. As soon as something becomes a cow, I release it right away, very quickly. I consider that a victory. Suppose I am building a practice center. If, in the process of building it, I feel that it is depriving me of my joy, freedom, and well-being, then I will let it go. I don't need the practice center. You cannot say that I did not succeed in building the practice center, because I consider letting go a victory, in that I preserved my freedom, the most precious thing a monk has.

It is the same with fame. You can lose your freedom and happiness by getting caught up in fame. When you look into a person — whether he or she is ordained or a layperson — it is not difficult to see whether he or she is still free. You can tell very quickly. You cannot be a happy person without internal and external freedom — no matter if you are a millionaire, the head of a huge company, or hold a high position in the government. It is our freedom and compassion that make us happy, not other things. This is something you are going to learn with the fourteenth exercise for mindful breathing: "Contemplating non-craving, I breathe in. Contemplating non-craving, I breathe out."

I enjoy the steps I take. I enjoy my in-breath and out-breath. I enjoy a cup of tea with my students. I enjoy contemplating the sky and the mountains. I do so because I have freedom, and I cherish this freedom. I have to be a free person; otherwise, I cannot be your teacher. If I am affected by respect, fame, and fortune, I am not worthy of being your teacher. This is not something to speak of really, but rather something you can look into deeply and discover for yourself. I hope all of us can practice in the same way. If we do not have freedom, if we are not free from cows, fame, and fortune, happiness will never be ours. This applies to every one of us in the Sangha.

[BELL]

Question: This question came out of our group. We have heard no mention of the critical importance of accumulating good merit in this lifetime or the avoidance of bad karma and what implications this might have for future reincarnations. At my age, I'm wondering if I should try to make up for things by learning how to do "Present Moment" double-time.

Thây: When you practice breathing in, calming yourself, and smiling, you are acquiring a lot of merit. You become happy. Freedom, relaxation, and well-being are within you. Even if you aren't trying, you make the people around you happy. You make your ancestors, children, and grandchildren happy. You can acquire this merit every minute of your daily life. Reincarnation takes place in every moment. We are reborn in every moment. You may think you are old, but you are still very young; you have just been born. When I look at myself, I do not ask what I will become after I die and what form I will take, because just by looking deeply in this very moment, I know that I have already been reborn in many forms. Look at the monks, nuns, and laypeople practicing in the Sangha. I have been reborn in you all. You carry me within yourselves. I don't need to die to be reborn. I don't have to rush and accumulate merit now.

Someone told me that if your first three years as a novice are successful, then you can be a happy monk all your life. This is true in my case. The highest form of accumulating merit is not to think of earning it. Just live your life deeply and mindfully, cultivating your compassion, and you will be happy in your practice. The Buddha said, "My teaching is lovely in the beginning, lovely in the middle, and lovely at the end." This means that you don't have to practice for twenty years in order to see some results. The moment you begin to breathe in calmly and breathe out smiling, the fruits of your practice are born right away. It is not a matter of time. Because you are not thinking of accumulating merit, a lot of merit is accumulating. It is difficult to identify my reincarnations because they are many and they take different forms. You think I am sitting here, but that is an incorrect perception. I am a little bit everywhere at this moment in different forms. We need to look deeply to see that and not be fooled by our perceptions.

[BELL]

Question: Dear Thây, how do you look deeply? Is there a formula? Can you give us a few examples of how you would approach looking deeply at anger, pain, and impatience? What steps can we use after recognizing that they are there and embracing them?

Thây: Looking deeply is a phrase I like to use. We know that we can use not only our eyes but also our ears to look deeply. Using our ears is called deep listening. Whereas deep looking leads to deeper understanding and seeing, deep listening yields better understanding and insight. All of us have eyes and ears, but if we do not have the energy of mindfulness to empower them, we cannot practice deep looking and deep listening. Even with our eyes and ears closed, we can still continue to look deeply. For instance, looking deeply into the nature of our in-breath, we don't need our eyes or ears; mindfulness in our mind consciousness does the work of looking deeply. Looking deeply means being deeply aware of the object of our concentration. We have to use a lot of mindfulness energy to embrace the object and concentrate on it alone. Sometimes we use our eyes, sometimes our ears, and sometimes our minds — but we have to use the strength of mindfulness all the time. Without mindfulness, we cannot dwell long on the object of our concentration.

Sometimes we can even use thinking (*vitarka*, initial thought and *vichara*, applied thought). In many cases, thinking can lead us astray, and we can get lost. But sometimes, if we know how to handle our thoughts, thinking can help us see more deeply. The Buddha clearly guided us in the practice of looking deeply. Look in such a way, he taught, that you can touch the nature of impermanence of what you observe. It is not through saying, "This is impermanent" that you touch the root of impermanence. You may use your intellect and say, "I know this flower is impermanent," but that may be superficial. You have to touch the nature of impermanence in a deep way in order to go beyond the notion of impermanence and its root.

If we learn to really touch the nature of impermanence, we also touch the nature of interbeing and nirvana. All of us have had the experience of reading something and fooling ourselves or being under the illusion that we have understood it. But upon rereading it or referring back to it, we find that we have not really absorbed or understood it. The same thing is true with looking deeply. We may think that it is easy to see that this flower is impermanent. We accept the flower's impermanence. But that hardly changes our lives, because we are only on the surface and have not delved deeply into it. If we delved deeply, we would see the nature of nonself; we would see the nature of interbeing; we would touch the nature of no-birth and no-death. If we really touch the nature of no-birth and no-death, our sorrow and fear will vanish. As long as our sorrow, fear, and craving exist, we know that we have not really touched and peered into the nature of what is.

When we study the fourteenth exercise of mindful breathing, we look deeply at the object of our desire and craving, and, if we look deeply enough, find that it is not really the object of our desire. Our illusion brings about a lot of suffering. If we really understand the true nature of the object, it will cease to be the object of our desire and we will be liberated. That object may be fame, wealth, or sex. If we look into its nature, we will see clearly what will happen if we are trapped by it. If, in our incorrect perception, we continue to cling to our desire and believe that it alone will make us happy, we will bring suffering upon ourselves and the people close to us. Happiness will not be possible. We have not seen the true nature of the object of our desire. Its true nature can be gleaned only through the practice of deep looking.

When the Buddha gave teachings on impermanence, nonself, emptiness, interbeing, no-birth, and no-death, and proposed that the nature of these things is not a true object of our desire and not an object of clinging, he was helping us look deeply. If you look at these characteristics of reality — impermanence, nonself, interbeing, emptiness, no-birth and no-death — not as objects of desire, then you get the liberation you deserve. Sometimes you may use thinking, and sometimes you may just embrace the object of your observation; there are many ways. But the purpose is to witness this reality, go deep into it, and become one with it. This is the core of the practice called deep looking, vipashyana, insight practice. In order to do it successfully, you must cultivate your concentration and mindfulness, which are the strengths that allow you to go deeply into the nature of things.

[BELL]

Question: Dear Thây, in a loving relationship, the two partners become one. What does that mean? How important is it? And how can we ensure that the stronger of the two does not overpower the weaker one and swallow him or her?

Thây: As soon as the concept "one" appears, the concept "two" also appears. It's like right and left. Reality should transcend the concepts of "one" and "two." I'm sure if you put the teaching into practice, you will find the answer on your own. I know that question has come from the intellect, not a direct experience of the practice. The principle of the practice is equanimity, using the wisdom of nondiscrimination. The other day, I gave an example that was quite easy to understand. I said, "The right hand never tells the left that it is a good-for-nothing. The right hand does not discriminate against the left nor take pride in itself, because it deeply knows that it is at one or 'non-two' with the left hand. Every time the left hand needs it, the right hand comes and takes care of it without saying, 'I'm the right hand. I will now help you, and you have to remember to pay back my love.'" In a relationship, this wisdom of nondiscrimination is possible if we live inside that wisdom. When you are capable of living with each other like that, there is no stronger or weaker person, no taking advantage of the other. If there is a tendency to take advantage of the other, it means that the wisdom of nondiscrimination is not yet present.

Question: I came here with a health challenge. My doctors had outlined a course of action that I could not live with. So I thought about a lot of alternatives and natural healing and, interestingly enough, a psychic friend predicted that I wouldn't get in touch with my real healing until May 24th, the first day of this retreat. She had no idea that I was coming here. I am very, very grateful for your teachings and feel that I will be able to work through my health condition because of what you've shared with us. I had no idea that such healing was going to be in store for me here or that such a wealth of information existed that could save my life and put me in touch with my real issues. There have been so many compelling stories told about people who were literally saved after being told they had two weeks to live. There are a lot of strong messages here that I don't feel are reaching the people in the U.S.

I was wondering if you had thought about compiling books specific to health issues. Have you thought of a book that would help people with major health ailments? It could be titled *Breathing Took Me Back to Life.*

Thây: I think I'll count on you to write that book for me. [laughter] Each of you should be a living book. We bring our torches and receive light from the Buddha. Each of us has to take our torch home and try to use that light to help the people around us. So please write that book with your own life and not just words. You have been exposed to the teaching, you know the value of the practice, and we are counting on you to help the people around you.

[BELL]

CHAPTER FIFTEEN

Happiness Is Not an Individual Matter

Dear Sangha, today is the eleventh of June, 1998, and we are discussing the Third Prostration.

Interbeing

When we touch the earth, we look deeply into our body and realize that we are not caught in it. Our body is wonderful. It contains the whole cosmos. As we already know, all of our ancestors, our children, and their children are present in our body. We feel their presence in every cell. They are within us and are also around us. It is the same with the elements. We can touch earth, fire, water, and air within us and also outside of us.

We can see ourselves as a wave on the surface of the ocean. We know that one wave is made of all the other waves. The one contains the all and the all is found in the one. That is the nature of interbeing. The rising and falling of the waves does not affect us. The dissolution of our body does not affect us. Nothing is created, nothing dies. We should be able to see this when we touch our body, and we throw away the idea that this body is me, myself. We should also throw away the idea that our life span is only sixty or seventy years.

Before our so-called birth, we have already been here in other forms. After our so-called death, we continue to be in other forms. It is not only the life spans of the Buddhas and bodhisattvas that are infinite. The life span of a leaf or a candle is also infinite. When we are practicing walking meditation and we step on a leaf, our mindfulness helps us see deeply into the nature of the leaf. It seems to be dying, disintegrating into the earth. In fact, this is just an appearance. If we look deeply into the nature of the leaf, we can see that the leaf is one with the tree. There is a moment when the leaf pretended to be born and a moment when it pretends to die. These are just appearances. Deep in its nature, the leaf is free from birth and death. It is a manifestation.

Throwing Away Notions

In the *Diamond Sutra* (in Sanskrit, the *Vajracchedika Prajñaparamita Sutra*), the Buddha advises us to remove our four notions: of self, human beings, life span, and living beings. Removing these four notions helps us to touch the nature of nirvana deeply and be liberated from fear. In the *Diamond Sutra,* there is a pattern that is repeated several times: "…what are called wholesome actions are in fact not wholesome actions. That is why they are called wholesome actions." This formula, "'A' is not 'A,' that is why 'A' can really be 'A,'" forms the dialectic of the *Diamond Sutra.*

When we look into a flower, we realize that it is made only of non-flower elements. At that moment, we touch the real flower. If we see that "A" is not "A," we see exactly what "A" is. Often, we are caught by the thought that "A" can only be "A," it cannot be "B." We are caught by the idea of identity. But in the dialectic of the *Diamond Sutra,* it is different. If we look into "A" deeply, we discover that "A" is only made of non-"A" elements. This dialectic helps us see into the true nature of reality.

When we look at ourselves, we identify a self. If we know how to look, we find that we are made of nonself elements: parents, ancestors, air, earth, clouds, heat, food, education, etc. Everything that we touch in ourselves can be called nonself. We are not afraid of using the word "self" if we are free from the notion of self. The Buddha used the words "I," "you," and "self." He asked his attendant, the noble Ananda, "Ananda, would you like to climb the mountain with me? We will enjoy climbing together." He used the words "you," "me," and "we," and he was not caught in the idea of self.

When I first offered the gatha on listening to the bell, "Listen, listen, this wonderful sound brings me back to my true self," many practitioners were hesitant to use it because of the word "self." That kind of attachment to words and concepts is dualistic. If you nourish the insight that self is made only of nonself elements, you can freely use the words "self," "I," "you," and "we," with the wisdom of nondiscrimination that helps us to be free from fear and attachment. The dialectic of the *Diamond Sutra* is a guide for us to practice looking deeply.

The first notion that the *Diamond Sutra* advises us to throw away is the notion of self. This can be done by looking in the same way as in the *Diamond Sutra.* A bodhisattva who thinks that she is a bodhisattva is not a true bodhisattva, because thinking implies discrimination by the mind. When you help living beings, and you feel that you are helping them, you are not really helping them. You are helping yourself. If you make a donation with the idea that you are the donor and the other person is the recipient of the donation, it is not a true donation in the spirit of the perfection of giving *(dana paramita).* Paramita means "crossing over to the other shore." To practice giving is one of the six ways to cross the stream of birth and death, of ill-being, in order to arrive at the shore of well-being. The gift should be made in the spirit of equanimity. This is the emptiness of giving: no discrimination between the giver, the gift, and the receiver. You are one with the receiver of your gift and the receiver is one with you and with the gift, also. It is like when I talked about the emptiness of transmission of our body from our ancestors, or our right hand helping our left hand when it is hurt.

In a loving relationship, the actions of offering happiness, removing pain, and being joyful are all done in the spirit of equanimity. There is no me or you, we belong to the same wonderful reality. If we give something in the spirit of equanimity, with the wisdom of nondiscrimination, it is truly dana paramita. It brings us to the other shore right away, because the spirit of equanimity and nondiscrimination is very powerful. It transcends all notions of self and nonself.

Psychotherapy tries to help people have a healthy self. If we look deeply, we can see that psychotherapy points in the same direction as meditation. Both help people to have awareness of the self. You have to observe yourself to some extent in order to become aware of your presence. Without recognizing your own presence, how can you recognize the presence of others? Some of us are incapable of recognizing the presence of other people because we are not really here. We don't practice being aware of our body, feelings, and so on.

A second aim of psychotherapy is to cultivate empathetic awareness of others. We recognize ourselves as being here, as the base. After we are fully present, we recognize the presence of others around us. This is not only awareness of the physical presence of others, but an empathetic awareness. We know that we are living beings, with sorrow and pain, and we recognize that other living beings also suffer. We understand something about ourselves and begin to understand something about others.

A third aim of psychotherapy is to have compassionate relationships with others, not to exploit or make use of them, fight them or destroy them, but have the energy of compassion for them. You know that if your relationships are compassionate, there will be less suffering and more happiness for you and others. All psychotherapists agree with these three goals. In the practice of mindfulness, we cultivate these three aims through knowing how to breathe mindfully and walk mindfully. Breathing in and breathing out mindfully, we become aware of our body, our breathing, and our feelings. We know that we have suffering, afflictions, and hope. This is awareness of the self. We gain this through our capacity of touching ourselves deeply with mindfulness. When we do this, we are able to recognize other living beings around us with their sorrow, fear, suffering, and hope. This is an empathetic awareness of others. With this awareness, compassion is possible.

The method offered by the Buddha is to remove suffering and cultivate well-being. Well-being can be described as mental health. When we have low self-esteem, mental health is not present. Psychotherapists try to help people cultivate the opposite of low self-esteem. But what about high self-esteem? [laughter] High self-esteem is also a form of mental illness. You have lost contact with reality, and you imagine things about yourself.

Human beings look down on other living beings. We think animals are created for us to eat, and that we can do whatever we want with animals, vegetables, and minerals. We are not very healthy in that respect. There is another type of esteem, not an inferiority or superiority complex, but the idea that we are all completely equal. In the teachings of the Buddha, that is also a sickness, because it is based on the notion of self. "I am equal to him. I am not less good than him." It sounds OK, no low self-esteem or high self-esteem, but it is a sign that you are still caught in the notion of self.

In the teachings of the Buddha, considering yourself as higher than another person, as lower than another person, or as equal to another person are all wrong perceptions. The correct notion of equality is called the wisdom of *samata.* According to this wisdom, you share the same ground of being with all other living beings. If one person has the seed of Buddhahood, you also have it. If one person has the capacity of becoming completely enlightened, you also have that capacity. If one person has the capacity of loving and being happy, you also have it, because you share the same ground of being.

We should not have an inferiority complex. If we look deeply, we realize that we are a Buddha. In the historical dimension, we might think that we are a non-Buddha, but in the ultimate dimension, we are already a Buddha, because since the non-beginning, we have established ourselves in the world of no-birth and no-death. I said earlier that a wave is also water. We cannot take the wave out of the water or the water out of the wave. In the ultimate dimension, our nature is nirvana. Nirvana is the nature of no-birth, no-death, of full enlightenment. This is samata. Samata means the nature of nondiscrimination, the nature of absolute equality. It is not the same as the equality complex that is caught in the notion of self. It's quite different. We can only touch our ground of being, samata, after we have thrown away the notion of self. If the notion of self is still there, and we are caught in it, we have not touched the ground of samata.

[BELL]

Nondiscrimination

According to the Buddha's teaching, the way to remove all our symptoms of mental illness is by looking into ourselves and other people to see the true nature of equality, that self is made only of nonself elements, that happiness cannot be an individual matter, that everything inter-is with everything else. This makes compassionate relationships possible.

If you are caught in the notion of self, compassion is not possible. Understanding your own suffering and happiness, having the energy of compassion within, liberates you slowly from the notion of self. Then you can relate to other living beings and touch the nature of samata, sameness, within yourself and everyone. Psychotherapy can explore this. True mental health and happiness can only be obtained if we throw out the notion of self and relate to people in the light of interbeing. There is a lot for us to explore.

The second notion that the *Diamond Sutra* advises us to throw away is the notion of a human being. Looking deeply into a human being, we find that humans are made only of non-human elements: animals, vegetables, and minerals. The moment we see this, we see human beings as a reality, not a wrong perception. When we look at non-human elements, we see ourselves. If we see ourselves in the realms of animals, vegetables, and minerals, we will do everything to protect them and be kind to them. We cannot protect human beings unless we protect non-human elements. The *Diamond Sutra* can be considered the most ancient text on ecology. It encourages us to protect all species, because humans cannot be without non-human elements. This is because that is; if this is not, then that will not be. This insight helps us realize the need to protect our environment, because our environment is ourself. When we realize that humans are made of non-human elements, we have a true perception of reality, we have wisdom.

The third notion that the *Diamond Sutra* advises us to throw away is the notion of living beings. Living beings are made from so-called non-living elements. Animals are made of vegetables and minerals. If we damage vegetables and minerals, animals cannot exist. This practice leads us to the wisdom of nondiscrimination. When you stand in front of a tree and practice mindful breathing, you realize that you and the tree inter-are. You know that if the tree is not there, you cannot be here. This kind of wisdom leads to the end of all wars and discrimination. People of all faiths need to cultivate this wisdom. It is not something to just talk about. It is something that we can live in every moment of our lives. Through deep looking, practicing the art of mindful living, we touch the reality of nondiscrimination in each moment. When we touch the reality of nondiscrimination, anger and discrimination are not born, and do not lead to words and actions that destroy our relationships.

We need teachers, therapists, and others to look deeply into this and put it into practice in their own lives. Therapists can explore this and apply their insight to helping people be free of mental illness. We need to educate our young people so they can live according to the principle of interbeing. We learn a lot in school. It is stressful. There is so much to learn, to push into our heads, and yet we do not learn the most important things. Our hope is that schools will offer students the opportunity to learn how to be aware of themselves, how to look at themselves, to recognize their suffering, hope, and happiness, so that they can recognize other living beings' suffering, happiness, hope, and despair. Then compassionate relationships are possible. This can only be done with the cultivation of the wisdom of interbeing.

Living beings are made of so-called nonliving elements. If we look deeply into the nature of rocks, minerals, and vegetables, we discover that they are not inanimate. The French poet Lamartine asked the question, "Inanimate objects, do you have a soul?" I say, yes. If we look into the true nature of an electron, we see that it is not inanimate at all. It is very alive. Our notion about living beings and nonliving beings is a wrong perception. We need to transcend this wrong perception to arrive at the wisdom of nondiscrimination, which helps reality manifest itself.

The last notion that the *Diamond Sutra* recommends we throw away is life span. We have already learned that our life span is infinite. It is not true that we begin to exist at the moment of our birth and cease to be after our so-called death. The life span of a leaf is also like this. If we touch deeply the nature of no-birth and no-death of a leaf, we know that we cannot rely on our perceptions alone. We all share the infinite life span of the living Buddha, the living Christ, of God, because our ground of being is nirvana, no-birth and no-death. We don't have to look for nirvana or enter nirvana, because we are already there. A wave doesn't have to enter the water, because the wave is the water. She only has to touch herself deeply for that wisdom to reveal itself.

Non-Craving

We have learned about the Three Dharma Seals: impermanence, nonself, and nirvana; and the Three Prostrations, which are concrete ways to practice contemplating impermanence, nirvana, and letting go. There is one thing left for us to inquire about: the fourteenth exercise, contemplating non-craving. Non-craving means the nature of reality. Because we have wrong perceptions, reality cannot reveal herself to us. Breathing exercises thirteen to sixteen help us remove our wrong perceptions so that reality is revealed. Because perception is always perception of something, we need to inquire about the nature of our perception and the nature of reality as the object of our perception.

The Buddha advised us to look into the nature of the object of our desire so that reality can reveal itself strongly, and then we will no longer be caught in a wrong perception. Each of us has objects of desire, of craving. We believe that if we cannot get what we want, we cannot be happy, and we chase after these objects. The Buddha advises us to look deeply into that object, using mindfulness and concentration, so that it reveals its true nature. This is the aim of the exercise, "Experiencing non-craving, I breathe in." We might desire wealth, believing that if we don't have a lot of money, we cannot be happy. Those of us who have a lot of money know that it can make us very unhappy. Money is not an element of our happiness. With money, we may feel that we have power. That power can bring us a lot of suffering because it is often linked with notions of self, discrimination, delusion, and ignorance. Looking deeply into the object of our desire, our craving, we see that it is not really an object to chase after.

If we are addicted to alcohol, we think that we cannot feel good without it. We need to look deeply into its nature; how it is made; what it is going to do to us and the people around us; what the relationship is between liquor and our liver, heart, feelings, and consciousness. If we look deeply enough, we see that the object of our craving is not an element of our happiness. We can suffer tremendously because of alcohol, or die because of it, yet we have chased after it for a long time.

The Buddha used the image of a man who is thirsty who sees a glass. The water looks very cold, fresh, and sweet, but there is poison in it. Someone warns the man not to drink the water, "If you drink it, you could die or be close to death. Don't drink it, I warn you. Look for something else to drink. Use anything to quench your thirst, but don't drink this." But the man is so thirsty and the water looks so appealing that he decides that dying is OK. He drinks it and thinks, "I'll die later." And he suffers.

It is the same with wealth, fame, sex, and food. If there is food on the table and you crave it, thinking that you cannot be happy without it, even if someone tells you that you will die or suffer a lot from eating it, you will still eat it. You are so hungry and you think that happiness is not possible unless you eat it. You think, "All right, I'll die, because I have to eat it." Many of us have this attitude.

I know a woman who received the Five Mindfulness Trainings a few years ago. Later she met a man at school and they fell in love. He told her, "I'm not happy with my wife, and when I see you, I know you are everything I want," and he cried. He was married and had a child, yet he wanted to have an affair with her. He didn't realize that if he went ahead, he would cause a lot of suffering to her, himself, his wife, and his child. Because the woman had received and was practicing the Third Mindfulness Training, she said, "No, I cannot have a relationship with you." But she still wanted to have the relationship very much. Finally, after graduation, he returned to his country. She felt alone, and she began to hate the Five Mindfulness Trainings. She said, "Because of the Five Mindfulness Trainings, I did not have a relationship with him, and he was exactly what I wanted. Both of us have clean consciences, but I still hate the Third Mindfulness Training."

I'm certain that if she had gone ahead and had a relationship with him, she would have created a lot of suffering for herself, for him, and for many other people. Because she did not experience that suffering, it was possible for her to hate the Third Mindfulness Training. We have to look deeply into the object of our craving to see how it has come about and what it will do to us and the people around us. If we have real insight into its origin and outcome, we will not want it, because we will see how it will bring us a lot of suffering.

Intention and desire, volition, is the third kind of nutriment we learned about. As I mentioned before, the Buddha offered the image of a man abducted by two strong men. The man wants to live. He doesn't want to die. Yet the two men carry him off with force and intend to throw him into a pit of fire. The man screams, "No, no, I don't want to die! I want to live! Don't throw me into the fire." Yet the two men continue and throw him into the pit. The Buddha said that the two strong men are your desire, your volition. You don't want to die, you don't want to suffer, but because of your desire, you are dragged into the realm of suffering. Looking deeply into the nature of the object of your desire with mindfulness and concentration, you discover the true nature of your desire, and you stop chasing after it.

Nowadays, people fish with plastic weights. They don't use live insects anymore. The fish see the bait. It's very appealing. They bite on it, and the hook inside cuts them. We behave in much the same way. We have a wrong perception about the object of our desire. We think that life will have no meaning, and we will not be happy if we don't have it. There are a million ways to be happy, but we don't know how to open the door so that happiness will come. We just chase after the objects of our craving. Many of us have experienced the reality that the more we chase after the object of our craving, the more we suffer.

I have a nice story to tell. Imagine a stream of water descending from the top of a mountain. She's very young; she wants to run. Her goal is the ocean. She wants to get there as quickly as possible. When she reaches the plains and fields, she slows down. She becomes a river. When you are a river, you cannot run as quickly. Flowing slowly, she begins to reflect the clouds and the sky. There are many kinds of clouds, with different forms and colors, and the river spends all her time chasing after them, one after another. But the clouds don't stay still. They come and go. The river cries a lot, because none of the clouds stay with her forever. Things are impermanent. She suffers because of her attitude and behavior.

One day, a strong wind clears away all the clouds and the sky is desperately blue. There are no clouds at all. The river thinks that life is not worth living anymore. She does not know how to enjoy the blue sky. She sees it as empty, and feels that life has no meaning. That night she wants to kill herself. How can a river kill herself? From someone you cannot become no one. From something you cannot become nothing. During the night, she cries a lot. This is the sound of the water lapping against the riverbank. This is the first time she has gone back to herself. Until now, she has only run outside of herself. She thought that happiness was outside, not inside. The first time she goes back to herself and listens to the sound of her tears, she discovers something. She did not know that a river is made of non-river elements. She had been chasing after clouds, thinking she could not be happy without them, and had not realized that she was made of clouds. What she was seeking was already inside her. Happiness is just like that. If you know how to go back to the here and the now and realize that elements of your happiness are already available, you don't need to run anymore.

Suddenly the river realizes that there is something reflecting on her riverbed: the blue sky. She sees how peaceful, solid, free, and beautiful the sky is. She has not noticed it before. She knows that her happiness should be made of solidity, freedom, and space. She is filled with happiness, because, for the first time, she knows how to reflect the sky. Before, she had only reflected clouds and had ignored the sky completely. This was a night of deep transformation. All her tears and suffering were transformed into joy, solidity, and freedom. The next morning there is no wind. The clouds return. Now she reflects them without attachment, with equanimity. She says "hello" every time a cloud appears. When the clouds leave, she is not sad. She has found freedom. She knows that freedom is the foundation of her happiness. She has learned to stop and not to run anymore. That night, something wonderful reveals itself. The image of the full moon is reflected on her back. She is very happy holding hands with the clouds and the moon, practicing walking meditation to the ocean. Each step, made together with the clouds and the moon, brings her a lot of happiness.

Each of us is a river. We begin as a stream of water descending from the top of the mountain, wanting to run as quickly as possible. Then we learn how to slow down a little, and we begin to chase after the object of our craving. We suffer. Sometimes we suffer so much that we don't want to exist anymore. Then we have a chance to go back to ourselves and reflect deeply. We realize that the object of our desire is the cause of our despair and afflictions. All the elements of happiness are available in the here and the now. We have everything we need. Suddenly we get the kind of freedom that we have never had, and we are capable of living each moment of our daily life deeply. Because we have become a happy river, we can help many rivers around us to be happy, also.

The Buddha said that the object of our craving is not our happiness. He used many images to help us see this. First, he said the object of our craving is like someone holding a torch against the wind. The fire from the torch burns our hand. The same is true of the object of our desire. If we handle it, it will burn us. The second image is a piece of bare bone. There is no meat on the bone, but the dog desires it. He spends all day chewing the bone, but he gets no nutrition at all, no satisfaction. The object of our craving is like the bone.

It is also like a pit of burning fire. People who have leprosy itch all over their body. They are not allowed to stay in the village with the other people. They have to go to the forest and live there as a separate community. They make a fire pit there. Every day, they put their arms and legs on the fire, because it feels pleasant. The more they itch, the more pleasant the fire feels. They call this happiness. The Buddha said that you only consider the object of your craving to be happiness when you are sick. If you do not have leprosy, putting your arms and legs on a fire is a form of torture. Only sick people feel satisfaction from tossing their body on a fire.

It is like a small bird stealing a piece of meat and flying up into the sky. A big bird sees it and follows the small bird. If the small bird does not give up the meat to the big bird, the big bird will kill it. Our object of desire can kill us. During mindful breathing, we look directly at our object of desire and look deeply into it. If we succeed, we will be free from it and will look for happiness in other places, in the here and the now.

Each one of us has to study and practice this. We have to help our young people study and practice it, too. What is true happiness? Is happiness possible? Are the elements and conditions for happiness available in the here and the now? Do we need to chase after happiness in the future? All these questions are helpful. Therapists, teachers, politicians, everyone should learn about this, because we all want happiness and we all want to reduce suffering. Let us come together, practice looking deeply, and offer our collective insight to our community and nation. There is a way out of suffering. There is a way to build well-being. It is to look deeply into the nature of our suffering. When we can identify the elements that have brought us suffering, we can see the way out.

[BELL]

CHAPTER SIXTEEN

Practicing the Six Paramitas

Dear Sangha, today is the twelfth of June, 1998, and it is the last day of our twenty-one-day retreat. Because we don't want to stay on the shore of anger, I have offered you ways to cross to the shore of well-being, non-anger, and joy. We want to leave the shore of jealousy for the shore of equanimity and love.

Giving

We can practice crossing over to the other shore in our daily lives through the Six Paramitas. We can cross over at any time, because we have been taught how to do it. I like to present the Six Paramitas as a flower with six petals. In the middle, we can write "mindfulness." The petals are giving, diligence, mindfulness trainings, inclusiveness, meditation, and insight, and the substance of each petal is mindfulness.

Dana paramita is the practice of giving. When you give, you suddenly find yourself on the other shore. When you are angry at someone, you suffer because of that person. If you practice giving, your anger will disappear, and you will suddenly find yourself on the shore of non-anger and well-being. Think of making an offering that will make him or her happy right now. It's strange how easy this practice is. Deep in your heart and mind, you know that you have the seed of generosity and the willingness to make the other person happy. These things have always been there. When you are angry, you offer non-joy and non-peace. So go back and touch the seed of your love. At the beginning of a relationship, you make the deep commitment to make your beloved happy. Maybe now you are doing the opposite. Go back to your original mind, touch your seed of love, and do what you originally said you would — make your partner happy.

You don't have to go to the store to buy your beloved a gift. There are many gifts that you can give right now — a smile, a loving look. Are you capable of giving? Can you give your joy, your stability, and your freedom? Breathing in, you know that you are alive and that your beloved is alive in front of you. With this insight, you smile beautifully, and your anger disappears. That smile, that joy, that capacity to cherish your own and your beloved's presence is a great gift, which will take you quickly to the other shore. The fruit of the practice is instantaneous; you don't need to practice for ten years to achieve it. If you practice breathing in and out with mindfulness and solidity just once, you can transform the situation. You simply allow your mind of love to manifest. This is the gift of dana paramita, the kind of giving that takes you and your beloved over to the shore of well-being. Please try it.

You can also give your freedom — freedom from anger, sorrow, and forgetfulness, freedom from the past and from the future. You are capable of being a free person in the here and the now. This is the greatest gift. You can say, "Darling, I offer you my freedom." If we share this freedom, happiness becomes possible.

When we are bound to our anger, afflictions, and worries, we are not free, and happiness is not possible. During this retreat, we have learned the art of letting go, of releasing our cows. We have learned many ways of reclaiming our liberty. As a free person, we can make the best gift to the other person. That person may be our partner, our son, our daughter, our friend, or our enemy.

Through the practice of giving, we can transform an enemy into a friend. It is very effective.

The Buddha said that when you are still angry at someone, even after you have tried to get rid of your anger in many ways, try giving him or her a present. I would also like to recommend this practice. When you are not angry at him or her, prepare a present. Wrap it with loving kindness, with all your heart. Think, "I am preparing this gift for him. My heart is full of love. My every gesture is motivated by love and the desire to make my beloved happy. In the future, in maybe a week or two, I may be angry at my beloved, and I resolve to send him this gift then." You do this with the awareness that your love is impermanent. The gift that you are preparing may one day restore your love. When you are angry at him, go to the post office and mail it. You will feel much better. Have you tried this? Please do.

There are several other ways to practice dana paramita. When we receive the Five Mindfulness Trainings and live according to them, we protect ourselves and our loved ones. This is a precious gift that can take us to the shore of safety and well-being. Giving is a very deep practice, and you don't need to be rich to give. You are a lot richer than you think. You can make many people extremely happy by practicing dana paramita. You need only go back to yourself, practice mindful breathing, and recognize that you have a treasure of happiness and other elements that can make people happy. If you know how to use your time, your energy, and your smile, then you can make people happy. When you make others happy, you are also happy. While practicing mindfulness and helping people practice mindfulness, you generate the energy of the living Dharma. This is a gift called *Dharma gift.* After having touched the nature of no-birth and no-death, you realize non-fear. Helping people remove fear from their heart, you offer *the gift of non-fear,* the most precious gift.

You have been offered the teaching on the emptiness of giving. You give with the spirit of nondiscrimination, unconditonally. This is the highest form of giving. If you give as a bodhisattva, the outcome will be tremendous, and the happiness created enormous. Please learn more about giving. The more we give, the happier we become, and we make so many people around us happy. The teaching on giving is wonderful.

Diligence

Diligence, in the form of selective watering, is the second practice to help you cross to the other shore. As I have mentioned before, we have many types of seeds in our consciousness, both negative and positive. We need to have the time and energy to go home to ourselves and water the wonderful seeds of joy, peace, love, and forgiveness every day. This is the practice of true diligence.

Arrange things in your daily life so that you have time to water your positive seeds. Ask your loved ones to practice in the same way. Say, "Darling, if you really care for me, please water the good seeds in me every day. I am capable of loving, understanding, and forgiving, and I need your help to practice these in my daily life. I promise to recognize the positive seeds in you, as well, and to do my best to water them every day." This is true love.

On the other hand, we do not want to water our negative seeds of mistrust, anger, hatred, and discrimination. We do not want our loved ones to water them every day either, because that will make us suffer. If we suffer, they will suffer, too. The practice is: "I vow not to water my negative seeds. I am determined to consume mindfully so that my negative seeds will not be watered. I promise to refrain from watering my beloved's negative seeds. If I water them, they will grow strong, and my beloved will be unhappy. His or her unhappiness will also overwhelm me." We are alert and committed. This is intelligent practice.

We can all sign a peace treaty with our families. There are moments when we are on good terms with each other, when we can enjoy a cup of coffee together. In those moments, we take the opportunity to sign the treaty for our own happiness and the happiness of our children, our friends, and our parents.

Diligence means, foremost, that negative seeds should be left alone and not watered. If they manifest, we embrace them and help them return to their seed form. When our negative seeds are lying still in the depths of our consciousness, we allow them to lie still; we don't touch or water them. If one or two of them are watered and they manifest on the upper level of our consciousness, we take care of them and help them return to their original place — to our store consciousness — as soon as possible. If we entertain them in our living room for a long time — in our mind consciousness — they will cause a lot of damage.

Our positive seeds also live in the bottom of our consciousness. We try our best to touch them every day so that they have a chance to manifest on the upper level of our consciousness. Once they manifest themselves, we invite them to stay as long as possible and entertain them in our living room. The longer they stay in our mind consciousness, the stronger their base in the bottom of our consciousness will be. Diligence is not an abstract word; it is a concrete practice. We practice with our parents, our children, and our society. By practicing selective watering, we cross over quickly to the other shore. This is also called transformation at the base.

Now let us look back on everything we have learned. In this twenty-one-day retreat, we have had the opportunity to allow our beautiful seeds to be watered. Everything I have offered you is already within you in the form of seeds. The Sangha and I have only helped water those seeds. We have all been exposed to a Dharma rain that has penetrated deeply into the soil of our consciousness, and, because we were open, has reached our positive seeds. Many of us have experienced happiness and increased confidence in the practice as a result. This is thanks to the Sangha that nourishes and supports us.

Organizing a retreat creates the conditions for Dharma rain.

All of us benefit from this rain. Even if we don't strive to do anything — just allow the Dharma rain and the energy of the Sangha to penetrate and water the seeds in us — it is good. Transformation will take place and a miracle will happen. That is why we have to organize retreats more often, regardless of their length. One day or even half a day of mindfulness — when people belonging to the Sangha come together and practice collective walking, sitting, and eating — can be of tremendous help.

[BELL]

Television Meditation

We can discuss with our children how to use television in an intelligent way so that their negative seeds are not watered. If your child watches a television program full of violence, craving, and fear — even if he is excited by the events shown in the film — he will be tired after an hour. You may like to talk to him then. Say you have something to discuss with him and propose that he turn off the television. Ask if he feels peaceful and happy after watching such a film. He will tell you the truth. Then you can both discuss an intelligent strategy for using the television set. There are many healthy programs available.

I know a family in Boston that has an intelligent policy regarding television; they select healthy programs and watch them together as a family. They put on their beautiful clothes — just as if they were going to the cinema — and watch a film selected by a family member. They don't turn on the television at just any time.

As I have mentioned before, I once had an interview with a magazine editor in Paris. The editor asked me to talk about some concrete practices, and I gave the example of a couple watching television. The lady tells her husband that she has something important to discuss with him. Out of politeness, he nods. Instead of watching television, she turns to look at him and asks, "Darling, do you think we are a happy couple? If not, why? Let us practice looking deeply to see what prevents us from being happy. Do we have enough material resources? Why are we not happy?" Meditation is looking deeply together to find out the cause of our unhappiness. You need to turn off the television set.

You are more than intelligent enough to practice looking deeply to find out why you are not a happy couple, to see what prevents you from being happy. Look into the suffering, find its causes — the kinds of nutriments that have been feeding your unhappiness — and then cut them out. Discuss a strategy for beginning anew as a couple. It is always possible to begin anew. Yesterday, a couple here began anew, and it felt like they had just gotten married. This is possible for anyone.

In the beginning, it is a pleasure to look at each other, and we say, "Your face is so beautiful. You are the object of my love." We spend a lot of time contemplating each other. But we do not know how to practice diligence, so we begin to water each other's negative seeds. We change. "You don't look as beautiful as you used to look," we say. "It has become unpleasant for me to look at you." We don't enjoy looking at each other anymore. That is why, in order to suffer less, we look at the television. This is a tragedy in many families. People want to forget their difficulties and unhappiness, so they try to evade them. Television is one way for us to do this. So turn it off, look at each other, and ask the real questions.

Some people think meditation means avoiding reality — that you pursue something transcendental and no longer care about practical things. But meditation, mindfulness practice, is concrete; you deal with reality instead of running away from it. You go back to your real problems and your real situation.

A warning similar to the one you see on cigarette packets — "Beware, smoking is hazardous to your health" — should be placed on every television set, because millions of people have become intoxicated by television programs. Only mindfulness can help protect us and our children. I think this matter has to be brought into the political arena. We have to develop a set of laws to protect us from a consumption that is intoxicating whole nations. So much violence, anger, craving, and hatred have been created by watering the negative seeds in us and our children. Diligence must be practiced on a national level. Politicians, writers, journalists, teachers, and therapists have to play their part in creating awareness so that proper measures may be taken to protect ourselves and our new generation.

Mindfulness Trainings

The third practice to help us cross over to the other shore is mindfulness trainings. The Five Mindfulness Trainings are a concrete practice created for our protection, the protection of our loved ones, our cities, and our nations. Recently, Sister Chân Không suggested that we send President Clinton a book on the Five Mindfulness Trainings and ask him how to implement them on a national level. If nations lived according to the Five Mindfulness Trainings, there would be a deep transformation resulting in less suffering and more harmony and happiness.

The Five Mindfulness Trainings can be presented as a nonsectarian, non-religious practice. Their substance is found in every spiritual tradition. If we live according to the Five Mindfulness Trainings and train daily in them, we are well-protected. We will arrive at deep transformation in our lives and also in our society. This is a great gift. When we practice the Five Mindfulness Trainings and manifest solidity, joy, compassion, and equanimity, we offer the best gift to our loved ones.

It is much easier to practice the Five Mindfulness Trainings as a Sangha. If everyone in your family lives according to the practice, you avoid making each other unhappy. The practices of deep listening and loving speech can instantly transform the atmosphere in the family. If the family practices well, it will have a positive impact on society. Children are also capable of this practice.

Inclusiveness

The fourth practice to help us cross over to the other shore is the practice of inclusiveness, *kshanti paramita* in Sanskrit, which means we exclude no one. If we train ourselves in the art of embracing, our hearts will grow stronger each day, and we will be able to embrace people and their difficulties. Remember the example of the earth and water. The earth is great, which is why it can receive, embrace, and transform whatever we pour onto it. Water is great because it is capable of receiving, embracing, and purifying. Please remember the image of a handful of salt poured into a bowl. Because there is little water in the bowl, the salt renders the water undrinkable. But if we pour the same amount of salt in a river, the river will absorb and transform it, and we can still drink from that river.

If we have understanding and compassion, we embrace things without suffering. Even if people say or do mean things, we don't suffer, because our hearts are large. We don't exclude anyone, and we can go very, very far. There are other ways of translating kshanti paramita — like endurance or forbearance — but if we look deeply into the nature of the teaching, we see that inclusiveness is a better term.

Meditation

The fifth practice to help us cross over to the other shore is meditation, which means mindfulness and concentration. In a difficult situation, if we go back to our mindful breathing and smiling, we can create miracles. With our solidity and freedom restored, we can easily overcome any difficult situation.

Suppose two young men are about to fight with each other. If one of them is capable of breathing in mindfully, he will know that once they start fighting, they may both end up in the hospital. He might say, "Do you really want to fight? We may injure each other." That insight will help the other person wake up. Instead of fighting, they may sit and talk to each other. A few seconds can make a great difference; a flash of awareness, one in-breath, is all that is needed for transformation to occur. If we train ourselves in the art of mindful breathing, we will be able to perform these miracles. We can intervene and stop a tragedy that is about to take place. We become bodhisattvas capable of restoring peace and reconciliation.

Meditation, the practice of mindfulness, helps us to be fully present and to touch the beauty and wonders of life, the refreshing and healing elements. By appreciating these positive things, we are able to release negative elements easily. It would be a pity if we didn't know how to benefit from the refreshing and healing elements available to us and allowed ourselves to be overwhelmed by feelings of anger, sorrow, and discrimination. We don't need to practice sitting meditation for ten years to cross over to the shore of well-being; we need only a few seconds. The practices of mindful walking and mindful breathing can produce miracles. We can produce awakening at any moment, and awakening is powerful. Looking at the blue sky, we take one deep breath and touch its immensity, solidity, and freedom. This is very nourishing.

[BELL]

Insight

Insight, prajña, is said to be the mother of all Buddhas. In India, they carve *prajñaparamita* in the form of a woman. Prajñaparamita, the insight that helps you cross over to the other shore, has produced many Buddhas and bodhisattvas. We are all her children. Through insight, we are born into the Dharma and grow up as a practitioner. Touching the seed of insight within us, we see what to do and what not to do, and suddenly find ourselves on the shore of well-being, non-fear, and loving kindness.

If we are about to have a dispute, we can practice hugging meditation. When you get angry at your beloved, you need the insights of impermanence and of interbeing. As I have mentioned before, you close your eyes and, looking deeply, ask, "In three hundred years, where will you be, my beloved? In three hundred years, where will I be?" This is touching the seed of the insight on impermanence in our store consciousness. If you breathe in and out and visualize yourself and your beloved three hundred years from now, you will be a different person when you open your eyes. Your anger will have vanished, and you will find that the only meaningful thing to do is to hug your beloved with the awareness that you are both alive. You touch the miracle of life by touching the seed of insight that exists within you. You don't need a teacher to give you this insight, this Buddha-to-be. If you know how to touch this insight within you, the Buddha in you will continue to manifest.

Buddha Eyes, Buddha Ears, Buddha Hands

I have transmitted to you the teaching on Buddha eyes, eyes that can look deeply. You have the seed of Buddha eyes within you. Every time you look with mindfulness and concentration, you are using your Buddha eyes. It is wonderful to look with your Buddha eyes, and it benefits all of us; if you can see deeply, you will not be trapped by your wrong perceptions. You will be able to understand yourself and others. Ask yourself whether you are using your Buddha eyes or your regular eyes. Please do not think that you do not have Buddha eyes. They are not an abstract notion. You have them within you.

I have also transmitted to you the teaching on Buddha ears. Please make use of them and listen deeply with compassion and understanding. When you use your Buddha ears to listen to someone, he or she feels wonderful. Maybe no one has listened to him or her like that before. Do not tell me that you do not have Buddha ears, because you do. Use them every day and listen to your children, your spouse, or your partner with them. Empower them with the energy of mindfulness, concentration, and wisdom. Just by listening, you can relieve someone's suffering.

I have also transmitted to you the teaching on Buddha hands. I often use my Buddha hands. This morning, my eyes were a bit tired because I did not get enough sleep. So I touched my eyes with my Buddha fingers, and I breathed in and out. I know that the Buddha is available to me at any time. With some mindfulness and concentration, our hands become the hands of the Buddha, and we can create miracles. Learn to touch your body, your feelings, and your heart with your Buddha hands. The Buddha is not out there, she is in every cell of your body. She is one of your spiritual ancestors. If you know how to touch, the Buddha will manifest and be available to you.

Remember when you were small and had a fever and felt so alone, your mother suddenly appeared like an angel. She touched your forehead with her hand, full of love and concern, and you felt wonderful. Even if your mother is no longer alive, if you know how to touch her, she will be born again within you. This is your hand, but it is also your mother's hand; your hand is a continuation of her hand. If you want to feel your mother's hand touch your forehead, go ahead. Your mother is alive within you.

This is a story told to me by a Vietnamese artist who moved to the United States forty years ago. His mother was illiterate. Before he left Vietnam, his mother said, "Son, when you are away, you will miss me and you will miss home. Every time you miss me, hold up your hand and look into it. I am in your hand." That is wonderful. For many years now, he has practiced looking at his hand so that he doesn't miss his mother. He still lives in the U.S.

With mindfulness and concentration, we can train ourselves to use our Buddha eyes, our Buddha ears, and our Buddha hands to touch the wonders available in the here and the now. Nothing has been lost, and there is nothing to restore. Everything is still here, intact. We just have to know how to reach out for it, and we will avoid making mistakes and be able to bring relief and happiness to people around us. Understanding and love are real energies that we can create at any time. We can produce miracles by being fully present and alive.

Walking mindfully is also a miracle. The famous Zen teacher Linchi said that walking on water or over fire is not a miracle; the miracle is walking on the Earth. Walking on the Earth, becoming fully alive and enjoying every step we make — that is performing a miracle. When I see you walking like that, I am motivated to walk in the same way, and life becomes real for us and for those we love.

Telephone Meditation

When you go home, you may find it difficult to readapt. There is a lot of noise and everything is fast-paced. People are not capable of dwelling in the present moment. But you can still continue to use your Buddha eyes, ears, hands, and feet to practice in your daily life. Practice telephone meditation. When the telephone rings, stay where you are and go back to your breathing. "Listen, listen. This wonderful sound brings me back to my true home." If you can practice with a brass bell, you can practice with the telephone.

In Plum Village, we practice telephone meditation. Every time the telephone rings, all of us go back to our true home, breathing in, calming, breathing out, smiling. Don't be afraid of making the caller wait; if he has an important message for you, he will not hang up before the third ring. Stay where you are and enjoy your breathing. Every time the telephone rings, we feel a bit nervous. We ask ourselves, Who is it? Is it good news or bad? Resist doing this. Stay where you are for three rings. Cultivate your solidity and freedom. Go back to yourself. After that, maybe you can do walking meditation to the telephone. Do it with majesty. You are still yourself. When you pick up the telephone, you are fresh, solid, and smiling. This practice is good not only for you, but also for the caller. You will have a good conversation.

If you are the caller, here is a short poem, a gatha, for you to use:

Words can travel thousands of miles.
May my words create mutual understanding and love.
May they be as beautiful as gems,
as lovely as flowers.

You can write your own gatha. Every time you make a telephone call, touch the telephone with your hand and practice breathing in and out. You can breathe in on the first line, out on the second line, in on the third line, and out on the fourth line. Now you are calm and ready to make the call. You know that your friend will not pick up the phone before the third ring because she is also practicing telephone meditation. Tell yourself, "She is breathing and smiling, why not me?"

There are plenty of occasions to practice. You may think that there is no room for the practice of mindfulness in your busy life. But daily practice is possible even in the busy city. If everyone in the city practiced telephone meditation, imagine how much more peace and happiness there would be. Encourage the people you know to practice this. I invented telephone meditation for your use, and many of us practice it throughout the world.

Mindful Eating

Please do your best to eat at least one meal a day with your whole family. This is important. Practice silent meditation, breathing in and out three times. Look at one another, recognize each other's presence, and eat silently for the first two minutes. You may like to recite the Five Contemplations:

This food is the gift of the whole universe,
the earth, the sky, and much hard work.
May we eat in such a way as to be worthy to receive it.
May we transform our unskillful states of mind
and learn to eat in moderation.
May we take only food that nourishes us and
prevents illness.
We accept this food in order to realize the path of
understanding and love.

The practice is easy. To be worthy of the food, we only have to eat it mindfully. If we do not eat it mindfully, we are not kind to the food or to the producers of the food. I like to remind myself to eat in moderation. I know food plays an important role in my well-being. That is why I vow to eat only foods that maintain my health and well-being. Both adults and children can practice in this way.

Eating a meal together, we cultivate more harmony and love as a family. Your little boy can learn the Five Contemplations by heart and recite the meditation for you. Or you can sing it together before eating. Make meditation pleasant. That is what I recommend. Use your talent and your art to make it pleasant for everyone.

A Room to Breathe

In your home, you can create a breathing room, the equivalent of a meditation hall. It need not be big. Some of us have a room for every activity — a dining room, a guest room, and a playroom. There should also be a room in every home where we can restore our peace and balance. We need only a small table in that room and a flower. The flower represents the best in us — the beauty of understanding and compassion. The breathing room does not need a lot of furniture, just a few cushions. It is very important to select the right kind of cushion for you. When a cushion fits me well, I can sit for two hours. Otherwise, I can only sit for thirty or forty minutes before I have to change my position. It is important to try different kinds of cushions and find one that allows you to sit with stability and pleasure for at least twenty minutes.

In this tiny meditation hall, we practice exactly as if we were in a monastery. Touching the doorknob, we breathe in. Opening the door, we breathe out. We step into the room as if we are stepping into the Kingdom of God, the Pure Land. Do it so your children can see, and ask them to practice, also. Make it a land of peace. Anytime you are disturbed, angry, feel shaky, or in a crisis, go to the breathing room and invite the bell to sound. Practice breathing in and out to take care of your anger and frustration. This is education for peace. If we do not do it, how will our children learn how to do it?

If you are a teacher, you can ask your students to practice, because they are subject to anger, fear, and pain. Think of your students as your own children and embrace them with your compassion. In school, if you walk, sit, and smile with compassion, your students will see it. Embracing them with your loving kindness, you will be able to help them suffer less and reconnect with their parents. Later on, you may like to engage the parents in a dialogue in order to help their children. The teacher is one end of the spectrum, and the parents are the other. If the two do not work together, it is more difficult to help the children. Teachers can get together to discuss the practice. You can produce a newsletter where teachers write about the fruits of their practice at home and in school. This would be helpful for many teachers across the country.

The same thing is possible for psychotherapists. Applying mindfulness practice with your family and with your clients, you can come together as a Sangha of therapists. You can practice together, support each other, and perhaps publish a newsletter to share your wisdom and success. This will help other therapists.

Please use your intelligence, skill, and creative mind to make the practice pleasant and beautiful.

[BELL]

In the evening, before your children go to bed, invite them to practice sitting with you for two minutes. Teach your child how to invite the bell beautifully. In retreats for children, I always teach them how to invite the bell. Sitting together, one sound of the bell is followed by three deep in-breaths and out-breaths, calming and smiling. If we practice with three sounds of the bell, we make nine in-breaths and out-breaths. Then we look at each other. After your child has invited the bell, she may then say good-night and go to bed. If you want to, you can continue for a few more minutes, but don't force yourself. There will be times when you need to sit longer to restore yourself. It depends on your needs. It is wonderful if you can do this practice every day.

In the morning, after breakfast, you can spend a few minutes in the breathing room. Sitting down and breathing in and out with the bell is a wonderful way to begin your day. If possible, before your child goes to school, practice three sounds of the bell with him or her, breathing in and breathing out. It will become a good habit, and the energy of that good habit will sustain you throughout the day.

If there is a pleasant path in your backyard or in your neighborhood, you can turn walking meditation into a delight for the whole family. You may combine a picnic with walking meditation and total relaxation on the grass. We can do five minutes of total relaxation in our home every day, because many of us are under stress. We lie down and someone sings to us, guiding us in releasing all of our muscles. We practice breathing and smiling for five or ten minutes. In the beginning, we might like to use a tape, but later on, each member of the family can take turns offering total relaxation. This is the kind of food and nutriment we really need. If a person does one session of total relaxation a day, he or she will be free from stress.

We can also organize half a day of mindfulness with much joy and relaxation. We can invite a few friends and children to come and share this event. Or we can ask our children to organize the event, with our guidance.

Building a Sangha

Try to build a small Sangha where you live, because the Sangha is a jewel. You cannot practice for long without its support. In my country, we say that when a tiger leaves the mountain and goes to the lowlands, he will be captured and killed by humans. In the same way, when a practitioner leaves the Sangha, she will abandon the practice in a few months. That is why it is crucial and wonderful to practice Sangha-building. As soon as you get home, think of a strategy to build a group of people around you who can support each other in the practice. Arrange to meet every week. Arrange an organized day of mindfulness from time to time. This is a refuge. "I take refuge in the Sangha." Every one has to take refuge in the Sangha. Our spiritual life depends on it.

During the past twenty-one days, we have been at this retreat as a Sangha. Now we have to take our Sangha home and continue it in many forms. During these twenty-one days, we have allowed ourselves to be penetrated by the Dharma rain. We know how precious the Sangha is. There are things that we are unable to do as individuals at home that become easy for us to do here with the Sangha. The support of the Sangha is crucial. "I take refuge in the Sangha" is not a matter of belief or faith; it is a matter of practice. When you go home, I hope that you can all build Sanghas for yourselves, your friends, and your children.

Closing Ceremony

My dear friends, it is time for the closing ceremony. I would like to ask all the monks and nuns to come up and invoke the name of Avalokiteshvara, to show our gratitude, so that the bodhisattva energy will protect us and keep us strong in the practice now and in the future.

[SMALL BELL]

[TEN BELLS]

Body, speech, and mind in perfect oneness,
I send my heart along with the sound of the bell.
May the hearers awaken from forgetfulness
and transcend the path of anxiety and sorrow.

[BELL]

Listen, listen.
This wonderful sound brings me back to my true self.

[BELL]

May the sound of this bell penetrate deeply into the cosmos.
In even the darkest places,
may living beings hear it clearly,
so that without any hardship,
understanding will come to their hearts
and they will transcend the realm of birth and death.

[BELL]

APPENDIX ONE

Discourses on the Full Awareness of Breathing

Section One

I heard these words of the Buddha one time when he was staying in Savatthi in the Eastern Park, with many well-known and accomplished disciples, including Sariputta, Mahamoggallana, Mahakassapa, Mahakaccayana, Mahakotthita, Mahakappina, Mahacunda, Anuruddha, Revata, and Ananda. The senior *bhikkhus* in the community were diligently instructing bhikkhus who were new to the practice — some instructing ten students, some twenty, some thirty, and some forty; and in this way the bhikkhus new to the practice gradually made great progress.

That night the moon was full, and the Pavarana Ceremony was held to mark the end of the rainy-season retreat. Lord Buddha, the Awakened One, was sitting in the open air, and his disciples were gathered around him. After looking over the assembly, he began to speak:

"O bhikkhus, I am pleased to observe the fruit you have attained in your practice. Yet I know you can make even more progress. What you have not yet attained, you can attain. What you have not yet realized, you can realize perfectly. [To encourage your efforts,] I will stay here until the next full moon day."

When they heard that the Lord Buddha was going to stay at

Savatthi for another month, bhikkhus throughout the country began traveling there to study with him. The senior bhikkhus continued teaching the bhikkhus new to the practice even more ardently. Some were instructing ten bhikkhus, some twenty, some thirty, and some forty. With this help, the newer bhikkhus were able, little by little, to continue their progress in understanding.

When the next full moon day arrived, the Buddha, seated under the open sky, looked over the assembly of bhikkhus and began to speak:

"O bhikkhus, our community is pure and good. At its heart, it is without useless and boastful talk, and therefore it deserves to receive offerings and be considered a field of merit. Such a community is rare, and any pilgrim who seeks it, no matter how far he must travel, will find it worthy.

"O bhikkhus, there are bhikkhus in this assembly who have realized the fruit of Arahatship, destroyed every root of affliction, laid aside every burden, and attained right understanding and emancipation. There are also bhikkhus who have cut off the first five internal formations and realized the fruit of never returning to the cycle of birth and death.

"There are those who have thrown off the first three internal formations and realized the fruit of returning once more. They have cut off the roots of greed, hatred, and ignorance, and will only need to return to the cycle of birth and death one more time. There are those who have thrown off the three internal formations and attained the fruit of stream enterer, coursing steadily to the Awakened State. There are those who practice the Four Establishments of Mindfulness. There are those who practice the Four Right Efforts and those who practice the Four Bases of Success. There are those who practice the Five Faculties, those who practice the Five Powers, those who practice the Seven Factors of Awakening, and those who practice the Noble Eightfold Path. There are those who practice loving kindness, those who practice compassion, those who practice joy, and those who practice equanimity. There are those who practice the Nine Contemplations, and those who practice the Observation of Impermanence. There are also bhikkhus who are already practicing Full Awareness of Breathing."

Section Two

"O bhikkhus, the method of being fully aware of breathing, if developed and practiced continuously, will have great rewards and bring great advantages. It will lead to success in practicing the Four Establishments of Mindfulness. If the method of the Four Establishments of Mindfulness is developed and practiced continuously, it will lead to success in the practice of the Seven Factors of Awakening. The Seven Factors of Awakening, if developed and practiced continuously, will give rise to understanding and liberation of the mind.

"What is the way to develop and practice continuously the method of Full Awareness of Breathing so that the practice will be rewarding and offer great benefit?

"It is like this, bhikkhus: the practitioner goes into the forest or to the foot of a tree, or to any deserted place, sits stably in the lotus position, holding his or her body quite straight, and practices like this: 'Breathing in, I know I am breathing in. Breathing out, I know I am breathing out.'

1. 'Breathing in a long breath, I know I am breathing in a long breath. Breathing out a long breath, I know I am breathing out a long breath.'
2. 'Breathing in a short breath, I know I am breathing in a short breath. Breathing out a short breath, I know I am breathing out a short breath.'
3. 'Breathing in, I am aware of my whole body. Breathing out, I am aware of my whole body.' He or she practices like this.
4. 'Breathing in, I calm my whole body. Breathing out, I calm my whole body.' He or she practices like this.

5. 'Breathing in, I feel joyful. Breathing out, I feel joyful.' He or she practices like this.
6. 'Breathing in, I feel happy. Breathing out, I feel happy.' He or she practices like this.
7. 'Breathing in, I am aware of my mental formations. Breathing out, I am aware of my mental formations.' He or she practices like this.
8. 'Breathing in, I calm my mental formations. Breathing out, I calm my mental formations.' He or she practices like this.
9. 'Breathing in, I am aware of my mind. Breathing out, I am aware of my mind.' He or she practices like this.
10. 'Breathing in, I make my mind happy. Breathing out, I make my mind happy.' He or she practices like this.
11. 'Breathing in, I concentrate my mind. Breathing out, I concentrate my mind.' He or she practices like this.
12. 'Breathing in, I liberate my mind. Breathing out, I liberate my mind.' He or she practices like this.
13. 'Breathing in, I observe the impermanent nature of all dharmas. Breathing out, I observe the impermanent nature of all dharmas.' He or she practices like this.
14. 'Breathing in, I observe the disappearance of desire. Breathing out, I observe the disappearance of desire.' He or she practices like this.
15. 'Breathing in, I observe cessation. Breathing out, I observe cessation.' He or she practices like this.
16. 'Breathing in, I observe letting go. Breathing out, I observe letting go.' He or she practices like this.

"The Full Awareness of Breathing, if developed and practiced continuously according to these instructions, will be rewarding and of great benefit."

Section Three

"In what way does one develop and continuously practice the Full Awareness of Breathing, in order to succeed in the practice of the Four Establishments of Mindfulness?

"When the practitioner breathes in or out a long or a short breath, aware of his breath or his whole body, or aware that he is making his whole body calm and at peace, he abides peacefully in the observation of the body in the body, persevering, fully awake, clearly understanding his state, gone beyond all attachment and aversion to this life. These exercises of breathing with Full Awareness belong to the first Establishment of Mindfulness, the body.

"When the practitioner breathes in or out aware of joy or happiness, of the mental formations, or to make the mental formations peaceful, he abides peacefully in the observation of the feelings in the feelings, persevering, fully awake, clearly understanding his state, gone beyond all attachment and aversion to this life. These exercises of breathing with Full Awareness belong to the second Establishment of Mindfulness, the feelings.

"When the practitioner breathes in or out with the awareness of the mind, or to make the mind happy, to collect the mind in concentration, or to free and liberate the mind, he abides peacefully in the observation of the mind in the mind, persevering, fully awake, clearly understanding his state, gone beyond all attachment and aversion to this life. These exercises of breathing with Full Awareness belong to the third Establishment of Mindfulness, the mind. Without Full Awareness of Breathing, there can be no development of meditative stability and understanding.

"When the practitioner breathes in or breathes out and contemplates the essential impermanence or the essential disappearance of desire or cessation or letting go, he abides peacefully in the observations of the objects of mind in the objects of mind, persevering, fully awake, clearly understanding his state, gone beyond all attachment and aversion to this life. These exercises of breathing with Full Awareness belong to the fourth Establishment of Mindfulness, the objects of mind.

"The practice of Full Awareness of Breathing, if developed and practiced continuously, will lead to perfect accomplishment of the Four Establishments of Mindfulness."

Section Four

"Moreover, if they are developed and continuously practiced, the Four Establishments of Mindfulness will lead to perfect abiding in the Seven Factors of Awakening. How is this so?

"When the practitioner can maintain, without distraction, the practice of observing the body in the body, the feelings in the feelings, the mind in the mind, and the objects of mind in the objects of mind, persevering, fully awake, clearly understanding his state, gone beyond all attachment and aversion to this life, with unwavering, steadfast, imperturbable meditative stability, he will attain the first Factor of Awakening, namely mindfulness. When this factor is developed, it will come to perfection.

"When the practitioner can abide in meditative stability without being distracted and can investigate every dharma, every object of mind that arises, then the second Factor of Awakening will be born and developed in him, the factor of investigating dharmas. When this factor is developed, it will come to perfection.

"When the practitioner can observe and investigate every dharma in a sustained, persevering, and steadfast way, without being distracted, the third Factor of Awakening will be born and developed in him, the factor of energy. When this factor is developed, it will come to perfection.

"When the practitioner has reached a stable, imperturbable abiding in the stream of practice, the fourth Factor of Awakening will be born and developed in him, the factor of joy. When this factor is developed, it will come to perfection.

"When the practitioner can abide undistractedly in the state of joy, he will feel his body and mind light and at peace. At this point the fifth Factor of Awakening will be born and developed, the factor of ease. When this factor is developed, it will come to perfection.

"When both body and mind are at ease, the practitioner can easily enter into concentration. At this point the sixth Factor of Awakening will be born and developed in him, the factor of concentration. When this factor is developed, it will come to perfection.

"When the practitioner is abiding in concentration with deep calm, he will cease discriminating and comparing. At this point the seventh Factor of Awakening is released, born, and developed in him, the factor of letting go. When this factor is developed, it will come to perfection.

"This is how the Four Establishments of Mindfulness, if developed and practiced continuously, will lead to perfect abiding in the Seven Factors of Awakening."

Section Five

"How will the Seven Factors of Awakening, if developed and practiced continuously, lead to the perfect accomplishment of true understanding and complete liberation?

"If the practitioner follows the path of the Seven Factors of Awakening, living in quiet seclusion, observing and contemplating the disappearance of desire, he will develop the capacity of letting go. This will be a result of following the path of the Seven Factors of Awakening and will lead to the perfect accomplishment of true understanding and complete liberation."

Section Six

This is what the Lord, the Awakened One, said; and everyone in the assembly felt gratitude and delight at having heard his teachings.

—*Majjhima Nikaya*, Sutta No. 118,
translated from the Pali

Translated from the Chinese by Thich Nhat Hanh from the *Samyukta Agama* (*Tsa A Han,* chapter 29, *Taisho Revised Tripitaka,* No. 99)

I

This is what I heard. At that time the Buddha was staying in the Jeta grove in Anathapindika's park in the town of Shravasti during the rainy-season retreat. At that time, many elder disciples were spending the retreat with the Blessed One. There were *bhikshus* staying all around where the Blessed One was, at the roots of trees or in caves. The number of young bhikshus present during that retreat was also quite great. They came to where the Buddha was staying, prostrated at his feet, and then withdrew and sat down to one side. The Buddha gave teachings to the young bhikshus on many subjects, instructing them, teaching them, enlightening them, and delighting them. After giving these teachings, the Lord was silent. When the young bhikshus had heard these teachings from the Buddha, they felt great joy. They stood up, prostrated to the Lord, and withdrew. After that the young bhikshus approached the elders. When they had paid respects to the elder monks, they sat down to one side. At this time, the elder monks thought to themselves, "We should take charge of these young monks and give them teachings. Some of us can instruct one monk, others can instruct two or three monks or even more." They put this idea into practice immediately. Some elders taught one young monk, others taught two or three young monks, and others again instructed more than three young monks. There were elders who guided and instructed up to sixty young bhikshus.

At that time when it was the end of the retreat and time for the Inviting Ceremony, the World-Honored One looked over the assembly of bhikshus and told them, "Well done, well done. I am very happy to see you doing the things that are right and fitting for bhikshus to do. Please continue to study and practice diligently like this, and please stay here in Shravasti for another month, until the full-moon day of the month of Kattika."

When many bhikshus who had been spending the rainy-season retreat scattered about in the countryside heard that the World-Honored One would stay at Shravasti until the full-moon day of Komudi, they performed the Inviting Ceremony, finished sewing their robes, and without delay took their robes and bowl and left for the town of Shravasti. When they came to the Anathapindika Monastery, they put away their robes and bowl, washed their feet, and went to the place where the Buddha was sitting. They paid their respects to the Buddha and then withdrew a little and sat down to one side. Then the World-Honored One taught the Dharma to the monks who had just arrived from the surrounding areas. He instructed them on many topics, enlightening and delighting them. When he finished, he sat in silence. When the monks from the surrounding areas heard the teachings, they were delighted. They stood up and prostrated, and then went to the elders. After they paid their respects to these monks, they withdrew a little and sat down to one side. At this time the elder monks thought to themselves, "We should also accept the monks who have just come from the surrounding areas, and each of us can instruct one monk, or two monks, or three monks, or more than three monks." They put this idea into practice immediately. There were elders who taught just one of the newly arrived bhikshus, and there were elders who taught more. There were even elders who instructed up to sixty newly arrived bhikshus. The elders did the work of instructing and encouraging the bhikshus who came from the surrounding regions, teaching them everything in order, putting first what should go first and adding later what should be taught later, in a very skillful fashion.

When the day of the full moon came after the Uposatha observances had been performed, the World-Honored One sat before the assembly of monks. After he had cast his gaze over the whole community of bhikshus, he said, "Well done. Well done, bhikshus! I am delighted to see that you have done and are doing the things that are right and fitting for a bhikshu to do. I am very happy when I see you have done and are doing the things that are necessary for a bhikshu to do. Bhikshus, the Buddhas of the past also had communities of bhikshus who did the things that are right and fitting for a bhikshu to do. The Buddhas of the future will also have communities of bhikshus like this community of bhikshus, and they also will do the things that are right and fitting for a bhikshu to do as you today are doing and have done.

"In this community of bhikshus, there are, among the elders, those who have accomplished the first *dhyana,* the second dhyana, the third dhyana, and the fourth dhyana. There are those who have accomplished the maitri samadhi (concentration of loving kindness), the karuna samadhi (concentration of compassion), the mudita samadhi (concentration of joy) and the upeksha samadhi (concentration of equanimity). There are those who have realized the limitless-space concentration, the limitless-consciousness concentration, the concentration of no thing exists, and the concentration of no perception and no non-perception. There are those who are always able to remain in one of these samadhis. There are those who have untied the three basic internal knots and have attained the fruit of stream-enterer. They have no fear of falling into the paths of great suffering and are firmly on the way to perfect enlightenment. They only need to return seven times more to be born in the worlds of gods and men before being liberated from the suffering of birth and death. There are monks who, after they have untied the three basic internal knots and have nearly transformed the three poisons of craving, hatred, and ignorance, have realized the fruit of once-returner. There are monks who have untied the first five internal knots and have realized the fruit of non-returning. They are able to reach nirvana in this life and do not need to be born again in the world, which is subject to birth and death. There are bhikshus who have realized the immeasurable miraculous intelligence and even in this world are able to use the divine eye, the divine ear, knowing others' minds, recollection of previous births, knowing others' previous births, and ending all the ashravas. There are monks who, thanks to practicing the meditation on impurity, have transformed the energy of attachment; thanks to the meditation on loving kindness, have transformed the energy of hatred; thanks to looking deeply at impermanence, have transformed the energy of pride; and thanks to the practice of conscious breathing, have been able to put an end to the [ignorance and suffering that arise in the fields of] feelings and perceptions.

"Bhikshus, what is the way to practice conscious breathing so that we eliminate the [ignorance and the suffering in the fields of] feelings and perceptions?"

—*Samyukta Agama,* Sutra No. 815
translated from the Chinese

II

"A bhikshu who practices the method of conscious breathing very diligently will realize a state of peace and calm in his body and in his mind. Conscious breathing will lead to right mindfulness, the ability to look deeply, and a clear and single-minded perception, so that he is in a position to realize all the Dharma doors that give rise to the fruit of nirvana.

"A bhikshu who lives near a small village or a town puts on his sanghati robe in the morning, picks up his bowl and goes into the inhabited area to seek alms. All the time he skillfully guards his six senses and establishes himself in mindfulness. After he has received alms, he returns to his place of abode, takes off his *sanghati* robe, puts down his bowl, and washes his feet. Then he goes into the forest and sits at the foot of a tree or sits in an empty room or out in the open air. He sits very straight, maintaining mindfulness before him. He lets go of all his cravings. He calms and clarifies his body and mind. He eliminates the five hindrances — craving, anger, dullness, agitation, and suspicion — and all the other afflictions that can weaken his understanding and create obstacles for him in his progress towards nirvana. Then he practices as follows:

1. 'Breathing in, I know I am breathing in. Breathing out, I know I am breathing out.'
2. 'Breathing in a long breath or a short breath, I know whether it is a long breath or a short breath. Breathing out a long breath or a short breath, I know whether it is a long breath or a short breath.'
3. 'Breathing in, I am aware of my whole body. Breathing out, I am aware of my whole body.'
4. 'Breathing in, I calm my whole body. Breathing out, I calm my whole body.'
5. 'Breathing in, I experience joy. Breathing out, I experience joy.'
6. 'Breathing in, I experience happiness. Breathing out, I experience happiness.'
7. 'Breathing in, I am aware of the feeling [that is present now]. Breathing out, I am aware of the feeling [that is present now].'
8. 'Breathing in, I calm the feeling [that is present now]. Breathing out, I calm the feeling [that is present now].'
9. 'Breathing in, I am aware of the mental formation [that is present now]. Breathing out, I am aware of the mental formation [that is present now].'
10. 'Breathing in, I make my mind happy. Breathing out, I make my mind happy.'
11. 'Breathing in, I bring right concentration to bear on the mental formation [that is present now]. Breathing out, I bring right concentration to bear on the mental formation [that is present now].'
12. 'Breathing in, I liberate the mental formation. Breathing out, I liberate the mental formation.'
13. 'Breathing in, I observe the impermanent nature of all dharmas. Breathing out, I observe the impermanent nature of all dharmas.'
14. 'Breathing in, I let go of all notions concerning dharmas. Breathing out, I let go of all notions concerning dharmas.'

15. 'Breathing in, I observe the nature of non-craving regarding all dharmas. Breathing out, I observe the nature of non-craving regarding all dharmas.'
16. 'Breathing in, I observe the nirvana nature of all dharmas. Breathing out, I observe the nirvana nature of all dharmas.'.

"Bhikshus, that is the practice of conscious breathing, whose function it is to calm the body and mind, to bring about right mindfulness, looking deeply, and clear and single-minded perception so that the practitioner is in a position to realize all the Dharma doors that lead to the fruit of nirvana."

—*Samyukta Agama,* Sutra No. 803
translated from the Chinese

III

At that time, the Venerable Ananda was practicing meditation in a deserted place. It occurred to him, "Can there be a way of practice if, when it is practiced to fruition, one will realize the ability to remain in the Four Establishments of Mindfulness, the Seven Factors of Awakening, and the two factors of wisdom and liberation?" With this in mind, he left his sitting meditation and went to the place where the Buddha was staying, bowed his head and prostrated at the feet of the Buddha, withdrew a little, and sat down to one side. He said, "World-Honored One, I was practicing meditation on my own in a deserted place, when the question suddenly occurred to me, 'Can there be a way of practice if, when it is practiced to fruition, one will realize the ability to remain in the Four Establishments of Mindfulness, the Seven Factors of Awakening, and the two factors of wisdom and liberation?'"

The Buddha instructed Ananda, "There is a way of practice which, if brought to fruition, will enable one to realize remaining in the Four Establishments of Mindfulness and, by remaining in the Four Establishments, the Seven Factors of Awakening will be realized. By realizing the Seven Factors of Awakening, wisdom and liberation will be realized. This way of practice is conscious breathing.

"How is conscious breathing to be practiced? A noble disciple practices as follows: 'Breathing in, I know I am breathing in. Breathing out, I know I am breathing out. Breathing in and breathing out, I know whether my in-breath and out-breath are short or long. Breathing in and breathing out, I am aware of my whole body. Breathing in and out, I calm my whole body.' While practicing like this, he dwells in the practice of observing body in the body, whether it be his own body or another body. At this point, the object of the bhikshu's observation that he follows closely is the body.

"A noble disciple practices as follows: 'Breathing in and out, I am aware of joy. Breathing in and out, I am aware of happiness. Breathing in and out, I am aware of the feeling [that is present]. Breathing in and out, I calm the feeling [that is present].' As he practices like this, he abides in the practice of observing feelings in the feelings, whether they be his own feelings or the feelings of another. At this point, the object of his observation that he follows is the feelings.

"A noble disciple practices looking deeply as follows: 'Breathing in and out, I am aware of the mental formation [that is present]. Breathing in and out, I make the mental formation happy. Breathing in and out, I bring concentration to bear on the mental formation. Breathing in and out, I liberate the mental formation.' As he does this, he abides in the practice of observing mental formations in mental formations, whether the mental formation is his own or that of someone else. At this point, the object of observation that he follows is mental formations.

"A noble disciple practices as follows: 'Breathing in and out, I observe the impermanent nature of things. Breathing in and out, I let go of all notions concerning dharmas. Breathing in and out, I observe the nature of non-craving concerning dharmas. Breathing in and out, I observe the nature of nirvana.' As he practices like this, he abides in the observation of phenomena in phenomena, whether they are phenomena in his own person or outside his own person. At this point, the object of his observation that he follows is phenomena.

"Ananda, the practice of conscious breathing to realize dwelling in the Four Establishments of Mindfulness is like that."

The Venerable Ananda asked, "World-Honored One, the practice of conscious breathing to realize dwelling in the Four Establishments of Mindfulness is as you have described. But how do we practice the Four Establishments of Mindfulness in order to realize the Seven Factors of Awakening?"

The Buddha said, "If a bhikshu is able to maintain mindfulness while he practices observation of the body in the body, if he is able to abide in right mindfulness and bind mindfulness to himself in such a way that it is not lost, then he is practicing the Factor of Awakening called right mindfulness. The factor of right mindfulness is the means that leads to success in the Factor of Awakening called investigation of dharmas. When the factor of investigation of dharmas is fully realized, it is the means that leads to success in the Factor of Awakening called energy. When the factor of energy is fully realized, it is the means that leads to success in the realization of the Factor of Awakening called joy, because it makes the mind joyful. When the factor of joy is fully realized, it is the means that leads to success in the realization of the Factor of Awakening called ease, because it makes the body and the mind light, peaceful, and happy. When the factor of ease is fully realized, the body and the mind are happy, and that helps us to be successful in the practice of the Factor of Awakening called concentration. When the factor of concentration is fully realized, craving is cut off, and that is the means that leads to success in the practice of the Factor of Awakening called equanimity. Thanks to the continued practice, the factor of equanimity will be realized fully [just as have been the other Factors of Awakening].

"When the noble disciple practices observation of the feelings in the feelings or observation of the mental formations in the mental formations or observation of phenomena in phenomena, he is also making it possible for the Seven Factors of Awakening to be fully realized in the same way as he does when he practices observation of the body in the body.

"Ananda, that is called the practice of the Four Establishments of Mindfulness with a view to full realization of the Seven Factors of Awakening."

The Venerable Ananda addressed the Buddha, "The World-Honored One has just taught the practice of the Four Establishments of Mindfulness that brings about the full realization of the Seven Factors of Awakening. But how do we practice the Seven Factors of Awakening in order to bring about the full realization of understanding and liberation? Lord, please teach us."

The Buddha taught Ananda, "When a bhikshu practices the Awakening Factor of mindfulness relying on putting aside, relying on no more craving, relying on cessation, he goes in the direction of equanimity, and then the strength of the Awakening Factor called mindfulness will help him realize fully the practices of clear understanding and liberation. When a bhikshu practices the other Factors of Awakening: investigation of dharmas, energy, joy, ease, concentration, and equanimity, relying on putting aside, relying on no more craving, relying on cessation and going in the direction of equanimity, the strength of these other Factors of Awakening will also help him to realize fully the practices of clear understanding and liberation. Ananda, we can call it becoming one of the different methods or the mutual nourishment of the different methods. These thirteen methods all advance when one of them advances. One of these methods can be the door through which we enter, and if we continue our journey after that using each of the other methods, we will arrive at the full development of all thirteen methods."

When the Buddha had finished speaking, Ananda was delighted to put the teachings into practice.

—*Samyukta Agama*, Sutra No. 810
translated from the Chinese

APPENDIX TWO

The Five Mindfulness Trainings

First Mindfulness Training

Aware of the suffering caused by the destruction of life, I am committed to cultivating compassion and learning ways to protect the lives of people, animals, plants, and minerals. I am determined not to kill, not to let others kill, and not to condone any act of killing in the world, in my thinking, and in my way of life.

Second Mindfulness Training

Aware of the suffering caused by exploitation, social injustice, stealing, and oppression, I am committed to cultivating loving kindness and learning ways to work for the well-being of people, animals, plants, and minerals. I will practice generosity by sharing my time, energy, and material resources with those who are in real need. I am determined not to steal and not to possess anything that should belong to others. I will respect the property of others, but I will prevent others from profiting from human suffering or the suffering of other species on Earth.

Third Mindfulness Training

Aware of the suffering caused by sexual misconduct, I am committed to cultivating responsibility and learning ways to protect the safety and integrity of individuals, couples, families, and society. I am determined not to engage in sexual relations without love and a long-term commitment. To preserve the happiness of myself and others, I am determined to respect my commitments and the commitments of others. I will do everything in my power to protect children from sexual abuse and to prevent couples and families from being broken by sexual misconduct.

Fourth Mindfulness Training

Aware of the suffering caused by unmindful speech and the inability to listen to others, I am committed to cultivating loving speech and deep listening in order to bring joy and happiness to others and relieve others of their suffering. Knowing that words can create happiness or suffering, I am determined to speak truthfully, with words that inspire self-confidence, joy, and hope. I will not spread news that I do not know to be certain and will not criticize or condemn things of which I am not sure. I will refrain from uttering words that can cause division or discord, or that can cause the family or the community to break. I am determined to make all efforts to reconcile and resolve all conflicts, however small.

Fifth Mindfulness Training

Aware of the suffering caused by unmindful consumption, I am committed to cultivating good health, both physical and mental, for myself, my family, and my society by practicing mindful eating, drinking, and consuming. I will ingest only items that preserve peace, well-being, and joy in my body, in my consciousness, and in the collective body and consciousness of my family and society. I am determined not to use alcohol or any other intoxicant or to ingest foods or other items that contain toxins, such as certain TV programs, magazines, books, films, and conversations. I am aware that to damage my body or my consciousness with these poisons is to betray my ancestors, my parents, my society, and future generations. I will work to transform violence, fear, anger, and confusion in myself and in society by practicing a diet for myself and for society. I understand that a proper diet is crucial for self-transformation and for the transformation of society.

Dharmacharya Shantum Seth, ordained by Thich Nhat Hanh, offers teachings and shares the practice of Mindfulness in different parts of India and the world. He also leads pilgrimages 'In the Footsteps of the Buddha'. Please visit: www.buddhapath.com

Practitioners of Mindfulness Meditation meet regularly at different locations in India to meditate and deepen their understanding of the Dharma. Please visit: www.ahimsatrust.org If you would like to attend please write to ahimsa.trust@gmail.com

For worldwise contacts and teachings of Thich Nhat Hanh, Please visit www.plumvillage.org